W9-BQX-980

Working with People

Working with People

THE HELPING PROCESS

Naomi I. Brill

Joanne Levine
Wichita State University

PEARSON

Boston • New York • San Francisco
Mexico City • Montreal • Toronto • London • Madrid • Munich • Paris
Hong Kong • Singapore • Tokyo • Cape Town • Sydney

Series Editor: Patricia Quinlin
Series Editorial Assistant: Annemarie Kennedy
Marketing Manager: Kris Ellis-Levy
Senior Production Editor: Annette Pagliaro
Editorial Production: Walsh & Associates, Inc.
Composition Buyer: Linda Cox
Manufacturing Buyer: JoAnne Sweeney
Cover Administrator: Kristina Mose-Libon
Text Composition: Omegatype Typography, Inc.

For related titles and support materials, visit our online catalog at www.ablongman.com.

Copyright © 2005, 2002 Pearson Education, Inc.

All rights reserved. No part of the material protected by this copyright notice may be reproduced or utilized in any form or by any means, electronic or mechanical, including photocopying, recording, or by any information storage and retrieval system, without written permission from the copyright owner.

To obtain permission(s) to use material from this work, please submit a written request to Allyn and Bacon, Permissions Department, 75 Arlington Street, Boston, MA 02116 or fax your request to 617-848-7320.

Between the time Website information is gathered and then published, it is not unusual for some sites to have closed. Also, the transcription of URLs can result in unintended typographical errors. The publisher would appreciate notification where these errors occur so that they may be corrected in subsequent editions.

Library of Congress Cataloging-in-Publication Data

Brill, Naomi I.
    Working with people : the helping process / Naomi I. Brill, Joanne Levine.—8th ed.
        p.   cm.
    Includes bibliographical references and index.
    ISBN 0-205-40184-8
    I. Social service.   2. Social workers.   3. Human services.   4. Helping behavior.
  I. Levine, Joanne.   II. Title.

HV40.B83 2005
361.3—dc22

                                                                        2004044743

Printed in the United States of America

10 9 8 7 6 5 4 3   09 08 07 06 05

To the memory of Naomi I. Brill
To my son Raphael

Brief Contents

1. Setting the Stage   1

Workers in the human services need to be aware of the context in which they practice, both in terms of the history from which the present has developed, and the present that is both shaping and being shaped by what they do. This chapter contains a historical survey and a look at the major trends in modern society that affect the definition and application of human service.

2. Understanding Ourselves   21

In dealing with people it is essential that workers possess awareness of themselves, their own needs, the ways in which they satisfy these needs, and the ways in which they use themselves in relationship with others. This chapter focuses on the development of such essential self-knowledge and ways to work toward those personal changes that contribute to more effective working relationships.

3. Understanding the Human Condition   43

Throughout the entire life experience, the processes of growth and development and socialization and resocialization are continuous and ever present. There are many theories attempting to explain how people develop both as individuals and as social beings. This chapter explains life as a dynamic process characterized by continual change in which people develop by adaptation to the demands of both their own inherent potential and the environment in which they live.

4. *Working with Ethnic Diversity in a Pluralistic Society*   71

People bring to the society not only their own uniqueness, but also expression of a culture that they share with some people. In so doing they can contribute to a stronger, richer totality. A healthy pluralistic society is made up of groups that encompass and express elements of their own group identities. To practice effectively, human service workers need to understand and be comfortable not only with the cultures of these smaller groups, but also with their give-and-take relationship with the larger society and, perhaps most important of all, their own membership in such minority groups.

5. *Developing and Maintaining Communication with People*   91

Meaningful and disciplined communication is the basis of all work with people. Workers need to know what they are communicating, how they are communicating it, how their communication is perceived and responded to by others, and how they receive and understand these responses. The use of the Internet and related electronic technologies has both expanded and challenged workers' abilities to effectively communicate with people. This chapter deals with the ways communication skills can be developed and used more effectively.

6. *Establishing and Using Helping Relationships*   117

Through communication and shared experiences and feelings, people develop relationships that can either help or hinder them in the realization of particular goals. This chapter is concerned with the meaning and content of working relationships and the ways in which workers can consciously utilize them as dynamic processes in effective practice.

7. *Using the Basic Problem-Solving Process*   129

Life is essentially a problem-solving process, and the so-called scientific method is a rational way of searching for solutions. We propose theories as to causation, collect and test data, take action in light of findings, evaluate, and revise and act. People, however, are also irrational beings. This chapter proposes a basic process for working with people that takes into account all aspects of their being.

8. *Developing an Eclectic Approach to Practice*   153

In no other field of endeavor is there greater need for a broad range of knowledge and skills than in the human services. The proliferation of theories has brought about a need for specialization in order to ensure competence, but such specialization must rest on a generalist base. This chapter presents a tool that workers can use in evaluating various practice theories in order to fit them into a coherent and meaningful totality.

9. *Utilizing Skills and Techniques* *175*

Basic research and development of theory often seem simple when compared with the difficulty of applying this knowledge to three-dimensional people in practice. In order to translate theory into practice, we develop skills and techniques that we adapt to unique individuals and situations. Their number is infinite, but this chapter examines selected skills and techniques in terms of how and when they can be used effectively.

10. *Working with People in Groups* *201*

Social groups are a crucial part of the life experience of people. They constitute a potent force for personal development and for prevention and remediation of personal and social problems, as well as a significant tool in the delivery of human services. This chapter deals with the basic knowledge essential for use of the group process in working with people both as clients and as colleagues.

11. *Dealing with Vulnerability, Dependency, and Resistance* *225*

There are certain groups of people within society who are more vulnerable than others. Often they are forced by circumstances into dependency that can become chronic and trigger responses of helplessness, rage, and personal deterioration. This chapter examines the factors of vulnerability, dependency, and resistance to change that are so significant in the practice of human service.

12. *Getting It All Together* *243*

The integration of values, knowledge, and skill into human service practice and the conscious use of self in their application constitute the major challenges of such work. The demands of continuous self-examination, continuous learning, and continuous flexibility in light of social change are heavy. This chapter speaks to these demands, of ways to deal with them, of ways to make human service what it can be—a most satisfying and meaningful career.

Contents

3. *Understanding the Human Condition*   *43*

6. *Establishing and Using Helping Relationships*   *117*

9. *Utilizing Skills and Techniques*   *175*

10. *Working with People in Groups*   *201*

11. *Dealing with Vulnerability, Dependency, and Resistance*   *225*

Tribute to Naomi I. Brill (1915–1999)

Over the past thirty years, the reassuring voice of Naomi Brill has guided students through the process of working with people. Her warm and engaging style and her ability to take complex ideas and make them accessible have stood the test of time. *Working with People* is now in its eighth edition—a classic text in the field of human services.

In the final analysis, perhaps the book's enduring appeal is due to the simple fact that it is about making a difference. *Working with People* inspires human service workers to make a difference, amidst the overwhelming morass of social problems confronting us nationally and globally, by using the requisite helping skills laced with self-awareness, compassion, and integrity. Loren Eiseley, a favorite author of Naomi Brill with whom she had many things in common (native Nebraskan, writer, professor, and naturalist), has best captured the spirit of her life and work in this brief story quoted from his book, *The Unexpected Universe:*

> A young man was picking up objects off the beach and tossing them out into the sea. A second man approached him, and saw that the objects were starfish.
>
> "Why in the world are you throwing starfish into the water?"
>
> "If the starfish are still on the beach when the tide goes out and the sun rises high in the sky, they will die," replied the young man.
>
> "That's ridiculous. There are thousands of miles of beach and millions of starfish. You can't really believe that what you're doing could make a difference!"
>
> The young man picked up another starfish, paused thoughtfully, and remarked as he tossed it out into the waves, "It makes a difference to this one."

Joanne Levine
Wichita, KS
November, 2003

Introduction

This current revision of *Working with People* has attempted to retain the vision of Naomi Brill, while acknowledging that social work practice is in a dramatic transition with new knowledge being added almost daily. The reader may be aware at times of stylistic differences between the two co-authors; two different voices providing unique, yet complementary, interpretations of the text's focus. Much of the seventh edition remains relevant because, as Professor Brill wrote in her introduction, in spite of our complex technology and our increasing dependence on it, people remain the same with the same basic needs. The role of the human service worker continues to be that of enabling people to make better use of the resources within themselves and in the society, as well as to create and/or improve such social resources as needed.

In light of the rapidity with which major changes are taking place and new knowledge is evolving, workers are faced with the demand for a lifetime of ongoing education. The basis on which this education rests remains the same—the intellectual process by which we approach the finding of solutions to our problems. The information revolution does not change this foundation—it only presents us with some new tools.

This book is designed to be a body of this basic knowledge and in so doing has three purposes:

1. To develop knowledge that will enable workers to approach their tasks in an orderly fashion with an awareness of what they are doing and why they are doing it.
2. To provide a knowledge base for additional education and training that will enable workers to practice in different fields and in a changing society.
3. To develop workers' consciousness of themselves in relation to their profession.

Primarily intended for professional social workers, this book can and has been used in allied professions having to do with the health and welfare of people and with their ability to function both as individuals and as members of groups.

While the style of this book is essentially unchanged, content has been reviewed, new material added, changes in emphasis made, and new reading references listed. The new edition also contains:

- An expanded and updated section on setting the stage for human services practice including information on managed care, privatization, and HIV/AIDS.

- The latest NASW Code of Ethics.

- Emphasis on the ethics of social workers with challenges arising from managed care and electronic information technologies.

- Inclusion of theories from feminist psychology and brief therapies.

- Discussion of changes in the delivery of human services through the use of the Internet and technology.

- Updated websites to supplement the material presented in many of the chapters.

Students are encouraged to explore on their own. A good starting point is the new *Social Work Dictionary* (4th edition; Robert L. Barber, ed., National Association of Social Workers, 1999). It contains terms, organizations, legislation, definitions, and content on various concerns—in other words, the nitty gritty. A good periodical index can open the door to current articles in such magazines as *Social Work, Social Work Education, Social Casework,* and so on, and the literature of allied professions. Extensive material from worldwide resources is available on the Internet.

Content continues to be organized in five major sections:

- Section I. Chapter 1 deals with the history of society's efforts to meet human need in light of changing times.

- Section II. Chapters 2, 3, and 4 are concerned with the makeup of human society, human development through the life cycle, and people—including workers—as purveyors of the culture.

- Section III. Chapters 5 and 6 are concerned with the two channels through which help flows—communication and relationship.

- Section IV. Chapters 7, 8, 9, 10, and 11 deal with the basic process workers use in planning and implementing human service.

- Section V. Chapter 12 recognizes the heavy personal demands that work with people places on practitioners and suggests ways of dealing with the inevitable frustrations, feelings of inadequacy, and burnout.

Finally, in spite of what has happened to the meaning of the word "enabler," which currently is frequently used to indicate those who support others in destructive behavior, this book considers the major role of human service workers to be acting as enablers. We are charged by the society with enabling others to function more effectively. In the performance of such work, many different roles are called for—teacher, counselor, nurturer, therapist, advocate, helper—but all are designed to fulfill the major role of the enabler—"one who provides the means or opportunity." Therein lies our great challenge.

While these roles are all essential to good practice, that of being the advocate for clients is assuming increasing importance with the development of managed care. The demands these systems place on the users to assess care that is offered and assure that it meets actual need often require knowledge and skills that many people do not possess. Knowledgeable and skillful workers can provide this.

Over the years, the various editions of *Working with People* have benefited from the work of editors and reviewers whose comments, criticisms, and suggestions have added greatly to both substance and method of presentation. Reviewers for this edition were Susan Claxton, Floyd College; Miriam Clubok, Ohio University; Richard Holody, Lehman College; and Yvonne M. Johnson, Rutgers University. To all of them we owe a debt. Heartfelt thanks also go to Janice Wiggins Clark and Chris Darnell.

Setting the Stage

Why is knowledge of both historical and current social trends important for human service workers?

What are the implications for planning and provision of human service of the three major recent social revolutions in American society?

a. The civil rights revolution of the 1960s
b. The women's revolution of the 1970s
c. The high-tech revolution of the 1990s

What are the implications of the changing age distribution and increased number of minority populations in the United States on the need for human services, housing, and products?

What are two major conflicting beliefs about the causes of human need, and how do they affect planning and delivery of human services?

What are the implications of managed care for the provision of health and human services?

Change is the essence of living—personally, socially, and naturally. Some changes come so slowly as to be almost imperceptible; others come with revolutionary speed. But whatever their tempo, changes are continuous and ever present. In change lives the opportunity and push for growth, development, and fulfillment of the potential with which all life is endowed.

When we look at history, which is in essence a record of changes, we can see the big trends that are sometimes lost in the press of day-to-day living. Perceiving these trends enables us to put present events into context and better anticipate the future. The present comprises the setting in which we live and work and both determines and is determined by the shape and direction of our endeavors. It is essential that we have knowledge of both where we came from and where we are. Such knowledge points a direction for the future.

The background of society's interpretation and acceptance of responsibility to meet the needs of its members is a checkered one marked by broad philosophical swings. The origins of altruism in people are unknown, although some scientists think that the development of this characteristic relates to human infants' long period of complete dependency. Their survival depends on having not only parents, but also a set of social supports to provide the care they need. With each birth producing only one or occasionally two or three offspring, it was important for species survival that all children survive. Based on studies of behavior patterns among primitive people living in areas with extremely limited resources, some scientists see a possible relationship between the existence of plenty and peoples' concern for others—those who have plenty can afford to be generous! Generally, it is accepted that people have both the capacity to care and the capacity to be selfish and that their life experiences will determine the direction in which they go.

Whatever the etiology, by the time people began to live in groups and leave some record of their existence, there was evidence of concern for the common welfare (which meant concern for all people) and of working together to ensure it, even if this cooperation involved nothing more than allocation of tasks on the basis of differential abilities. Obviously, this was not purely "disinterested benevolence," as the dictionary defines altruism. It was based on the need to have a group of strong members capable of banding together to gather food, fight off danger, and ensure the continuation of the group, for prehistoric people were prey rather than predator, weak creatures whose ability to survive in a world of wolves depended on group cohesiveness. The moral imperative to care for those in need came later with the development of organized systems of ethics. This primary duality of purpose remains today even in our complex technological society. We care for people both as a moral ought and as a pragmatic necessity.

This social concern was already well institutionalized in ancient times. It was seen in Babylon in the Code of Hammurabi, which mandated protection of the weak; in the teachings of Buddha; in the early Greek and Roman states, which made legal provision for the care of those in need; in ancient Jewish doctrine, which taught of giving as a duty and receiving as a right; in the teachings of Christianity, which follow the Jewish tradition emphasizing mercy and charity as cardinal virtues.

In the early years of the Christian church in Europe, from which came the roots of the U.S. welfare system, practice of these virtues was mainly through the giving of mutual aid. By the sixth century, however, it was obvious that some more formal system of charities was essential. Monasteries, craft guilds, and small towns began to provide such a structure as an accepted part of the feudal system. When this system broke down, people in need went wandering over the face of Europe, carrying with them disease, famine, extreme poverty, and general social disorganization.

As always, crises bring change. Laws were passed not only to control itinerant laborers, but also to provide help for the poverty-stricken. When voluntary donations proved insufficient, compulsory assessment of funds became an accepted mode of operation. In England these laws culminated in the Elizabethan Poor Law in 1601, which served as a basis for some provisions of modern U.S. public welfare legislation. The needy were classified as children, able-bodied, or impotent. Different provisions were made to deal with each group. Local units of government were charged with carrying out these laws.

This same pattern was followed in the American colonies when the need for a permanent and organized policy to deal with the poor, the sick, the retarded, the insane, widows, and orphans became obvious. Fortunately, there was a strong moral imperative to provide help; the philosophical stance of the time viewed those in need as a part of God's plan for humanity and the care of them as both a privilege and a responsibility. Care was provided on a local level. Residency requirements were established to prevent dependents' drifting from one colony to another. The principle was "we take care of our own."

When a federal government was established after the American Revolution, it was only a question of time until it became involved in helping care for needy people. Such involvement began when the federal government established the Freedmen's Bureau at the end of the Civil War to plan for the newly freed slaves. From there it moved into the health field in response to several factors: a series of national epidemics, the work of early reformers, and scientific discoveries relating to the causes of disease.

The latter part of the nineteenth century was a period of unprecedented growth and expansion in the United States. The nation expanded across the country to take in the entire continent. Industry developed and prospered, and significant discoveries were made in science that enabled people to lead healthier, more fulfilling lives. But along with this came a return to the Puritan ethic—to attitudes equating affluence with morality; poverty and need were considered indicative of a flaw in moral character. Public charity was thought to be pauperizing. Human need was viewed not as inevitable but as controllable and eradicable. There was a strong movement toward the development of private charities that emphasized internal factors as causes of human need and stressed personal counseling to deal with them.

Once the belief that people could better themselves was generally accepted, the need for special education and training for human service workers (who had previously been volunteers) became obvious. Beginning with apprenticeship and inservice training, pushed by study and by increasing knowledge of people and their problems, present-day training for human service workers has grown into a complex educational system. The practice of the human service professions has also developed; today, practice is based on an increasing body of knowledge, directed by an accepted code of ethics, and practitioners are licensed both formally by society and informally by their clients.

The present knowledge base, however, is not concerned purely with individual causation of need, be it illness, poverty, or handicap. Historically, there have always been those who traced causation of need to social conditions, the environment, and circumstances over which people often had no control. This duality of causation is currently reflected not only in educational programs, but also in the extensive structure of human service organizations supported by local and federal tax funds as well as by private contributions.

From the 1930s until the 1990s there was a gradual movement from local, to state and regional, and finally with the development of the so-called welfare state, to federal planning and funding and control of major programs designed to deal with human need. This trend changed with the passage of the Personal Responsibility and Work Opportunity Reconciliation Act of 1996 (PRWORA). Beginning in the 1980s, a strong effort was made to return such programs to the state and local governments and to the private sector. Questions were raised about public welfare grants perpetuating dependency and encouraging "illegitimacy." This debate is ongoing and current federal legislation has returned many welfare functions to the states. Public assistance grants are now time limited and work is required of most recipients. The question of jobs for such often untrained workers has yet to be dealt with.

Two facts are obvious from this overview: (1) We have not arrived at any consensus on dealing with our social problems, and (2) it is possible to find individuals and groups within the total society who are operating on the basis of the philosophical stances of each of these four centuries (Table 1.1). As a part of society, human service workers are exposed to these philosophical differences in their own lives and reflect them in their attitudes toward themselves and their clients. The philosophy dominant at any one time will determine not only the resources available to workers, but also how these resources are used.

The changing attitude toward human need is not the only current trend affecting human services. The human service workers of today are primarily products of the years following the Vietnam War, which have seen extremely volatile social change. These changes have not come easily. They reflect questioning of established values and upsetting of accepted patterns of thinking and behaving. They determine not only the kind of education required, but also those areas where the greatest need for service exists and where the greatest numbers of workers will be concentrated.

Limited knowledge and awareness of our world are no longer sufficient. Developments in transportation and communication make our planet ever smaller and more interdependent—socially, economically, financially, scientifically, and militarily. That which affects one affects all. The worldwide AIDS epidemic is a clear example of this; worldwide drug use still another. And worldwide economic situations influence all things. Such far-reaching events not only affect the nature of the problems with which we deal, but also the resources available to deal with them.

Such changes often require developing and using new knowledge and different skills. The first step is thoughtful awareness of what is happening and its impact on people. There are several trends in our society that we will further consider because they have special import in the planning and delivery of human services:

1. Increasing size and changing makeup of the population.
2. The permanent face of pluralism.
3. The psychosocial impact of HIV/AIDS.
4. The changing healthcare scene and managed care.
5. Changes in the family.
6. Continuing poverty and the growth of the working poor.
7. The impact of the Internet and electronic information technologies.
8. The trend to privatize human services.
9. The indelible mark of terrorism.

Increasing Size and Changing Makeup of the Population

In 1798, Thomas Malthus published his *Essay on the Principles of Population,* in which he theorized that population increases faster than the means of support. Since that time, improved nutrition and healthcare have helped boost growth. In 1998, there were approximately 270 million people living in the United States, with about 20 million having been added since 1990. The projected size of the population in 2005 is about 283 million and in

TABLE 1.1   The Background of Human Service in the United States

Precipitating Event	Organizational Response	Underlying Philosophical Stance
1600 to 1700		
Poverty and hardship of pioneer society; Indian battles; isolation of colonies leading to sense of community and responsibility for selves	Residency laws—each colony cared for its own; help on personal basis by individuals in their homes; apprenticeship for children	Humans need a natural and inevitable order of a divinely ordered universe; helping others a duty to God and to the community
1700 to 1800		
French and Indian Wars; problems with England culminating in the American Revolution; establishment of a loose federal government; opening of the West resulting in personal mobility; results of wars, broken families, displaced people, poverty, epidemics	Separation of church and state resulting in many sects that cared for their own; emphasis on states' rights left programs largely local but with some state support; development of both public aid and organized private philanthropy	Development of a class society with growing feeling that in such a land of affluence, people should be able to care for themselves, that poverty and unworthiness were equated, that poverty need not exist; emphasis on the Puritan ethic
1800 to 1900		
Expansion across the continent; rapid urbanization; increasing wealth; Industrial Revolution; Civil War; resultant lack of sanitation in new cities; epidemics; poverty of workers who lost their jobs; broken families; displaced people; growth of unions	State funds extensively used; custodial and institutional care increased; Freedmen's Bureau brought federal government into the care of people when local facilities did not suffice; public health movement; development of "scientific charity" requiring highly trained professionals	Causes of human need are understandable and preventable; poverty and need are an individual matter and people are responsible for their own plight; public services to which people have a "right" are pauperizing and destructive
1900 to 1980		
World War I; economic depression and dust storms; World War II; Korea; Vietnam; increasing involvement in world politics and economics; movement from an agricultural to an industrial to a technological society; civil rights movement; increasing affluence; women's rights movement; recession	Increasing involvement of federal government in social services; federal job programs; unemployment insurance; Social Security Act; mental health movement; war on poverty; welfare state	Human need can and should be eradicated for the welfare of all and this can be achieved by laws and extensive social programs

continued

TABLE 1.1 Continued

Precipitating Event	Organizational Response	Underlying Philosophical Stance
1980 to 1990		
Increasing international involvement; increasing affluence and increasing poverty, hunger, and homelessness; high-tech revolution	The New Federalism and the "trickle down" theory of economics with a so-called "safety net" for those on the bottom; reaction to cost of social programs with return of federal to state funding; phasing out of programs	Return to the Puritan ethic and local, state, and private responsibility; limitation of the role of federal government in dealing with social problems
1990 to the present		
Ghetto areas in cities marked by poverty, drug use, unemployment, poor housing, health problems, family breakups; increasing concern about public education, law enforcement, healthcare systems; concentration of wealth in the hands of the few	Social revolution designed to do away with social programs and centralized government of the Roosevelt era; Welfare Reform Act passed in 1996, based on grants to states to design their own programs requiring work; social programs seen as too expensive	Welfare programs create dependency and immorality; responsibility should be returned to the states and private industry

2015, the population is projected to be 310 million (Ameristat, 1998). These projected figures may vary depending on such things as mortality rate, immigration, and number of live births. But however you measure it, the actual number of people whose welfare we need be concerned about is increasing, and there is serious concern about the planet's ability to support worldwide population growth regardless of our technological miracles.

There also are trends that will change the makeup of the U.S. population that have many implications for individuals, families, and governments. These are the increasing numbers of elderly—especially the oldest-old (85+)—due in large part to the aging of the Baby Boom generation and the changing racial and ethnic composition of the population. Hispanics, for example, will soon be the largest minority group in the United States. By the year 2050, it is projected that 25 percent of the population will be of Hispanic descent, representing 1 in 4 Americans (U. S. Department of Commerce, 1999).

The significant challenges resulting from these trends are, in most instances, fundamentally interrelated—it is difficult to consider them separately. For example, the increasing numbers of people living to advanced age present special health problems and may strain healthcare systems; they may add to family pressures by creating the "sandwich" generation of middle-aged adult children who are attempting to simultaneously care for their own young children and aging parents; the financial difficulties from not working and living on a meager fixed income may lead to poverty and poor housing. Costs for programs such as Social Security and Medicare may escalate, however, as the proportion of people needing care increases and the proportion of people in their working years contributing to such programs decreases. As the organization of older people into political action groups in their own interests becomes effective, the social stresses inherent in the situation become greater.

Analogous problems may also arise from changes in the racial and ethnic composition of the population. There may be exacerbated racial tensions; the need for bilingual services and workers may reshape the job force; and people unable to compete in a multicultural society may fail to thrive economically, placing greater demands on social welfare programs. These sorts of relationships need to be kept in mind when considering the specific trends.

The Permanent Face of Pluralism

Given the changing makeup of the population discussed above, diversity is a concept that increases in relevancy. Most of us are still taught in grade school, through the media and our civic organizations, that the United States is the "great melting pot" wherein diverse people come together and are blended into a whole, contributing to, and sharing equally in the benefits of society. In reality this has never been true. Certain groups have always been excluded, and the civil rights movement of the 1960s embodied recognition of this fact. Various minority groups express the need and desire to retain their own cultures to some extent and at the same time participate freely in the benefits of society. They have developed solidarity and strength in working toward this goal. In rapid succession African Americans, Hispanic Americans, Native Americans, and, most recently, Asian Americans have moved toward unity within their own cultural groups and toward status as one equal and distinct part of the totality.

However, the basic changes that entail embracing diversity in personal attitudes and behaviors and in social institutions do not come easily, evenly, or without conflict. Hate crimes, which are criminal acts motivated by bias against another person's race, religion, disability, sexual orientation, or ethnicity, are but one reflection of these conflicts. Sadly, it has almost become commonplace to view the media's coverage of hate crimes in those places traditionally considered safety zones—schools, workplaces, daycare centers, places of worship. Since 1990, the FBI has been designated by the Attorney General to collect data on hate crimes. These statistics confirm that victims unfortunately come from all beliefs, races, religions, and sexual orientations. Clearly, bias-motivated crimes have become a serious issue and all human service workers are challenged to combat their destructive impact on the personal, professional, and political levels (Federal Bureau of Investigation, 1997).

A major strength of our society lies in its diversity, but only as this can be embraced rather than used as a means to hate and abuse. This tremendous diversity represents limitless potential and promises much in the enrichment of life and resources. This diversity also demands major changes in the recruitment, preparation, and practice methods of human service workers so they may optimally assist those in need.

The Toll of HIV/AIDS

The changing face of the AIDS epidemic is also affecting the current healthcare scene. HIV and AIDS now affect all types of people, and they are no longer seen solely as diseases of homosexual men with little social status. As a result of new treatments, the progression has been slowed from HIV to AIDS and from AIDS to death for people infected with HIV. However, while these advances have resulted in the United States seeing a decrease in the total number of AIDS cases, in 1996 more than 48,000 women had died of AIDS in the United States and more than 100,000 women were infected with HIV; 44 percent of U.S. teenagers newly diagnosed with this disease were women. HIV is now the leading cause of death among African American women of child-bearing age. We also cannot forget the larger picture of the AIDS epidemic: 91 percent of all AIDS deaths in the world occur in 34 developing countries, mostly located in sub-Saharan Africa. Of the 30 million persons in the world currently infected by HIV/AIDS, 26 million (85 percent) reside in these 34 countries (World Health Organization, 1998).

The AIDS epidemic continues to dominate the healthcare scene. AIDS extracts a devastating cost from U.S. society through tremendous personal and economic losses. It is estimated that the U.S. economy has absorbed over $55 billion in annual productivity losses due to illness and premature deaths caused by this catastrophic disease (Karger & Stoez, 2001). AIDS therefore remains of great significance in the modern healthcare picture, both at the national and international levels. Although there are increasingly effective treatments that are a cause for optimism, science has yet to find a cure.

The Changing Healthcare Scene and Managed Care

The late eighteenth and nineteenth centuries in this country were marked by nationwide epidemics of smallpox, cholera, influenza, diphtheria, typhoid, tuberculosis, and polio. With the development of a national public health movement, these diseases have become controllable and bacterial epidemics are almost a thing of the past. Currently, there are other events of significance in the modern healthcare picture, which is plagued with problems and inconsistencies. How as a society do we eliminate the differences in life expectancies for men and women and for those who are African Americans, and decrease the number of AIDS cases for women and women of color? How do we help the over 40 million uninsured Americans, of whom 10 million are children under the age of 18 (Karger & Stoez, 2001) obtain health insurance while at the same time containing the escalating costs of healthcare?

These questions might seem paradoxical given that the United States has the highest per capita medical expenditures in the world—healthcare costs 40 percent more than in any other industrialized nation. Yet, despite the dramatically increasing cost of providing healthcare over the past twenty-five years, of all the developed countries the United States still has the smallest percentage of people covered under publicly subsidized healthcare programs. Also consider the following: Despite leading the world in development and use of medical technology, there also continues to be different life expectancies for men, women, and those who are minorities; unequal access to healthcare; and devastating emotional, social, and financial impacts of AIDS, cardiovascular disease, cancer, mental illness, emphysema, arthritis, and diabetes. Many of these diseases are often long term and catastrophic in terms of life expectancy, cost of treatment, and effects on family and society (Wallace, Green, Jaros, Paine, & Story, 1999).

The negative effects of these problems are reflected in life expectancy projections for the United States, which show striking variations by sex and ethnic group. For example, the average life expectancy for white females born in 1996 is 79 years and for white males 73 years. However, for African American females born that same year, the average life expectancy is 74 years while African American males have an estimated life expectancy of 66 years. Similar differences are also seen in the projected average life expectancies for those born in the year 2010. White females are estimated to live 82 years, white males 76 years, and African American females 76 years. It is discouraging to see that African American males' life expectancy is actually projected to decrease from 66 to 65 years. We see in these life expectancy projections for people of color the toll taken by the unrelenting stressors of racism, poverty, and the lack of access to healthcare and related services (Ameristat, 1998).

The changing healthcare picture reflects the impact of its increasing cost, complexity, and inaccessibility juxtaposed with massive efforts to contain healthcare expenditures while maintaining the quality of services. Managed care, now over a decade old, has emerged as the major effort to accomplish these goals.

The term *managed care* refers to a variety of healthcare financing methods and delivery systems. Managed care is a healthcare insurance system that contracts with a network of hospitals, clinics, and doctors who agree to accept fees for each service as flat payments per patient. Broadly defined, managed care now covers two-thirds of all privately insured Americans, and many federal and state governments are encouraging (and in some cases requiring) Medicare and Medicaid beneficiaries to join managed care plans. Table 1.2 shows an overview of types of managed care plans.

TABLE 1.2   Overview of Managed Care Plans

Health Maintenance Organization (HMO): A prepaid or capitated insurance plan in which individuals or their employers pay a fixed monthly fee for services instead of a separate charge for each visit or service.

Preferred Provider Organization (PPO): A type of HMO whereby an employer or insurance company contracts with a select group of healthcare delivery providers to provide services at preestablished reimbursement rates. Consumers have the choice of whom to contact to provide the service. However, if the doctor is not on the provider list, higher out-of-pocket expenses will result.

Exclusive Provider Organization (EPO): A type of HMO that has large numbers of independent doctors who are in private practice. Physicians are paid a fixed fee for treating IPA members but can also treat patients who are not members of the plan.

The Network Model: Multispeciality groups of doctors have contracts with more than one HMO. Doctors work out of their own offices.

Point of Service (POS): An option that can be offered by any type of HMO. If patients use doctors in their HMO network, and if referrals are made only by the primary care physician, only nominal fees are charged. If patients use doctors outside of their HMO's network, the cost is higher.

Physician-Hospital Organization (PHO): Organized groups of doctors who are affiliated with a particular hospital and provide services to patients who enroll in their plan as they would in an HMO.

Many questions arise from the growing influence of managed care. Most importantly, people must ask: Can providing accessible, comprehensive, continuous, and effective services be realized while recognizing that resources are scarce and cost efficiency is needed? Many feel these are competing and incompatible goals that engender many ethical conflicts. For example, managed care has introduced routine reviews of treatment services, ostensibly to reduce the provision of redundant, ineffective, or unnecessary services. These reviews have given rise to limitations in the relationship between the patient and the healthcare provider, including the length of time allocated for treatment, the number of times they can meet, and the types of services eligible for reimbursement. For those who provide mental health services, in particular, this is a big change. Prior to managed care, the counselor and the client would together decide how many times they would meet and for how long (Wernet, 1999).

These review systems in managed care can also cause ethical conflicts for social workers and other caregivers who strive to maintain patient confidentiality. While older third-party billing systems required the disclosure of minimal client information, review systems under managed care require the disclosure of traditionally confidential information to numerous people who are not directly involved in the client's care. Most often they are employed by a managed care company contracted by the client's employer. Because so many people see the patient's information, it is therefore impossible to guarantee confidentiality of a person's sensitive medical, social, and psychological information. Social workers and others who work in the helping professions must now make this clear to their clients from the start.

Vigorous debates rage about the benefits to clients as a result of these cost containment efforts. Each of us who works in the helping professions must become familiar with the issues to maintain our professional values and be most helpful to our clients. It is a given that managed care is clearly shaping U.S. medicine. A challenge continues to loom about how to achieve a balance between containing costs while increasing the access to and improving the quality of care for an economically and culturally diverse population.

Changes in the Family

Two factors leading to limitation of opportunities for women—the obvious discrepancies between wages paid men and women for the same work and the definition of complementary roles for men and women both within the home and outside—made women a natural group to participate in the civil rights movement of the 1960s. The era was characterized by efforts to raise social consciousness of inequities and of legal definitions in the Constitution that ensure the rights of minorities, women, the aged, the mentally ill, the handicapped, children, as well as the right to alternative lifestyles. These struggles have produced burning issues, often with moral and religious as well as economic connotations, and have resulted in the sometimes extreme polarization of supporters and opponents.

The subsequent redefinition of women's roles caused by the civil rights and women's movements led, in turn, to a reevaluation of the work and family roles of both sexes. A natural outgrowth of this reexamination of personal and family roles, of sex role stereotyping, as well as changing sexual mores, has been the emphasis on the right to alternative lifestyles. People are now considered to have choices, more or less socially accepted, of not marrying at all, of traditional family life, of single parenting, of living in various types of communal family organizations, and of living openly in homosexual relationships.

While many of these changes in the family are positive, they also have engendered stress. Violence and abuse within the family are increasingly visible, a not-unexpected occurrence given the stress of change and increasing openness about matters previously concealed within the closed-family system. The major purposes of the family are seen as nurturing of children and acting as the primary source of socialization. But children, the most vulnerable members, have suffered as a result of the changes taking place, and the processes of socialization have broken down. Statistics on the lives of many children in the United States are appalling. In 1999, about 22 percent of the children in this country, nearly one-fourth, lived in poverty; half a million were living in foster care; one in every eight was not covered by health insurance; the teenage birth rate reached more than half a million births to girls 15 to 19; homicide was the third leading cause of death for children 5 to 14, and the number of 10- to 17-year-olds using firearms to commit murder continued to rise (Wallace et al., 1999).

As well, changed economic conditions have hit the family hard. Loss of jobs by the breadwinners due to industrial change can result in personal demoralization and homelessness. The "feminization of poverty," wherein one-parent families headed by women are particularly hard pressed, is another reflection of conditions that can undermine the economic and social foundations of family life. Consider, for example, that in 1995, 20 percent of children were living in families with incomes below the federal poverty level; 64 percent lived in families headed by a single parent; and four out of five infants and toddlers and one older child in five lived in poverty. Additionally, children in families headed by single mothers, African American children, and children living below 150 percent of the federal poverty level are much more likely to be in poor or fair health than children in two-parent families, white children, and children living in more affluent families (Karger & Stoez, 2001). It is also sobering to consider that despite the massive expenditures for healthcare in the United States, it still ranks 25th among industrialized countries in reported infant mortality rates (Wallace et al., 1999).

Clearly, families in the United States today are characterized by extraordinary socioeconomic, ethnic, and cultural variations. During the last third of the twentieth century there were enormous demographic and economic changes that affected families, including the increased incidence of single-parent families; increased maternal employment outside the home; declining labor market prospects for less skilled, especially male workers; and the increased incidence of childhood poverty, both within their families and in their neighborhoods. These changes have had a tremendous impact upon families and their most vulnerable members—the children.

Continuing Poverty and the Growth of the Working Poor

Despite significant changes for families that have evolved over the past several decades, for many there has been a constant theme—poverty. Clearly, the problem of poverty haunts many families, a self-perpetuating social blight, the destructive effects of which can be seen in every aspect of the lives of the poor. Former Vice President Hubert Humphrey (Vice President from 1965 to 1969) said, "The moral test of government is how it treats those who are in the dawn of life—the children; those who are in the twilight of life—the aged; and those who are in the shadows of life—the sick, the needy and the handicapped."

In addition, the so-called welfare state has grown older and presents many of the problems of aging systems. There are those, too, who believe that poverty and unemployment are built into our present economic system and that only major changes in the system itself will control and—partially, at least—eradicate it. However we regard it and whatever we consider the better way to deal with it, widespread poverty and its destructive impact on all people—those who experience it and those who escape its immediate effects but are a part of the system that produces it—cannot be ignored.

Widespread poverty, of which children bear a disproportion burden, remains a major concern of modern society. In 1963, when Michael Harrington wrote *The Other America: Poverty in the United States,* his conclusion that one-fourth of the people of this, the wealthiest nation in the world, lived in poverty as a result of unemployment, underemployment, and inability to work for a variety of reasons came as a shock. Most people thought that the passage of the Social Security Act in 1935, with its system of benefits for children, the elderly, and the disabled, had cushioned the vulnerable against some of the unavoidable tragedies of living.

Over the years social welfare laws had continued to be interpreted liberally, with amendments to the original act to make its provisions better meet actual need up until the 1980s. The War on Poverty in 1964 represented a massive effort to ensure that all people shared in the benefits of society according to their need. The rationale was that every citizen has a right to become or remain a part of our society, because if this right is denied, it impoverishes us all.

In the early 1980s a growing disenchantment with the welfare state and economic conditions in general was reflected in an effort to dismantle the federal system of grants and aids, to repeal laws, and to return programs to state and private resources. The economic theory on which these efforts were based was the "trickle-down" system of economics, in which money, resources, and tax advantages were designated for business, industry, and the wealthy on the supposition that the investment of capital and the development of new business would, in time, offer jobs and prosperity that would take care of the poor.

This approach to meeting human need represents a major philosophical change in attitude toward those who must have help. It resulted in widespread unemployment, actual hunger as a national problem, and suffering and deprivation as federal programs on which people depended were curtailed or phased out. Private agencies and state programs, hard pressed themselves, were unable to meet the growing needs. In 1996 came passage of the Personal Responsibility and Work Opportunities Act (PRWOA). Considered to be one of the most important pieces of policy legislation since the Social Security Act of 1935, this act included deep cuts in basic programs for low-income children, families, and elderly and disabled people. Major welfare programs were replaced with the Temporary Aid to Needy Families (TANF) program, which allowed each state to determine which families receive assistance and under what circumstances. TANF is a block grant program based on workfare, time-limited benefits (maximum of five years), and strict work participation rates (Karger & Stoez, 2001).

The ranks of the poor in the United Status fluctuate. One important dimension is the growing size of the so-called "underclass" of poor people with poor education, poor health, and few job skills who tend to create a self-perpetuating group. In the 1990s, poverty reached its highest level since 1984. Nearly 15 percent of Americans were living below the poverty line in 1993. By 1997, the poverty rate had dropped to around 11.5 percent. However, the 2002 Census Bureau's American Community Survey showed that the total percentage of people in poverty increased to 12.4 percent from 12.1 percent in 2001 and totaled 34.8 million. At the same time, the number of families living in poverty went up by more that 300,00 in 2002 to 7 million from 6.6 million in 2001. During this same period, the number of children in poverty rose by more than 600,000 during the same period to 12.2 million. For the youngest group of children, those under 5, 19.8 percent were found to live below the poverty line in 2002. This was an increase from 18.8 percent the year before (Clemetson, 2003). It is clearly of great concern that these figures are found in one of the richest countries in the world. At the same time, other troubling dimensions to the overall problem assumed greater prominence and continue to haunt us in the twenty-first century.

Another group in poverty is the working poor—families or individuals who are in the work force (full or part-time) but are still at or below the poverty line. Apart from those groups unable to work—children, the aged, or disabled—the number of working individuals (ages 22 to 64) who are poor has escalated sharply, increasing more than 50 percent between 1979 and 1991. This is despite the common misperception that most poor people don't work. In fact, 41 percent of all poor people actually do work at some time during the year. This rise in the number of working poor is attributable to a complex array of many factors that include the replacement of high-paying industrial jobs with low-paying service jobs, the low minimum wage, the failure of the private sector to create the kind of jobs necessary to raise low-income workers above the poverty line, and severe cutbacks in federally funded job training programs (Karger & Stoez, 2001).

Finally, another important dimension is the international turmoil, unrest, famine, and loss of natural resources, resulting in increasing numbers of displaced people. They seek refuge both legally and illegally, creating additional pressure on already overstressed welfare systems. Though the United States takes in thousands of such persons each year, this is only a fraction of those seeking to leave their troubled homelands. Estimates in 1999 were that over 14 million people worldwide are refugees and asylum seekers in need of protection. These people are diverse and come from over 40 countries spanning the globe, from every continent except for North America and Australia (U.S. Committee for Refugees, 2000). Much debate has arisen in the United States about how many resources can be allocated to meet the complex and varied needs of those who are able to start new lives in this country. Policies to address both legal and illegal immigrants raise some of the most difficult social, ethical, and legal questions as the influx of these displaced persons have major social and economic impacts upon U.S. society.

The Impact of the Internet and Electronic Information Technologies

In the past hundred years this country has moved from a predominantly rural, agricultural society through an industrial revolution into a technological society, a nuclear age. We are living in what is now the information society. The Internet and related technologies have transformed society by creating new economic opportunities, facilitating personal and professional communications locally and globally, and exponentially expanding the opportunities for accessing and disseminating information. It is estimated that the World Wide Web adds 25,000 new sites each month, an estimated 3.4 trillion email messages were delivered in the United States in 1998, and 2.1 billion email messages are sent daily by U.S. users. Clearly, the Internet and related technologies are some of the most significant technological advances of the twentieth century (Karger & Levine, 1999).

Human service workers are not only a part of this information revolution, they are both affected by and affecting it. Over the past decade human service providers, agencies, and hospitals have steadily increased their use of computers and other electronic technologies. Many hospitals, for example, now use the Internet for a wide range of functions including communicating patient information, sharing techniques, data sharing with other institutions and providers, advertising, and communing both within and without the hospitals. Managed care companies routinely utilize electronic data collection and storage of patient information to facilitate the reimbursement process. There is also growth in the use of telehealth—electronic technology to deliver health-related services, including counseling and psychological services (Levine, 2000).

But all change has its price, and the diffusion of electronic information technologies into the human services is no exception. While using the Internet and related electronic technologies (i.e., fax, videoconferencing) may be cost effective and efficient, serious questions are raised about ensuring the privacy of the electronic storage and transmission of highly personal information. Unfortunately, both privacy safeguards and privacy rights legislation have lagged in this area. As a result, human service workers are confronted with new legal and ethical dilemmas and few guidelines or precedents to help in their resolution (Linzer, 1999). The guidelines are in the process of being defined through legislation, case law, and the mandates of professional associations.

It is therefore imperative that human service workers and their clients actively enter the debate about how to better regulate the virtual world of electronic data collection and storage yet not stifle the free flow of information that characterizes a democratic society. Only then will the core values of the human services—service, social justice, and the dignity and worth of the individual—be incorporated into formal policies and legislation (Karger & Levine, 1999).

The Trend to Privatize Human Services

An important theme running through the human services landscape is privatization. This term refers to having the private sector finance and deliver social services. Human service workers are conflicted about privatization of human services, though many acknowledge that the private sector can play an important role in service delivery. Privatization has figured most prominently since the 1980s when government was downsized because of the dominant conservative political influence at that time. Downsizing of the public sector resulted in a greater responsibility for service delivery placed upon the private sector. Underlying this shift was dissatisfaction by many with the quality and cost of services when delivered by the public sector. As well, this shift underscored a belief by some that the private sector was more efficient and cost effective than the public sector in providing human services (Karger & Stoez, 2001).

Those who think that privatization is the best way to help the needy in our land cite many benefits, including the quick ability to raise funds for services through commercial loans and issuance of stocks, access to private sector innovations that can be used for the good of the disadvantaged, and access to financial resources and managerial talent that can promote the professional practice of human service endeavors.

Privatization of human services often happens today on a local level. Many human service workers, including licensed masters-level social workers, psychiatric nurses, and licensed professional counselors, engage in private counseling practices either on a full- or part-time basis. These private practitioners provide affordable mental health services to middle- and working-class clients who cannot pay the higher fees often charged by psychologists and psychiatrists. These clients may be some of the 40 million Americans without health insurance or with coverage that does not provide enough benefits to cover the cost of mental health services, necessitating paying out of pocket for help. Clearly, the affordable nature of these private practitioners meets a need.

There are also benefits for the private practitioners, including higher salaries than those in most public and nonprofit settings, autonomy from the policies of traditional agencies, specialization reflecting the individual practitioner's abilities and strengths, and control over work schedules. Research on licensed masters-level social workers engaged in private practice report that they experience fewer psychological and health strains than those in agency practice. When human service workers feel satisfied with their working conditions and valued for the jobs they do, they are better able to serve clients (Karger & Stoez, 2001). Opponents feel the traditional values of human services—service to the community and disadvantaged—are not reconcilable with privatization. Reasons underlying this perspective arise from concerns about privatization, which include commercializing human need to generate financial resources and capital for providing services and programs, an emphasis on selecting clients who are financially remunerative and "dumping" poor clients who are not, and utilizing outcome measures that may place emphasis on the quantity of clients served versus the quality of services provided. Privatization is felt to reinforce the "two-tier" system of service provision in this country where those who can privately pay receive better care than those who cannot. The "dumping" of poor clients by the private sector service providers onto the public sector service providers is felt to unfairly tax these already stressed systems. Ultimately, opponents of privatization believe the reasons above only serve to further marginalize our most vulnerable members and reinforce the inherent inequities found in our society—antithetical to the mission and values of the human services. Human service workers struggle to provide services when the needs of their clients are immense and the resources our society allocates are relatively small. Privatization may be seen as one attempt to help those in need. However, human service workers need to think deeply about how privatization may challenge the fundamental notion that government is the primary way through which the welfare of our citizens—even the most needy and disenfranchised among us—should be cared for. It is only through this examination that the values of human service workers can help us to take what is efficient, yet humane, from privatization and use this to help the needy among us.

The Indelible Mark of Terrorism

The September 11, 2001, terrorist attacks on the United States had immense social, economic, emotional, and political implications not just in this country but around the world. On that one day about 3,000 people were murdered, leaving behind grieving family and friends, young children and infants; some born after this heinous event, never to meet their parent. The heroism of those who first responded, including firemen, policemen, and other emergency workers, have been both a source of pain and pride. In New York City, about 300 firemen died on September 11th, and it is estimated their actions contributed to at least 20,000 people being saved from death in the World Trade Center.

Prior to September 11th, Americans, for the most part, had been insulated from the impact of terrorist attacks in their homeland. Their experience lies in sharp contrast to the experiences of people in other regions of the world, such as the Middle East, where terrorist attacks have unfortunately long been a part of daily life. September 11th has left an indelible mark.

There have been a range of governmental responses in the United States to the events of the September 11th attacks. There has been the creation of the Department of Homeland Security and the passage of the USA Patriot Act in October 2001. This Act expands the authority of federal officials to track and intercept communications for foreign intelligence gathering purposes and creates new crimes and new penalties for terrorists. As this Act has come to be implemented, many have contended that some provisions go too far. We are left, as a nation, to ponder a central question: How do we safeguard civil liberties yet provide the government with the latitude it needs to obtain information vital for protecting our national security and interests? The article, Two Years On (see Box 1.1), was published in the *New York Times* at the second anniversary of September 11th. It explores the question above and also forces each one to ask: How do I define patriotism?

Summary

The human services do not exist in a vacuum. They are an intrinsic part of a vital, changing social system shaped by and shaping the day-to-day changes that make up history. To be a meaningful part of these changes, we need to know what is happening in our segment of the world in relation to all other segments. Only as they are aware of what is taking place, of its impact on themselves and the people with whom they work, will human service workers be able to play a constructive role as the changes and trends discussed above unfold. As well, they need to equip themselves personally and professionally to make the most of the changes that take place. Ultimately, this will affect the well-being of clients—the ultimate goal of human service workers.

The enthusiasm with which we have seized on the idea that science and technology can find a solution to all human concerns merits consideration, because today's solutions are often tomorrow's problems. Already we are concerned about some of the side effects of electronic devices in spite of the tremendous assets that they obviously represent. They can be destructive as well as constructive.

As we move into this new age, we need to keep in mind that unless we learn to get along with each other and to control our burgeoning population as well as our overuse of

Two Years On

Even as the twin towers were falling, we wondered what kind of world we would find ourselves living in in the future. The trauma of that day led us to expect an abrupt demarcation in our lives and in the life of the nation. How abrupt, how tragic it has been for many people cannot be overemphasized. But coming into this second anniversary, our response is more measured; there is a recognition that we are now living among the uncertain ripples thrown out by that collision of worlds. The purity of our first reactions has been eroded by time and by some of the uses that have begun to be made of 9/11.

Any two years in which America fought two wars would be memorable in their own right, the wars themselves capable of shunting our sense of other events to one side. The first war, in Afghanistan, rose right out of the ashes of the World Trade Center. Its logic, if not its conclusion, was clear. But the reasons for the second war seem muddier now than when the conflict began. For many, there seemed to be a connection between Saddam Hussein and the terrorists who crashed into the Pentagon and the Trade Center. That connection was encouraged by President Bush and his administration and taken on faith by much of the country. It is worth reminding ourselves, on this day particularly, that we come no closer to understanding the significance of 9/11, at home and abroad, if we use the memory of what happened that morning falsely and vainly.

It seemed as if two great tides emanated in response to the tragedy of that Tuesday. One was a sense of generosity, a deep compassion that expressed itself in immediate acts of cooperation and support. The other was a sense of patriotism, a strong consciousness of our American identity. When those two tides overlapped, as they often did in the months after 9/11, the result was impressive and profoundly moving. But we have also seen, in the past two years, a regrettable narrowing of our idea of patriotism. It has become, for some people in some ways, a more brittle expression of national sentiment—a blind statement of faith that does more to divide Americans from one another than to join them together.

We need to fear and temper that kind of rigidity. It is not the least bit unpatriotic to question some of the arguments that led to war in Iraq. No national purpose is served by losing our sense of political and historical discrimination in an upwelling of patriotic fervor. Much as it may seem logical that the horror of the morning of Sept. 11, 2001, is inextricably linked to the other terrorist horrors around the world, the fact is that the connections are not all clear. The final answers must be as the evidence—not political will—determines.

One of the hardest parts of living with 9/11 may be learning to understand the ways in which it was a local and particular, rather than universal, event. Watching a disaster of those proportions gradually become scaled to a broader historical context does not come easily to those of us who witnessed it in one form or another. But that is what history will do and what we must accept.

For two years, and for many more years to come, we have had a chance to watch how individuals, communities and institutions have absorbed the shock of 9/11. It has illuminated all of us, thrown us all into a peculiar relief. It has taught us important things about who we are, what our government is, and who our elected leaders are and what they make of us. Whether it is the debate over the war in Iraq or over the proper memorial for Lower Manhattan, the memory of 9/11 should provide us with a standard of judgment, of moral assessment, based on our own behavior and on that of others, that is not easily faulted or compromised. Those buildings did not fall or their occupants die to become symbols in an incoherent argument. That outpouring of strength and consideration was never meant to serve as the pretext for false conclusions. The day will slip away from us as time passes, but not the clarity of the actions we took together in response. The purest patriotism we have in us to express was expressed in the common generosity of that moment.

Source: Copyright © 2003 by The New York Times Co. Reprinted with permission.

finite natural resources, the answers of science and technology may well be unable to rescue us from the consequences of our own actions. The basic question for human service workers is, as always, how the changes in society affect people and how we deal with them.

Major trends, such as managed care, will continue to shape the role of the human service worker. The philosophical base and the values on which these trends rest will determine the social sanctions that are extended to human service. The fundamental trends in society will influence the policies and programs that are designed as well as the amount and kind of financial support provided. If these trends result in the adoption of values opposed to those on which human service is based, workers will need to be cognizant of this, be able to analyze their own positions in regard to it, and be ready to determine where and how they will stand and act. Clearly, workers must be vitally concerned with the ethical problems that arise out of the advance of knowledge and changing social conditions. Because human service workers are people, yet serve people, and these are people problems, they need to think about matters of concern such as:

- How should we deal with overpopulation?
- Is healthcare a right or a privilege?
- Should ours be a multilingual society?
- How do we contain the high costs of care yet provide high-quality services?
- How can we safeguard people's highly personal information yet not stifle the free flow of information in this age of electronic data transmission?
- Do people have the right to die in the manner they choose?
- What is happening to the vulnerable members of our society?
- What are the roles and responsibilities of human service workers as we face the threats of terrorism and bioterriorsm?

SUGGESTED ASSIGNMENTS

1. Arrange for students to interview those below about their experiences working in a managed care environment. Have students explore what is different about their jobs now versus before managed care, what they like and dislike about working in a managed care environment, what they think benefits and doesn't benefit both the workers and the patients; and how they feel cost containment has effected the quality of care in their setting:
   a. nurse
   b. doctor
   c. social worker and/or other mental health professional
   d. physical and/or occupational therapist
   e. hospital administrator

2. Arrange a classroom debate on the pros and cons of privatizing one or more of the major governmental welfare programs such as Social Security or the delivery of public welfare systems. Students shall document factual reasons for the stands they take, not merely express opinions.

3. Assign students in pairs to visit one of the social organizations designed to deal with one of the major current social problems to observe the setting, talk with workers and, as far as possible, the clients, and report back to class on what they found. Suggested sites are
   a. A nursing home
   b. A public health clinic or an emergency room in a hospital that serves indigent people
   c. A public housing project in a low-income area
   d. A public welfare office
   e. A public school suffering from major problems with violence
   f. A police department
   g. A hospice for AIDS patients
   h. A local government or nonprofit agency responsible for disaster planning

4. Have students read the USA Patriot Act of 2001 as well as recent opinions about the implementation of the Act. Have students debate which parts of the Act they feel conflict or are congruent with the National Association of Social Workers' Code of Ethics and/or other codes of ethics for other helping professionals.

5. Have students write a reaction paper to the article, Two Years On (see Box 1.1).

REFERENCES AND RELATED READINGS

Ameristat Population Reference Bureau and Social Science Data Analysis Network. (1998). Available online: http://www.ameristat.org

Clemetson, L. (2003, September 2). Census shows ranks of poor rose in 2002 by 1.3 million. *The New York Times,* pp. A1, A4.

Federal Bureau of Investigation Justice Information Series. (1997). *Uniform Crime Reports Hate Crime Statistics 1997.* Available online: http://www.fbi.gov/ucr/ucr.htm.

Harrington, M. (1963). *The other America: Poverty in the United States.* New York: Scribner.

————. *The New American poverty.* (1984). New York: Holt, Rinehart, and Winston.

Karger, H., & Levine, J. (1999). *The Internet and technology for the human services.* Boston: Addison-Wesley.

Karger, H., & Stoez, D. (2001). *American social welfare policy: A pluralist approach* (4th ed.). Boston: Allyn and Bacon.

Levine, J., (2000). Internet: A framework for ethical analysis in the human services. In J. Finn & G. Holden (Eds.), *Human services online: A new arena for service delivery* (pp. 173–192). Binghamton, NY: Haworth Press.

Linzer, N. (1999). *Resolving ethical dilemmas in social work practice.* Boston: Allyn and Bacon.

Malthus, T. (1999). *An essay on the principles of population.* Amherst, NY: Prometheus.

Moffett, G. D. (1994). *Cultural masses: A global population policy.* New York: Penguin Books.

Pipher, M. (1997). *The shelter of each other: Rebuilding our families.* New York: Ballantine Books.

Trattner, W. (1988). *From poor law to welfare state: A history of social welfare in America* (6th ed.). Chicago: Free Press.

United Nations. (1998). *Revision World Population Estimates and Projections.* www. undp.org/popin/ wdtrends/wdtrends.htm.

U.S. Committee for Refugees. (2000). *World Refugee Survey 2000.* Washington, DC: Immigration and Refugee Services of America.

U.S. Department of Commerce, Economics and Statistics Administration, Bureau of the Census. (1999). *Aging in the United States—past, present, and future.* Available online: www.census.gov.

Wallace, H., Green, G., Jaros, K., Paine, L., & Story, M. (1999). *Health and welfare for families in the 21st century.* Sudbury, MA: Jones and Barlett Publishers.

Wernet, S. (1999). *Managed care in the human services.* Chicago: Lyceum Books.

World Health Organization. (1998). *Report on the global HIV/AIDS epidemic—June 1998.* Online: http://www.who.itn/emc-hiv/global_report.

SELECTED RELATED WEBSITES

Civil Rights
http://www.civilrights.org

Federal Government Resources on the Web
http://www.lib.umich.edu/govdocs/federal.html.

Northern Lights Managed Care Information
http://www.nhionline.net/

September 11, 2001 Victims Memorial
http://www.september11victims.com/september11victims/

U.S. Committee on Refugees
http//www.refugees.org

U.S. Department of Homeland Security
http://www.dhs.gov/dhspublic/index.jsp

U.S. Department of Justice: Terrorist and Emergency Attack Information
http://www.usdojgov/ag/terrorismaftermath.html

U.S. Government and Grant Resources
http://psyche.uthect.edu/ous/Govt.html

The USA Patriot Act of 2001
http://www.findlaw.com

World HIV and AIDS Statistics
http://www.avert.org/worldstats.htm

Understanding Ourselves

Why is self-awareness a particularly important characteristic of human service workers? What personal qualities contribute to it, and how can they be developed?

How does the dichotomy within the four major value systems in the Western world regarding people and their society affect the practice of human service?

How does knowledge of the process and use of the skills of assertiveness contribute to the effectiveness of people who work with people?

How can conflict lead to growth and change?

Richard Leakey, the eminent paleontologist, tells the story of excavating the grave of a Neanderthal man who, by radiocarbon techniques, was dated as being more than 60,000 years old. Analysis of pollen around the body revealed that it had been laid on a bed of oak, pine, juniper, and ash branches with green reeds and blue and white flowers arranged around it.

Such loving care of an individual body reveals that even among primitive peoples, long thought to be concerned simply with survival, there were, in spite of hard and often brutal lives, ideas of the importance of self and the uniqueness of the person. As cultures advanced, as languages were recorded first in symbols and later in letters, the burning ethical question asked by philosophers, religious leaders, and thinkers of all ages, as well as by ordinary individuals, concerned this self in relation to other people and to the natural world in which we live.

What kind of creature am I? Where do I come from, and where do I go? How can I understand and control myself, my own behavior, my relationships with others, my life, and my future?

As cultures became complex, responsibility for such matters was relegated to religious leaders, and it became dangerous for the rank and file to question established ideas or even to read the books of a society. But the free mind cannot be denied, and in spite of threats of death, of being forced to recant, of personal destruction in many forms, the search for both questions and answers goes on, and knowledge about people and their world gradually accumulates.

Such development, exchange, and testing of ideas are of tremendous importance, particularly at this time in our history. We have reached heights of technological development that should enable us to provide a healthy, good life for all. We have attained sufficient self-awareness to realize that the major factor preventing us from approaching this ideal more closely is our lack of understanding of ourselves and a lack of motivation to develop a healthy interdependence based on such understanding. We stand at a crossroads, from which one direction can lead to a better life for all and one to the end of all life on the planet.

It is often difficult to see oneself realistically in relation to such global problems; it is equally difficult to know and to understand ourselves. This undertaking is one at which the best thinkers of all time have not been too successful, one at which we will spend our entire lives working. The paradox is that someone else, however knowledgeable, however well intentioned, cannot do this for us. Each must conduct this lifelong search, with help perhaps, but essentially alone. The first step is to provide ourselves with some ideas, some tools for thinking.

The Nature of Human Service

The unique factor in human service is that its delivery requires knowledgeable and disciplined use of the worker's self. Working with people is a transactional process in which there is inevitably both give and take between and among the people involved. The effectiveness of the best program can be minimized when the worker through whom it is channeled is unaware and cannot or will not deal with harmful aspects of self in relation to others or does not know how to capitalize on strengths.

A good example of the importance of this comes from research on the effect of the expectations of classroom teachers who believe that certain children are of less worth than others or cannot learn as well. When a teacher is handicapped by personal bias or a tendency to stereotype particular groups of students on the basis of race, creed, color, physical condition, social status, wealth, or poverty, his or her ability to teach and the students' capability to learn can be damaged. With more accepting teachers, such children may be able to learn, each according to his or her own innate capacity and to the opportunity provided.

People who aspire to use themselves effectively in a knowledgeable and disciplined manner in relationships with others must strive to develop a personal objectivity based on such qualities as:

- Awareness of self and personal needs, weaknesses, and strengths.
- Cognizance of and ability to deal with their own personality patterns, with the "garbage" from previous life experiences that cloud their ability to relate freely.
- Openness and freedom to perceive with clarity and relate with honesty—regardless of how different or similar others may be.
- Ability to perceive and evaluate values, attitudes, and patterns of behavior of the groups of which they consider themselves a part.
- Ability to differ and stand alone when necessary.

Learning to Know and to Use One's Self

There is an old definition of education, the origins of which are obscure, but which is nonetheless valid and applicable to the process of self-learning: "Education is the progression from freedom, through discipline, to greater freedom."

People are endowed with both the need and the capacity to relate meaningfully to others. There is little indication that this is not a free and open endowment with potential for development and effective use, provided the basic needs of the developing individual are met and inhibiting experiences are minimized. Unfortunately, few people develop under optimum conditions, and human service workers find themselves handicapped by how they meet their own needs as well as by ways of thinking, feeling, and behaving that are not conducive to the creation of effective open relationships with others.

To free themselves to better use their innate capacity to relate, workers often face an experience in reeducation. Initially, they must be not only capable of accepting their own imperfections, but also motivated and convinced that they can change. Few people are so smug or so rigidly defended that they have not, at times, questioned their own contribution to relationships. However, it is one thing to recognize one's shortcomings and another to change them. We are often impelled to respond to others in undesirable ways for reasons that lie buried beyond recall in the past. Workers who are successful in liberating themselves from these influences can begin to enjoy and utilize their full capacity for human interaction.

Attitudes and behaviors are learned in response to a need to react to particular circumstances. They tend to become internalized and invested with an emotional component that may have little relationship to their true significance. The progression moves somewhat like this:

1. Situation that demands a reaction from the individual.
2. Response on a trial-and-error basis or on the basis of precept.
3. Learning that a particular response is effective.
4. Development of feeling that this is the "right" response because it works in this situation.
5. Reinforcement of this "right" response by support of significant others.
6. Development of feeling that people who respond differently are "wrong."

This learning process begins at birth, and by the time children are ready for school, they have a pretty good idea of what is "right" and what is "wrong" for them.

Mary was only 5 years old that summer when she sat on the back steps and watched her neighbor pressing clothes out on the terrace. After regarding the woman soberly for a while, she commented, "My mother irons indoors." The neighbor explained that she liked being out of doors on a nice day, and Mary listened patiently. But when the neighbor finished, Mary repeated with emphasis and finality, "My mother irons indoors." For her, at 5, there was already a right and a wrong way, and the person who deviated from her pattern was automatically wrong.

The Impact of Culture

Cultures dictate patterns or ways of behaving in response to a specific situation, and these patterns are imparted to the child through the family, the school, the church, other social institutions, and the peer group. In this process, the reasons for selecting a particular way of behaving may be lost. The behavior becomes invested with an almost ritualistic and emotional significance—the accepted way for that particular culture. The person who deviates from this norm is usually punished in some way by becoming an outcast, being designated as "strange" or "different," becoming the subject of sanctions, or—in extreme cases—being killed. The form of the punishment is prescribed by the culture.

Cultures also define significant roles and set up expectations of the behaviors that accompany them. When these role definitions become rigid, they tend to be counterproductive, because both individuals and social groups are constantly in the process of change and adaptation to the differences that are part of life. For the young child, knowing what is expected can contribute markedly to feelings of security. However, if expectations are too rigid, it can also be inhibiting to growth and lock in the developing individual so that full use of potential for adaptation to change is impossible. We can see much rigidity operating in the sex-role definitions that have been so inhibiting to women's use of their potential for achievement; we see these roles operating in families where the accepted expectations for husband-wife and parent-child roles may be such that individuals cannot adapt to people whose expectations differ from theirs.

The Nguyen family had only recently come to the United States from Vietnam, but with the help of relatives they found a home and both parents got jobs. Although language was a difficulty, the teenage daughter made friends and got along well in school. However, her brother, Cang, age 14, gravitated to an already formed gang whose membership requirement was shoplifting. He was picked up quickly and referred to juvenile court. The worker preparing the case met strong resistance to even discussing the problem. Although obviously frightened, Mr. Nguyen felt the worker's presence to be an unnecessary intrusion on his role as head of the family.

The Impact of Personal Needs

Finally, attitudes and behavior develop in response to unconscious needs and drives for protection from pain, preservation of personal integrity, allowance for essential growth, and assistance in dealing with reality. Coping mechanisms—denial, projection, regression, fantasy, and so on—relate to their source of stimulus and may seem inappropriate to the observer. Selection of the particular mechanism used is strongly influenced by the culture and setting as, for example, a family that supports the use of humor to deal with painful feelings. People universally use these mechanisms, and they can be an effective part of the process of dealing with the demands of living. They can also be ineffective when used rigidly or unrealistically.

Beryl Chessman used denial and, to a certain extent, fantasy in reacting to her husband's physical abuse. Although this had been going on for many years, she not only denied the violence, but also took refuge in the fantasy that the behavior would improve. It was only when the abuse was extended to their 10-year-old daughter that she was able to overcome her fear, face the reality of her situation, and try to make use of help to end it.

Whatever the dynamics or origins of particular attitudes and behavior, human service workers must be aware of both their existence and the fact that one may not realize how deeply these attitudes can affect one's feelings toward oneself and one's behavior toward others.

We need to begin by accepting that what we are will affect what we can do and then striving to develop a self-awareness that will enable us to understand and, if possible, change attitudes and feelings and control our behavior in working relationships. Almost all of the human service professions provide some sort of education and training in awareness of self in relation to others, ranging from personal analysis to the encounter and sensitivity groups popular in the 1970s, 1980s, and 1990s. These groups are designed to sensitize people to themselves and their own feelings and actions and to increase awareness and understanding of others and of the impact on each other of the two persons involved in transactions. Short of these formalized efforts, however, there are some concrete steps that workers can take to help them to deal with themselves in what is, after all, a very personal struggle. They can ask themselves some very basic questions:

- How do I think and feel about myself?
- How do I deal with my own fundamental needs?
- What is my value system, and how does it define my behavior and my relationships with other people?
- How do I relate to the society in which I live and work?
- What is my lifestyle?
- What is my basic philosophy?
- What do I present—and represent—to those with whom I work?

How Do I Think and Feel about Myself?

Probably the most important factor about all individuals is how they feel about themselves. A person may be physically or intellectually handicapped or whole; old, young, or middle-aged; wealthy or poor; fat or thin; of any color or race. Whatever the case may be, if one likes oneself, one can usually succeed in life and relate well to other people. A variety of factors contribute to the development of one's self-image, but it is principally a matter of how one feels about oneself. Though extraordinary sensitivity to and acceptance of one's own strengths and needs may be a part of individual endowment, life experiences tend to determine people's attitudes toward themselves; within these experiences, the attitudes of other individuals and groups are of paramount importance.

During their development, it is important for children to be accepted as they are and not as people would like them to be. Unrealistic expectations can be destructive; realistic expectations are essential in promoting healthy growth. Early experiences that enable children to value and like themselves can form a firm foundation on which they can depend during subsequent crucial life stages, particularly adolescence and old age, when people tend to be most vulnerable to self-doubt.

A major value in modern society is success in athletics, but for every "winner" there are many "losers." The self-image of young children who are losers can be seriously damaged, particularly when parents buy into this situation. Such a child was Bobby, whose family valued participation and success in competitive sports highly. His physical coordination was not outstanding, and when pressure was exerted after a couple of failures in soccer, he tended to give up and began to overeat and to gain weight. His father's anger, his mother's scarcely concealed disappointment, and his brother's scorn left him feeling a failure and was reflected in his growing inability to relate to other children and in failure in his school work. Recognition of the right to be a unique individual is essential to healthy development.

Just like other facets of personality, self-acceptance is not static. It is a matter of degree and is subject to change according to circumstances and situations. Adolescence, with its questioning and search for identity, is often a period of intense discomfort and self- deprecation. The child who was at 10 fairly comfortable and happy-go-lucky may at 14 find herself at odds with parents who are having trouble accepting her growing up; she may feel concerned and unhappy about herself as a person in a society that seems to frown on her, her ideas, and her feelings.

In old age, the negative social impact is often equally strong, because many of the adaptive mechanisms of aging lack status in modern society. Certainly the tendency to slow down, to be more conservative, and to narrow one's circle socially, economically, and physically are contrary to the values of the lively ones in our fast-moving technological society. The impact of this impatience and disapproval may help to intensify the older person's feeling that he or she lacks worth and importance.

Thus the all-important ability to be comfortable with oneself is based on the following factors:

- The awareness of and ability to accept oneself as a fallible individual with strengths and weaknesses.
- The development of a flexible adaptive pattern that does not demand perfection of oneself and hence does not expect it of others.
- The capacity to recognize and deal with the impact of negative attitudes and behavior of significant individuals within the life experience, including social groups and the society as a whole.
- Acceptance of the fact that self-liking is not static or unchanging.

Self-acceptance and liking involve a continuous process of awareness, assessment, and flexibility.

How Do I Deal with My Own Fundamental Needs?

Certain fundamental human needs must be met if we are to survive; the way in which we meet them determines how healthy we are and how we develop and function as total persons. These needs can be considered in two overall categories: the need for security and the need to accommodate the drive toward growth. Each of these categories encompasses five subcategories of needs. A dynamic interrelationship exists in which each type of need is continuously affecting and being affected by the others, and there is no real and complete understanding of what is happening in one area without understanding what is happening in the others.

Emotional feelings are subjectively experienced and often difficult for the outside observer to give credence to. It is only within the past hundred years that we have even begun to understand the significance of the emotional part of an individual, particularly its effect on functioning in the other areas. Now we recognize the tremendous power of the emotions and are beginning to understand the part they play in determining the individual's ability to utilize other capacities.

The *physical,* or material, structures of the body and its organic processes are easier to study because of their manifest natures, but much is yet unknown, particularly about the way physical factors affect and are affected by other aspects of the individual.

The field of holistic health stresses the importance of focusing on health rather than illness, prevention rather than cure, good nutrition, and a wholesome life in its total aspect. Research in areas such as nutrition and behavior, exercise and well-being, and the impact of stress on the protective mechanisms of the body, as well as exciting findings in human genetic research are bringing new insights about the physical aspects of functioning and also the totality of good living.

The *intellectual* refers to the capacity for rational and intelligent thought, the power of knowing, and relates to the ability to develop, understand, and master knowledge and skill. One of the vital and as yet incompletely answered questions in this area is how people learn and how they can utilize this capacity to its maximum extent.

Social pertains to the need and capacity for relationships with other people. Survival of the newborn infant is impossible without an initial relationship with caring people. The capacity for relating meaningfully with others is a developing thing in a healthy person and, while subject always to individual variation, maturation brings expansion of the boundaries in which such relationships occur. The loner who is lacking in them is often a very disturbed person. The word "people," however, is a limiting one. We are more and more aware that we must also exist in a state of ecological balance with other vital elements in nature. The attitudes and feelings that arise out of respect for self and other people also involve regard for the integrity of nonhuman forms of life.

Spiritual pertains to the animating or vital principle that gives life to physical organisms. As such, the origin, function, and expression of spiritual needs are not totally understood. It is obvious that people are more than a conglomerate of physical, social, intellectual, and emotional needs and drives and that there is a spiritual component of each of these areas. Over the centuries, organized religion has attempted to provide a medium for expressing these spiritual needs, but unfortunately, particularly in its sectarian aspects, it has tended to compartmentalize rather than unify. To ignore or deny spiritual needs because we do not completely understand them is to deny the totality of the individual.

The Basic Human Needs.   Security, the first category of basic human needs (Figure 2.1) runs the gamut from the material needs to sustain life—food, clothing, and shelter—to less concrete needs for loving and being loved, for meaningful association with others, for a milieu that provides acceptance of ideas and feelings regardless of whether they conform to the cultural norms, and for reward for risk. Healthy security provides the firm floor on which individuals can stand with confidence and assurance as they grow. They can depend on this essential base and can move from it to try new ways; they can return to it when faced with failure, to regroup and start again. This can be simply illustrated by observing children who are learning to walk—they pull themselves up, try, fall, weep with frustration over failure, try again, and eventually totter a few steps for the first time. How much simpler this task if the child has a solid surface on which to experiment, together with encouraging, supporting parents to provide a focus for these efforts. How much more difficult if the floor is slick or unsteady, or the parents hostile, indifferent, or over-protective.

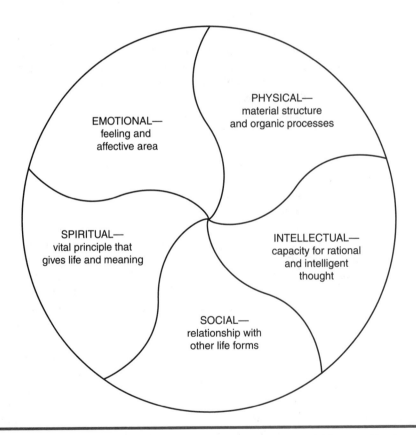

FIGURE 2.1   The development of the individual rests upon fulfillment of basic needs.

Growth is a continuous and essential concomitant of the life process. All individuals are endowed at conception with a maximum potential for growing and developing in every area of self and, throughout their lifetimes, mature toward the point that is their maximum capacity. Because genetic endowments and maximum potentials differ greatly from individual to individual, the idea of equality has caused some problems. For our purpose here, equality lies simply in the fact that each of us possesses the drive to grow. To illustrate this concept in its most apparent form, one individual may possess much greater potential than another for developing physical dexterity. Though capacity for development in all areas may not be at equal levels, there is some evidence that the exceptionally well-functioning person tends to operate well as a total individual. Normally, however, individuals develop one area to its highest peak—perhaps at the expense of the others.

In a sense, one's potential lies dormant until it is stimulated by the interaction of internal impulses for normal growth and development with external experiences that are taking place in the environment. We must remember that environment begins at conception and that what happens to the developing infant within the mother's body has a major impact on present and future development.

People require stimulation to trigger development in all life areas, but it must be in a good balance, determined by their needs at a particular time. Overstimulation, which is so often present in young families attempting to move upward on the economic and social scale, can be as inhibiting as understimulation can be stultifying. Timing is of great importance. There is some evidence, for example, that the child who is not stimulated during the time when early coordination is developing to use muscles and nerves in even so simple a task as catching a ball will be unable, even with subsequent exercise, to achieve the peak potential for physical development. Growth and development take place in accordance with an internal timetable that follows a general pattern but is unique to the individual.

There are many roadblocks in this process of developing potential, and the relationship between security and growth in any individual is seldom completely understood. Occasionally, we see someone who flowers in conditions of adversity that are totally destructive to others, but such a person is the exception. The sad statistics on mental retardation in our enlightened society lend credence to this statement. Nine percent of all children in the United States are considered retarded, but only 5 percent are born that way—the others achieve this state by age 13 as a result of their life experience. Three-fourths of these children come from poverty areas.

In general, we could say that in the physical area we need a basic minimum of material supplies, stimulation, opportunity for physical development at crucial points in the developmental timetable, and basic health services that are one of the benefits of our modern society. In the area of intellectual development, we need stimulation and the opportunity to acquire and master knowledge, each according to his or her own capacity. In the area of emotional development, we need fulfilling relationships with significant other people and the ability to accept and be at peace with ourselves. In the area of social growth, we need the opportunity to become socialized on an increasingly wider scale with an expanding capacity to relate meaningfully and effectively with people who are different from ourselves. In the area of spiritual development, we need the stimulation and opportunity to find a meaning in life that transcends the mere satisfaction of needs and gives purpose and direction to the total experience.

In summary, we can say that in looking at ourselves, our own basic needs, and the ways in which we meet them, workers in the human services must keep in mind the following factors:

- Everyone has a need for security and dependency.
- Everyone also has a need for growth and independence.
- Everyone is a unique individual and has a unique potential for development in each of the living areas.
- The varying aspects of an individual's potential exist in a dynamic interrelationship that constitutes the whole, and no one aspect can be considered as separate from the others.

Workers who are aware of the existence of these needs within themselves can then look at ways in which to meet them—for meet them they must. The drive for growth and expression will not be denied, and if it cannot be channeled in a positive and healthy direction, it will take an undesirable course. One's purpose in considering one's own needs is to avoid utilizing working relationships to meet those needs rather than those of the clients. While helping relationships can be a source of personal satisfaction that is normal and useful, human service workers whose personal lives do not fulfill their own needs may find themselves manipulating those with whom they are working, making them overly dependent, using them to satisfy needs for power, prestige, or self-fulfillment. This does not mean that workers get no satisfaction from their successes, no pleasure—and frustration!—from their working relationships. Rather, it means that the satisfaction derives from the client's freedom to develop and be successful as a person apart from the worker.

What Is My Value System, and How Does It Define My Behavior and My Relationships with Other People?

Cultural groups tend to establish certain values and standards of behavior as significant and binding for their members. These values and standards are internalized and emotion laden, and they have become so much a part of one's attitudes, feelings, thinking, and behaving that one is often unaware of their existence. Effective workers must learn to avoid judging their clients' attitudes and behaviors according to their own personal value system.

In Western society, dominant philosophical values regarding people and society can be traced to four different sources:

1. *Judeo-Christian doctrine,* with its concept of the integral worth of the individual and one's responsibility for one's neighbor.
2. *Democratic ideals,* which emphasize the equality of all and the right to "life, liberty, and the pursuit of happiness."
3. *The Puritan ethic,* which says that character is all, circumstance nothing, that the moral person is the one who works and is independent, and that pleasure is sinful.
4. *The tenets of social Darwinism,* which emphasizes that the fittest survive and the weak perish in a natural evolutionary process that produces the strong individual and society.

Even the casual reader will see that a dichotomy exists within this value system. We hold that people are equal, but that those who do not work are less equal. In his novel, *Animal Farm,* George Orwell says sardonically, "All animals are created equal, but some are more equal than others," and certainly this applies here. We hold that the individual life has worth, but that only the fit should survive. We believe that we are responsible for each other, but that those who depend on others for their living are of lesser worth.

This dichotomy affects both workers and clients in their attitudes about themselves and each other and in their capacity to relate. We see physicians struggling to retain life while stating that both the individual and the society would be better off if the patient were dead. We see workers in public assistance programs administering financial aid to needy people with the grim conviction that their clients should not be supported if they cannot sustain themselves. We see legislators drafting legislation and voting funds to be used for programs to sustain the lives and serve the needs of people whom they are convinced are undeserving. We see teachers working with children whom they feel are unteachable. This dichotomy is particularly significant in helping relationships because, of necessity, there exist elements of dependence and independence, implications of superiority and inferiority, a need to give and a need to receive. Recognition and reconciliation of this value conflict is one of the primary personal tasks of the worker.

While the four value sources listed previously constitute the major origins of values in our society, there are other significant sources. The development of this country from rural to urban (which has taken place with almost unbelievable swiftness within the past fifty years), along with the corresponding moves from agriculture to industrialization to computerized technology, has resulted in changes in the basic institutions and structure of society. Old values and standards are questioned and discarded; new ones are not yet fully defined. For example, at the end of the Russian Revolution, group daycare centers were established for children of working mothers, contrary to the cultural pattern of U.S. society, which dictated that mothers should remain in the home and care for their children.

Today, eighty years later, daycare is booming in the United States. Mothers seek employment outside the home in increasing numbers, as economic and social pressures force them to leave their children and go to work with curtailed consideration of whether this is the best solution in the individual situation.

An even greater, more significant, and more widespread social change is taking place that will have a major impact on our definition of the value of the individual—the growing scarcity of resources. Food and energy are increasingly in demand with an expanded population and, we realize fully for perhaps the first time, are finite. The world's wealth is unevenly divided, and those possessing the larger part of it are unwilling to share. Already we see evidence of the impact of scarcity in discussions concerning who shall be kept alive, our ability to afford to keep a Social Security system in this country, and who shall be accorded expensive medical procedures.

To complicate matters still further, there is no uniform pattern of values throughout the country, although developments such as mass production of clothing, books, movies, and so on tend to push toward such conformity. A value that is generally accepted and lived by in the urban ghetto may be completely intolerable in the neighboring suburbs or in the isolated, rural communities of the West and South. Differences in race, religion, education, economic standards, and the definition of necessities for survival all work toward the development of differences in values and behavioral norms.

Recently, concern over social conditions and crime has resulted in renewed efforts to define common values that can govern behavior that will contribute to a more stable society, but this is no easy task. Behaviors about which greatest concern is voiced have to do with work, irresponsible sexual behavior, lack of respect for differences among people, and violence as a means of gaining ends or relating to each other. But different people define the values in these areas differently for many reasons, and change will not come easily.

People who help, in general, are of middle-class origin. Although in recent years people from all walks of life have been encouraged to enter human services work, studies indicate that most of these jobs are still filled from the middle class. This situation has given rise to the frequently heard accusation that workers tend to impose their own middle-class values on their clients, values generally related to cleanliness, conformity, hard work, and sexual behavior.

Part of the responsibility of workers is to help their clients to be effective in the society in which they must live. This calls for a certain degree of adaptation to the dominant value system, even while possibly working to change it.

Sometimes, in order to survive, those whose values run contrary to those of the larger society need to adopt a different way of living. The effective worker, however, cannot force or impose these changes. Society imposes the need for them—the worker's role is to help the client assess the nature of this imposition and decide how to adapt to it in a way that is not self-destructive.

A simple example of this is the value that our entire industrial system characteristically attaches to time, punctuality, and regular, consistent effort. When concerted effort is made to include people from the hard-core poverty culture as employees, it is often necessary to make special provisions for getting them to work regularly and on time. Anglos often complain of the lack of time sense in African Americans, Hispanic Americans, and Native Americans, without recognizing the differing cultures and value systems within these minority groups.

The worker must have sufficient self-awareness to be able to differentiate between value changes that are essential for good social functioning, those that are dictated by a personal value system, and those that are so internalized that the individual is often unconscious of the reasons for adopting and using them as a basis for judging effectiveness of behavior. We see, for instance, the worker who believes that drinking is wrong saying of the man who stops for a beer on the way home from work, "He drinks!" Old social agency records are filled with notations of home visits in the morning where the mother is "still in her nightgown with the breakfast dishes unwashed, is drinking coffee, smoking, and watching television"—ergo, she is sloppy, dirty, and a poor mother.

Thus, effective workers must:

- Be aware that they are a walking system of values that is so much a part of them that they are scarcely aware of its existence even though they have considerable feelings about the rightness of it.
- Use all means possible to become conscious of what their biases are. One of the most useful tools in this struggle is becoming sensitive to one's use of the paranoid "they." "They" always wear bright colors and talk too loudly; "they" do not mow their lawns;

"they" do not support their families; "they" cheat on their income tax; "they" get pregnant out of wedlock—and so on, ad infinitum. Workers who are aware of doing this have taken the first step toward overcoming their biases when they recognize their own "theys."

- Strive to evaluate themselves and their values objectively and rationally, look at the origins of their values and the purpose they serve, and try to think about whether they will also serve this purpose for others.

- Strive to change those values that, on the basis of this evaluation, need changing; try to differentiate between those that dictate personal style of living and those that leave clients "free to step to the tune of a different drummer," if such meets their needs and is not destructive.

How do workers accomplish these objectives? If they are comfortable with themselves and have sound, healthy resources for meeting their own basic needs, they will probably not find it too difficult to respect other people's differences. They might begin by getting their own houses in order. They might try to create and live within a climate of openness and honesty where questions and differences are not only tolerated but are an integral part of the richness of life. They might begin to know and appreciate, through literature, art, music, and personal experience, as many different kinds of people as possible and to understand and value the various approaches to life among them.

In *Understanding Human Values,* Milton Rokeach (1979) proposes two classes of human values: terminal (those related to desired end states) and instrumental (those related to desired ways of reaching desired end states). He postulates that there are a limited number of basic values, and he reports a study that tends to substantiate the theory that people can and do change values as they perceive the dichotomy between what they profess and what they do in terms of implementing values. The importance of this kind of knowledge for human service workers is great, for both their own personal equipment and the kind of personal and social changes they are attempting to implement. The role of values in human functioning is paramount.

Whitney Young, one of the great African American leaders of the twentieth century, commented that children who grow up without knowledge of and ability to relate to and work with people different from themselves are handicapped. Many of us grow up bearing this handicap, but it does not necessarily mean that we must carry it with us throughout our lives.

There is no substitute for personal contact in learning to relate to people who are different from yourself—as all people are to a certain extent. Such opportunity should be available to all children and young adults, who are usually more open to differences and not yet handicapped by preconceived ideas or by conscious and unconscious biases and fears. However, older people can also learn to see others differently.

Margaret, a 60-year-old social worker, tells the story of attending a Quaker meeting where a young man identified himself as a practicing homosexual and asked for support for a newly formed gay group. Margaret had been troubled for some time about her own feelings about the gay people who came to her groups. The product of an orthodox religious background and a fairly conservative midwestern family, she had never known a person who was openly homosexual on a personal basis, and she was uncomfortable being with gays.

She liked the openness of the speaker and at the end of the meeting talked with him. She wondered how he might feel about her and on impulse asked how he felt about women. He laughed and put an arm around her shoulders and said, "Would you have me abandon half the human race?" In being comfortable with him, she was able to begin to look at her fears and her stereotypes and to more comfortably relate to gay people she knew, from the young men and women who flaunted their differences to the troubled middle-aged person with a spouse and children just becoming aware of self.

How Do I Relate to the Society in Which I Live and Work?

Human service workers, like all other people, hold membership not only in diverse small groups, but also in the larger society. Group participation and social relationships have a profound influence not only on the way we see ourselves as individuals, but also on how we see ourselves in relationship with other people. Workers must be conscious of the positions they occupy in society and in the groups of which they are members. What roles do they fill, and what statuses do these roles carry? With what particular subgroups do they identify? How do they relate to the power structure within the group and the society? How do they relate to people in general at levels different from their own? Do they relate as effectively to people who are higher on the scale as to those who are lower?

Society tends to relegate individuals to certain positions, to exert pressure for conformity, and to punish members who deviate from group standards and norms. How do workers—whose task is essentially to act as a change agent when social pressures become destructive to people—deal with these pressures in their own lives? Can they, if necessary, tolerate and deal with social disapproval in order to attain important objectives?

What Is My Lifestyle?

In the process of living, each of us develops his or her own style, tempo and rhythm, way of thinking, feeling, and behaving, set of personal values, and sense of personal identity—in other words, own way of life. Individual differences set us apart from each other and create a gap that must be bridged. In part these differences arise from the fact that every person is endowed with a developmental pattern and a biological rhythm that is unique. And in part they are the result of those life experiences that establish certain ways of behaving and reacting.

Not only does the worker react to each client's unique totality, but clients also react to it in the worker. The incompatibility between worker and client that can result from this uniqueness derives from two sources: the difficulty we have in understanding and accepting people who are different from ourselves, and the transference of attitudes and feelings from previous experiences with persons who have displayed similar personality patterns. The person who brings to a helping relationship memory of a happy experience with a blunt, outspoken, dominating, but warm and loving parent may have no difficulty in relating to another person with similar personality patterns, whereas someone else might shrink from such assertiveness and never perceive the worker's underlying warmth. Similarly, one helping person might have trouble working with a questioning, querulous, complaining old lady if his or her childhood had been scarred by such a grandmother. Another with a similar background may have carried over the memory of ways of relating to such a person that would help in the new relationship. The worker must be aware of both the assets and the liabilities that arise from personality and from prior experience, and he or she must learn to assess their effects on other people.

Human service workers must also learn to assess the impact of their personal lifestyle on others and weigh its importance against that of the objectives they wish to achieve. Workers must develop a way of living that leaves them free to avail themselves to others. Sometimes it will be necessary to modify lifestyle in order to simply survive. Many long-accepted standards in areas of life to which deep emotions are attached, such as sex, the family, religion, and even personal appearance, are being challenged. Workers who opt to be personally in the forefront of these movements for change will need to consider the possible impact on their professional effectiveness. In an isolated community, workers who flout accepted patterns of living will probably be unable to function.

What Are My Feelings about Conflict?   Conflicts are an inevitable part of life—personally, professionally, nationally, globally. This is especially true in the human services, where conflicts are normative by-products of helping people with problems and working to create change on personal, societal, and political levels.

Yet, a major problem for many workers is their inability to disagree, to present differing points of view, to refuse a request, to discuss an emotionally loaded issue, or to say "no" in ways that are constructive. In part this arises from early training in the home, the school, and the church, which may emphasize not discussing painful issues, not questioning points of view or authority, or not confronting differences honestly and openly. Because of these feelings workers may handle loaded situations with evasion, with attack, or with false passivity. However, as discussed earlier, conflict is a normative occurrence. It is therefore crucial for workers to honestly ask themselves: "Am I comfortable with conflict? Do I know how to handle conflict in constructive ways that can lead to change and growth?"

Because of their involvement with conflict, human service workers often take on a mediator's role, which facilitates reconciliation, settlement, compromise, or understanding among two or more conflicting parties. Mediation is a problem-based process that focuses on problem solving—not behavior or personality issues. Personal changes are a secondary outcome of agreement seeking (Fisher & Ury, 1991).

A suggested framework for mediation interventions by human service workers is as follows (Parsons, Jorginsen, & Hernandez, 1998):

- Separate the people from the problems.
- Focus on interests instead of positions.
- Create options that satisfy interests of the participants.
- Select criteria for choosing alternatives.

Mediation is seen as helping clients make use of available resources and influencing organizations to provide responsive services. Mediation is empowering for clients because they are encouraged to use available adaptive and coping resources of their social and physical environments. Mediation is also empowering because agreements are voluntary and reached by the conflicting parties through consensus (Cloke, 1994).

Negotiating Conflicts across Cultural Boundaries.   Given our multicultural society, human service workers also need to increase their awareness about the role of cultural differences in how conflict is perceived and handled. Successfully negotiating conflicts with people of diverse backgrounds starts with an honest appraisal by the worker of any prejudices or misinformation he or she might have about other cultures.

Geert Hofsteade, a Dutch sociologist, has developed a theory called individualism–collectivism, which helps illuminate the role of cultural differences in social behaviors such as conflict (Hofsteade, 2000). This theory states that some cultures are strongly individualist and others are strongly collectivist. Individualist cultures, found in most northern and western regions of Europe and North America, are those where individuals place their goals ahead of the goals of any group of people with which they may be associated. Collectivism can be characterized as individual people holding their goals as secondary to those of a group of people to which they belong. Cultures in which a collectivist orientation predominates are found in Asia, South America, and the Pacific (Ady, 1998).

When thinking about conflict resolution and culture, it is critical to understand whether the conflicting parties' cultures have an individualist or collectivist orientation. This will greatly impact how the conflict is expressed and what type of resolution will be acceptable. For example, a person from an individualist culture who is extremely unhappy in her marriage finds divorce to be an acceptable solution because this best meets this person's individual needs. Conversely, a person from a collectivist culture may never get divorced—even if living in a strife-ridden marriage—because he believes keeping the family together is more important than his individual happiness.

Assertiveness Training.   Assertiveness training is another tool workers can use to develop the ability to deal with conflict and constructively express their points of view. Its thesis is that individuals have a right to be different, to express and defend different ideas and points of view, and that they have the right to be heard.

In assertiveness training, differentiation is made among these three traits:

1. *Nonassertiveness,* in which people deny the right to be assertive and do not express their own thinking and feelings, which contributes nothing to enhancing the situation and can destroy self-confidence and self-respect.
2. *Assertiveness,* in which people express their feelings and thinking in ways that show respect for the right to personal worth and to equal self-expression for those with whom they are interacting; this can be constructive to both participants.
3. *Aggressiveness,* in which people exercise their right to express their own feelings and thinking, but in a way that attacks those with whom they are interacting; this mobilizes aggression in others.

A young couple comes to the door, introduces themselves as members of a religious sect, asks to leave literature, and solicits contributions. The householder, who does not support the group and thinks their beliefs are contrary to the beliefs of a free society, might respond:

1. Nonassertive: "Oh, all right, I'll take the literature and here's a dollar."
2. Assertive: "I don't agree with the aims of your movement and don't want to support it in any way, but I'd be glad to explain my reasons for this stand if you wish."

3. Aggressive: "You people have got a nerve coming around here knocking on people's doors with that trashy literature. I've got my own church."

Because assertiveness does not attack others and does express respect for their right, too, to be different, it does not mobilize hostility but creates an open climate in which differences can be discussed and compromises reached.

What Is My Basic Philosophy?

The nature of the human service worker's beliefs about life, the individual, society, and their interrelationships forms a vital part of the capacity to work effectively with people. It provides the rationale and motivating force for the worker's efforts and gives the worker a personal significance—what we believe strongly we tend to try to put into practice. Figure 2.2 shows a sample "Bill of Rights."

A Bill of Rights

1. You have the right to refuse requests from others without feeling selfish or guilty.
2. You have the right to feel and express anger and other emotions.
3. You have the right to feel healthy competitiveness.
4. You have the right to use your judgment in deciding your own needs.
5. You have the right to make mistakes.
6. You have the right to have your opinions and ideas given the same respect and considerations others have.
7. You have the right to ask for consideration, help, and/or affection from others.
8. You have the right to be treated as an adult.
9. You have the right to tell others what your needs are.
10. You have the right on some occasions to make demands on others.
11. You have the right to ask others to change their behavior.
12. You have the right to be treated as a capable adult and not be patronized.
13. You have the right to not automatically be assumed wrong.
14. You have the right to take time to sort out your reactions—to use your time space rather than others' time space.
15. You have the right not to have others impose their values on you.

FIGURE 2.2 A Bill of Rights (based on material taken from a workshop on assertiveness training by Patricia Jakubowski-Spector, July 1974, University of Maryland). There are almost as many bills of rights as there are people working in this area, each with its own particular emphasis. All emphasize the right of the individual to be oneself, to be different, to self-expression, to respect and consideration. Most of them emphasize an equally basic essential, the responsibility to extend the same rights to others. This old bill covers these fundamentals and is still relevant today.

The overall philosophical base of the human services lies in these beliefs:

- The individual is a social animal.
- The individual exists in interrelationship with other people and with all other life forms. This relationship may be defined as one of mutual rights and responsibilities.
- The welfare of the individual and of the group cannot be considered apart from each other.
- Each person and all living things possess intrinsic worth.
- Each person and all living things are characterized by a need to grow and develop toward the realization of a unique potential.
- The individual and the society can be understood.
- The individual and the society possess the capacity for change as a part of their intrinsic natures.

Workers who are committed to this philosophical base with a personal conviction that is both ethically and pragmatically sound will not only be motivated to search for ways to make it operational, but will also get maximum satisfaction from their efforts and in so doing greatly increase their capacity to achieve.

The personality of the worker in human services is probably the single most significant factor in determining effectiveness in dealing with other people. Workers who can feel genuine warmth and concern for others and therefore can empathize with them, who are honest, open, and loving, who can face the reality of living comfortably, and who are at peace with themselves will tend to be effective in enabling people to use the strengths they possess for living well.

What Do I Present—and Represent—to Those with Whom I Work?

We must not only know ourselves; we also need to know what we present to others with whom we work. We must be aware that we may be perceived differently from the way we are in reality. This has particular significance in initial contacts, but it must also be kept in mind in ongoing work with clients. We are constantly giving verbal and nonverbal cues to what we are and what we represent, and these cues may be misread. We need to be sensitive to the reactions of others and get feedback from them as to what is getting across. Essentially, we present ourselves initially as a set of latent characteristics (such as a particular race, age, sex, and appearance) to which people will often react, unfortunately, on the basis of preconceived attitudes.

We give hints by our behavior as to the all-important self-image we carry with us, and we set ourselves up for reactions from others by communicating our self-image to them—people react by attacking when we communicate helplessness; they resent us when we communicate indifference, lack of sensitivity, or actual hostility; we are treated contemptuously when we communicate inefficiency or dishonesty.

The values and attitudes we present embody what we think is important: for example, respect or lack of respect for other people and their ideas, commitment to implementing change or retaining the status quo, and so forth. We are often judged by the reference groups—social, religious, and fraternal—with which we are identified, each of which exposes certain values.

Finally, we present ourselves as representatives of a professional or work group. All professions and many occupations have codes of ethics to serve as guidelines in working situations both with clients and with colleagues. When such codes are flouted, as by the worker who makes sexual advances to a client or uses racial slurs, the members of the entire group will be judged thereby. When a profession is perceived as punitive or self-serving, its representatives are perceived in the same way.

We need first to be sensitive to and aware of what we present and represent to others in our working situations; we need to be able to evaluate these qualities realistically in terms of their validity and importance; we need, as far as is possible, to correct the misconceptions and establish ourselves as we are. This can be accomplished much more effectively by deeds than by words, although each has its place.

No longer able to continue her part-time work, Rachel Ullman applied for funds to supplement her income, although she hated "going on welfare." After a visit from a student worker, she called the supervisor and complained about his "sending a worker dressed in mink and driving a Cadillac."

The coat "never was very good rabbit," and the Cadillac was a used car, as "my husband thinks they are the best buy." When the worker discussed this undefensively with her client, it opened the door for needed expression of feelings by this independent woman about her increasing dependency and her having to ask for help.

Summary

Self-understanding can never be complete, but in human service work, where we are making use of ourselves in helping relationships with others, we need to strive for as much clarity and honesty with ourselves—and with others—as possible. We need to become sensitive to personal patterns of thinking, feeling, and behaving that hamper our ability to work effectively with others. While outsiders can help to change such patterns, basic responsibility for dealing with them rests with the individual worker.

SUGGESTED ASSIGNMENTS

1. Divide students into four groups and assign to each one of the listed values that constitute the philosophical base of human service:
   a. The worth of the individual
   b. The right of self-determination
   c. The right to share the benefits of society
   d. The mutual rights/responsibility relationship of people and their society

Each group will designate a reporter and spend 15 minutes or so discussing the meaning and significance of this value. The reporter will then summarize the group's findings and questions for discussion with the class.

2. Assign a culture paper in which students examine their personal attitudes and values with regard to deviance from generally accepted social norms—about such things as divorce, child abuse, dependency, crime, homosexuality, house husbands, and so forth. Try to relate them to students' abilities or inabilities to relate to people with different attitudes and lifestyles.

3. Assign pairs of students to role-play critical situations from their own experiences where assertiveness, nonassertiveness, or aggressiveness were involved. Have students change roles. The class will observe and critique.

4. Have the instructor go around to each student in the class and ask him or her to share the first word that comes to mind when hearing the word "conflict." The instructor writes these words on the blackboard as the students speak. After all the students have shared their word associations, the instructor facilitates a discussion about them; that is, how many of the words had positive connotations, how many have negative connotations, what are the students' thoughts about how conflict can lead to change and growth, and so on.

5. Have students interview people from the same and different culture groups regarding how they would handle conflict at work and in their personal lives. Relate these different approaches to the theory of individualism–collectivism.

REFERENCES AND RELATED READINGS

Ady, J. (1998). Negotiating across cultural boundaries. In T. Singelis (Ed.), *Teaching about culture, ethnicity, and diversity*. Thousand Oaks, CA: Sage Publications.

Anderson, R. E., & Carter, I. (1990). *Human behavior in the social environment*. New York: Aldine.

Bearley, A., & Bearley, M. (1995). *Managing assertively* (2nd ed.). San Francisco: John Wiley and Sons.

Cloke, K. (1994). *Mediation: Revenge and the magic of forgiveness*. Santa Clara, CA: Center for Dispute Resolution.

Fisher, R., & Ury, W. (1991). *Getting to yes: Negotiating agreement without giving in*. New York: Penguin Books.

Hofsteade, G. (2000). *Culture's consequences*. Thousand Oaks, CA: Sage Publications.

Joward, S., & Landsman, T. (1990). *Healthy personality: An approach from the viewpoint of humanistic psychology* (4th ed.). New York: Macmillan.

Leakey, R. (1993). *Origins reconsidered: In search of what makes us human*. UK: Time Warner Books.

Maslow, A. (1993). *The farther reaches of human nature*. New York: Viking.

Parsons, R., Jorginsen, J., & Hernandez, S. (1998). *The integration of social work practice.* Belmont, CA: Wadsworth Pub.

Reamer, F. (1995). *Social work values and ethics.* New York: Columbia University Press.

Rokeach, M. (1979). *Understanding human values.* New York: Macmillan.

Rogers, C. (1995). *On becoming a person.* Boston: Houghton Mifflin.

SELECTED RELATED WEBSITES

Conflict Research Consortium—Providing a Comprehensive Gateway to Information on More Constructive Approaches to Difficult Conflicts
http://www.colorado.edu/conflicts/

Institute of Conflict Resolution, Cornell University School of Industrial and Labor Relations
http://www.ilr.cornell.edu/depts/ICR/

U.S. Institute for Peace
http://www.usip.org/library.html

Washington State University Web Page on World Cultures
http://www.wsu.edu:8080/~dee/

Understanding the Human Condition

What are the differing basic assumptions on which the range of personality theories rest?

How has the women's liberation movement influenced approaches to understanding the psychological development of girls and women?

What are the major attributes that constitute socialization and from where are they derived?

What are the characteristics of social roles and what is their function in social groups?

What are the life stages and the tasks that accompany each?

There are almost as many theories of personality development as there are theorists who think about the nature of people and the human condition. These theories are tools that can be used to think about and understand people. Human service workers are best served by an eclectic approach to theory, enabling them to integrate ideas from many thinkers.

It is generally agreed that personality theories are also theories of behavior—personality is the individual system that determines for each of us our adjustment to the environment; behavior is the way in which this system manifests itself. There are eight basic assumptions on which personality theories rest:

1. People are knowable, behavior is natural, and the mind enables us to know ourselves and our world.
2. Cause-and-effect relationships exist; nothing in nature is happenstance.
3. Causation is multiple; many causes operate simultaneously.
4. Some causes are internal, and some are external; there is a constant interplay between the internal world and the external world to produce life functioning.
5. Causes are both fundamental and precipitating; the former are basic and ongoing, and the latter give rise to immediate interaction.

6. Purposes and motivations enter into behavior; these may be conscious, preconscious, or unconscious, and they may agree or be in conflict.
7. Behavior is affected by the context of the total situation as well as by the immediate circumstance.
8. Reality is always richer and more accurate than our mental picture of it; it is infinite in its detail and impossible to know in totality.

There are two major facts on which modern personality theories agree: Life is a dynamic process, and people develop by adaptation to the changing demands of both their own inherent potential and the environment in which they live. Viewed from this frame of reference, change is a categorical imperative, and once human service workers have accepted this, they will utilize the particular theories that will help to bring about specific desired changes.

What is the nature of an individual? Workers can find a very useful yardstick for measurement in the statement credited to the anthropologist Clyde Kluckhorn, who sees the individual as a totality of three different sets of characteristics: (1) those shared with all other people; (2) those shared with some other people; (3) those shared with no one else (Figure 3.1).

The Biological Heritage

Our biological heritage is the result of millennia of evolution and comprises those characteristics that we hold in common with all members of our own species, regardless of race, color, or various social and cultural patterns such as nationality or religion. Change in these characteristics comes through an evolutionary process once thought to be long, slow, and continuous. Presently, however, there is a generally accepted theory designated as *punctuated equilibrium,* which says that some changes in life forms can come relatively quickly

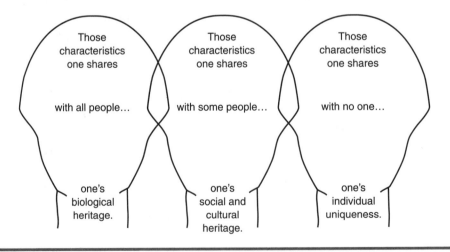

FIGURE 3.1　The three faces of the individual.

in response to changing events in the environment. Human biological entities possess certain needs that are common to all—the need to be nurtured and to have their basic physical needs met, to grow, to express their aggressive impulses, to realize the potential with which they are endowed, and to have meaningful relationships with others of their own kind. Biological existence is based on certain natural laws, disregard for which may lead to physical illness or destruction of the individual body and ultimately of the species. An ever-present example of such disregard is our current ecological dilemma, which we have created through our inability to perceive and to accept the interrelationship of all life forms. By upsetting delicate balances among them and disregarding the existence of nonhuman forms of life, we have succeeded in creating an environment increasingly hostile to our own continued existence.

Once conception has taken place, the genetic endowment of the individual is set and the heritage of constitutional strengths and weaknesses determined. From this point on, environment, both in utero and out, will be the decisive factor in how these strengths and weaknesses are developed and used. At present there is considerable and often controversial research going on in biology laboratories where experiments are being made with alteration of DNA, the "set of instructions" that determines what genes go into each individual person conceived. Many of these experiments are designed to alter the genetic heritage of individuals who carry defective genes that will cause problems in life, and these experiments have met with some success. Because individual biological endowment is one-half of the endowment—environment balance that determines the ability of people to function—we do have the responsibility to be aware of and responsive to the special needs it creates and its impact on behavior and on the expectations that can realistically be held for people. Fashions change from time to time in thinking about the relative importance to human functioning of endowment and environment, but the fact remains that both exist, and the interrelationship between them is significant in determining not only the ability of the individual to have a good life, but also the ability of the human service worker to provide help in achieving it.

The Social Heritage

We are able to alter the social heritage of individuals, and for this reason we must pay particular attention to what it is and how it becomes a part of the person.

The process of birth, by detaching the infant from the mother's body and establishing it as a discrete individual, introduces the task of learning to live with other separate individuals. This learning takes place within a balance of freedom and restraint—freedom to be oneself within the confines imposed by other people's freedoms. Such learning begins immediately with the response or lack of response to the infant's cry; its arena grows with the expanding life of the child, who must acquire knowledge of self and others in social interaction. This acquisition must be accompanied by enough security to allow a high degree of personal experience so that correction and adaptation to change can almost constantly be made.

Basic to all theories about socialization is the concept of the self developed through social interaction with others; this core self possesses certain attributes that will determine the effectiveness of the person in transactions with the environment. The War on Poverty, which was characterized by an effort to enable people to use resources within the system, defined the ultimate goal of socialization as "social competence," or the capability for full participation in society. Eight major personal attributes contribute to socialization:

1. A self-image that includes not only knowledge of self as a separate entity, but also acceptance of self and conviction that one is competent to deal with the demands of life.
2. Respect for the integrity of others and knowledge of the boundaries of personal rights and responsibilities in relation to the rights and responsibilities of others.
3. Knowledge of and ability to subscribe to or coexist with the values and norms of society.
4. Knowledge of the rules that govern behavior in given social groups.
5. Ability to assess alternative behaviors and probable outcomes realistically and to make choices in light of this reality.
6. Ability to deal with personal feelings constructively.
7. Ability to accept compromise and limitation.
8. Ability and flexibility needed to be active and self-motivating, rather than merely reactive to social situations, and to initiate and participate in change.

It is obvious that such a complex set of attributes in such an equally complex entity as a person requires learning from many different sources. This learning comes from the variety of social situations of which the individual is part from birth onward. The major ones are (a) the family or family surrogate; (b) the peer group; (c) the social institutions such as the church, synagogue, school, tribe, or cultural group; and (d) the professional or work group.

One of the best ways to understand the process of socialization is by looking at the theory of social roles. A *role* may be defined as the sum total of the behaviors expected from a person who occupies a particular position and status in a social pattern. *Position* is the place occupied in that pattern. *Status* is the rank or importance of that position. Roles have certain implicit characteristics:

1. Role implies action that is mandatory—the person filling that role is required to behave in a certain way.
2. Role implies transactions with others—the behaviors arise out of social interaction and are carried out in relation to another person or persons.
3. Role involves perception and expectation—perception by both the occupant and others of what behaviors are involved and expectation of how they will be carried out.
4. Role behaviors are defined by social norms—values, judgments, and feelings are involved as to the *right* way the occupant of a particular role *should* behave.
5. Roles tend to demand conformity and to lock the occupant into expected behaviors.
6. At any given point in time, individuals occupy more than one role, and there may be conflict among the expectations and behavior demands of the various roles.
7. In any social situation, the role demands placed on an individual may be incompatible with personal needs.
8. Changes in role are usually accompanied by stress for the individual involved. Structured social groups are systems made up of individuals who occupy a set of roles, each of which contributes to the essential balance of the group. Because of this, there is pressure for people to remain in their expected roles and not change them, but roles are not static and they do change. In one sense, life could be defined as a series of roles that provide the medium through which social learning takes place.

The Spiritual Heritage

People working in human services have also acknowledged the need to address the spiritual needs of those they strive to help. This is a challenging task because each person defines spirituality in a way that makes sense to him or her. Therefore, the meaning is different for each one of us and reflects many aspects of a person's existence and life experiences. It is this individual interpretation that makes spirituality so personal, mysterious, and unique. It also makes coming up with a standard definition such a difficult task. Edward Canda's (1980) definition of spirituality serves as one helpful effort to define this difficult concept:

> Spirituality is conceptualized as the Gestalt of the total process of human life and development, the central dynamic of which is the person's search for a sense of meaning and purpose through relationships with other people, the nonhuman environment, and the ultimate reality.

This definition helps us to understand that spirituality and religion are not the same thing. While religion may be an important part of a person's spiritual practice, religion may be defined as follows (Reese, 1996): "Religion—from the Latin 'religare' ('to bind fast')—typically refers to an institution with a recognized body of communicants who gather together regularly for worship, and accept a set of doctrines offering some means of relating the individual to what is taken to be the ultimate nature of reality."

Spirituality and religion may have areas in common, but a person can be spiritual without formally identifying with religious institutions. Human service workers should develop ways to incorporate a spiritual assessment (see Table 3.1) into their work with people. Helping people identify their spiritual needs also involves understanding the impact

TABLE 3.1   Areas for Enhancing Spiritual Competence

Spirituality and Religion	Understand the differences and similarities.
Spirituality and Culture	Develop awareness and knowledge about the wide range of spiritual practices across cultures.
Spirituality and Self-Awareness	Engage in self-exploration about one's religious and/or spiritual beliefs, sensitivity and acceptance of a wide range of other spiritual practices, limits of one's knowledge about other spiritual practices.
Spirituality and Counseling	Explore the role of spirituality in client's conception of problems and solutions, identify and respect spiritual themes during the counseling process.
Spirituality and Community Resources	Identify community resources for referral and education.
Spirituality and the Life Span	Develop knowledge and awareness of the impact of spiritual beliefs at various stages of the life span.

these spiritual beliefs have on decisions that people make about their care and how they handle crisis in their lives. Human service workers also should understand their own spiritual beliefs, educate themselves about the cultural contexts of spirituality, and increase their self-awareness about spiritual areas, including their own biases and lack of knowledge regarding the spiritual practices of other people.

> Nancy, a victim of rape, finally decided to seek out emotional support by confiding in two friends and another member of her church about what happened during a church retreat. The church member assured Nancy that nothing she said would leave the room. However, the church member told a counselor at Nancy's school and then went to Nancy's mother's workplace and told her. Nancy stated, "It ripped our lives apart." Nancy felt this betrayal of confidence was an assault on her spiritual self because she had lost control over how she chose to handle the aftermath of her rape. Nancy wasn't sure that reporting her rape to the authorities was the "right" way to handle what happened. However, the betrayal of her confidence resulted in her losing the ability to handle the impact of the rape based on her personal beliefs and ways of looking at the world. This incident was also a betrayal of trust in her church and its ability to take care of her spiritual needs. (GlenMaye, 1996).

The Family

Primary learning takes place within the family or the family surrogate (the increasing number of children who are not growing up within their biological families makes it essential to keep this in mind). Here individuals learn not only that they are separate individuals, but that they are separate people who must, of necessity, exist in a give-and-take relationship with other people. They also learn that there are certain norms of behavior and rules that govern ways of expressing feelings, of thinking, and of behaving. For example, first children, however much they might wish to, cannot destroy the second babies who have replaced them in that role. They learn that they must place limitations on their freedom if they are to survive.

Initially, this learning is enforced by outside authority, but gradually external enforcement is internalized and a personal imperative develops, which to a greater or lesser degree dictates the importance and rights of self and others. The significance of the early years cannot be overestimated. The old saw, "Give me the child for the first six years and it is mine forever," is to a certain extent valid, but a great deal of important social learning also takes place outside the immediate and extended family and in later years. Growing individuals are seriously handicapped, however, if the early years have not left them with a good feeling about themselves and with the capability to define and respect the rights of others.

There are many ways in which families can be destructive to the children who grow up within them. These can be summarized as (1) the overprotective family, where the child is shielded from difficult situations and given license to behave without regard for the rights of others; (2) the indifferent family, where the child is not accepted and loved as a unique person but only as he or she fulfills family expectations; (3) the divided family, where the child may be pulled in different directions by the significant people there; (4) the nonexistent family, where the child has no one to fill family roles; (5) the abusive family, where violence in both direct and subtle forms is visited on family members, particularly children; and (6) the dysfunctional family, unable to meet the nurture and socialization roles of its members. Whatever the situation, the family or family surrogate is the primary group for early nurturing, and its failure leaves an ineradicable stamp.

The current reality for many families now involves divorce. In fact, one of the most significant changes in our society is the increased number of divorces. Consider the following: in the 1960s, 90 percent of children grew up in homes with two biological parents while in 1996, 45 percent of marriages in the United States ended in divorce. In 1996, there were 1,150,000 divorces and about 1,000,000 children were affected (Bryner, 2001; Hetherington & Stanley-Hagan, 1999). There are many factors suggested as contributing to this trend, such as more accepting societal attitudes about divorce and having children out of wedlock.

The issue of how children adjust to divorce is clearly complex and involves many factors such as their age and developmental stage at the time of divorce, the amount of parental discord, and how the divorced parents handle the many emotional, financial, and social aftermaths of divorce. There is a growing body of research on the effects of divorce with varying findings about its impact on families. While divorced parents may struggle to cope with the many losses associated with divorce, it is their paramount responsibility not to involve their children in their pain or discord, but rather to provide them with stability, love, and support.

Andy and Sam were both in middle school when their parents divorced after a tumultuous marriage. Shortly thereafter, Howard (their father) remarried. Andy and Sam would spend every other weekend at Howard's house, where they became increasingly rude and argumentative with his new wife, Anna. Often, she would be in tears several hours into their visit and refuse to leave her bedroom. The boys would also forget important school books at their mother's house on the weekends they were scheduled for visits with their dad. He would then have to drive almost an hour each way to get the books so that the boys could complete homework assignments. After several more months, Andy's grades began to drop and Sam received detention for fighting with a classmate. Finally, Howard and his ex-wife Clara decided to seek out family counseling. The counselor met with Howard, Clara, Andy, and Sam as a group and individually with each boy. It soon became clear that Andy and Sam were wishing their parents would remarry and that Howard would "get rid of" Anna. Through counseling, the boys were helped to understand that while their parents would never remarry, both still loved their sons. Andy and Sam were further helped to understand that the divorce was not their fault. Over time, Andy and Sam began to feel less angry and guilty about the changes and losses that the divorce had wrought in their lives.

The Social Group

In modern society, children are exposed early to the tribe (a group of people of common origin who feel strong cultural ties), the religious group, and at an increasingly younger age, the formal learning group. Here they not only learn group expectations and behaviors, they also continue to define themselves in terms of the expectations of others. This definition can be constructive or destructive, depending on what these expectations are.

Bobbie is one of the Jones children, the fourth of eight. The Joneses are "no good." They "could at least keep themselves clean." That house "is just falling to pieces." They "don't even raise a garden." Mr. Jones "won't work if you offer him a job."

Mrs. Jones "just sits on the front porch—doesn't even do the dishes, wash the clothes, or cook a meal." "You should smell those children when they come to school—which isn't often!" "They just can't learn." "That 10-year-old is already fooling around with the boys."

In the social groups in the small town where the Joneses live, Bobbie has little opportunity to learn to define himself constructively. Unless there is an effective intervention, he will become what others expect him to become, and his potential for self-development will never be realized.

The Peer Group

As children move out from the family into a peer group and become a part of various social institutions, they often find themselves confronted with cultures that differ from those they learned in their family groups. The values and norms of these organized groups to which they are introduced are often rigid, strongly supported by rituals, and demanding of conformity if the individual is to survive and to use the group. These norms deal with simple situations (such as what to wear to school) and complex situations (such as the relationship among student, teacher, and parent); they are formal and openly stated (students must be in their classrooms by a certain hour) or covertly stated and accepted by the group (in spite of rules against leaving the campus, the "in-group" sneaks off and goes for lunch at a nearby drive-in). Presently, there is justified concern in neighborhoods and schools about gangs that often promote violence and antisocial behavior.

As part of socialization, the growing child must adapt to the differences between the family group and the peer or institutional group as well as among the subgroups within them. The elementary school years and adolescence are marked by this accommodation. When, early in adolescence, children begin to sit in judgment of their parents, they are also judging the values, norms, and supporting rules that they are being exposed to in the larger society. The importance of various groups changes according to the life stage of the individual. In contrast to the early years when the family is all-important, the school years—and particularly adolescence—are stages when the peer group is overwhelming in importance. (Young adults often "come back to the family" when they reach the age of 19 or so.) Adolescent delinquency, for example, has been defined as "a failure to comply with norms," and from this point of view such delinquency can rarely be treated effectively merely on an individual basis. The adolescent is responding to the normal expectations of the peer group, which at that stage of development is of primary importance. Many of our modern correctional programs make maximum use of the peer group in working with adolescent delinquency.

The Workplace

As developing individuals move through the formal educational world into the working world, they become a part of the profession, the trade, or the occupation through which they will earn their livings. Each of these groups has its own set of values, develops its own behavioral norms, and sets up its own role expectations, which may be formally or informally expressed.

Professions, which are the most organized of the working groups, tend to have specialized characteristics involving (1) a unique body of theoretical knowledge out of which specialized skills and techniques grow, (2) recognition by society of this unique expertise, (3) delegation to the profession of the authority to regulate itself, (4) development of a usually written and binding code of ethics, and (5) legal ability to control admission of new members to the profession.

Professions exist in a hierarchy, in which the older, more established ones are accorded major status and the more recent ones lesser status. Each develops its own culture and its own role expectations for its practitioners, and each stakes a claim to its own area of practice. They are exclusive, tending not only to shut people out, but also to shut them in. These factors may create problems between members of different professions, particularly when role boundaries are not clear, as well as between "professionals" and "nonprofessionals" who are frequently working together in the delivery of human services. The status accorded to certain professions as well as to certain roles within the workplace can be a problem, especially when workers become so accepting of the status hierarchy that they cannot question or legitimately challenge people or groups of higher status.

At present there are major conflicts within the workplace where human service workers function. These are related to three developments: (1) Delivery of human services is now "big business"; (2) human services are delivered primarily within bureaucratic structures; and (3) research and technology—particularly in the biological but somewhat in the social sciences—have advanced to the point where basic human processes can be altered and behavior controlled by external means.

These developments pose ethical problems for workers whose function is to intervene in the lives of others, make judgments, and take actions that will vitally affect their clients. Personal integrity and the highest degree of respect for the individual are essential. Workers are often placed in a double bind when the introduction of management techniques, efficiency and cost-effectiveness, and the profit motive become major considerations. In and of themselves, these are essential, but they are easily misused. We see such instances as a child protection worker disturbed because caseloads are so large that abused children cannot be safeguarded; physicians at odds with their practice groups because of requirements that they limit the procedures they use or the time they spend with patients; nurses in old people's homes or mental hospitals uncomfortable with the practice of administering to patients often excessive or insufficiently monitored drugs to limit patients' demands so that more can be accommodated, or to limit their behavior so they can be more easily controlled.

As the population increases, as expenses mount, as we learn more about how to control people, and as social and economic pressures increase, the use of such actions, which disregard the integrity of the individual, will probably increase also, and the pressure on workers to fall in with dehumanizing practices will become greater as they become the expected norm.

The code of ethics that governs a profession or occupation is of maximum significance when the profession's purpose is human service. The integrity of individuals, their right to self-determination insofar as possible, their right to "life, liberty, and the pursuit of happiness," and their right to the necessities to sustain life should be taken for granted, and yet all too often they are honored in the breach rather than in the observance. Sometimes even the acculturation process that takes place when an individual enters the human services results in workers developing a perception of clients as less than human, the object of research, or merely the means of earning a living.

Because of their special responsibilities for people and their lives, the human service professions place great emphasis on codes of ethics for their practitioners. The National Association of Social Workers (NASW), for example, adopted such a code in 1979 with the most recent revision in 1999 by the NASW Delegate Assemblies. The NASW Code of Ethics states: "[T]he primary mission of the social work profession is to enhance human well-being and help meet the basic human needs of all people, with particular attention to the needs and empowerment of people who are vulnerable, oppressed, and living in poverty."

This Code of Ethics includes six broad ethical principles based on social work's core values of service, social justice, dignity and worth of the individual, importance of human relationships, integrity, and competence. Presented below, these values and ethical principles are discussed in the Code as they apply to social workers' ethical responsibilities to their profession, clients, employers, employing organizations, and society (NASW, 1999):

Value: Service

Ethical Principle: *Social workers' primary goal is to help people in need and to address social problems.*

Value: Social Justice

Ethical Principle: *Social workers challenge social injustice.*

Value: Dignity and worth of the individual

Ethical Principle: *Social workers respect the inherent dignity and worth of the person.*

Value: Importance of human relationships

Ethical Principle: *Social workers recognize the central importance of human relationships.*

Value: Integrity

Ethical Principle: *Social workers behave in a trustworthy manner.*

Value: Competence

Ethical Principle: *Social workers practice within their areas of competence and develop and enhance their professional expertise.*

Human service workers need to understand that codes of ethics cannot resolve all ethical dilemmas or guarantee answers. They are guides that reflect the workers' commitment to uphold the ethics of their profession. Codes provide this guidance through offering a set of values, principles, and standards to guide decision making when conflicts arise. Ultimately, however, it is the informed judgment of the worker that will come into play. This judgment should be the result of having also consulted relevant information from legal sources, agency guidelines and research (NASW, 1999; Welfel, 2001).

The Importance of Socialization

Socialization is essential for survival and for social functioning, and membership in groups is essential for the good health of the individual. Groups are not perfect, but they can be a source of strength and support. They provide an antidote for what Phillip Slater calls "the pursuit of loneliness" in our modern multifaceted society. The person without family ties and without peer group identification, who has not found reference groups of which he or she can become a part, is very often a person who does not function well.

Socialization does not mean that the individual is a mindless conglomerate of conformity to existing patterns, a stereotype of a role. Life is a process that demands innovation and change. A need for these is built into people, who are subject to many different socializing agents at any time. For example, there has been a growing recognition of the existence of sexual stereotypes and the changing roles of both women and men in the past fifty years. This is reflected in society on many levels—personally, legally, and socially. An effectively socialized person can reconcile conflicting demands—such as being a mother, wife, and worker—but also can conform well enough to function in society.

The Person as an Individual

Ultimately, each person is unique—the product of a unique genetic heritage in continuous and dynamic interaction with a unique life experience. Change on a personal level comes more quickly than either biological or social change. While people are subject to the influence of both natural laws and social rules, the element of individual choice cannot be disregarded.

Personality Theories

Genetic, social, and individual factors combine to create the total personality; if we are to understand the human condition, we need to think about this complex entity. People have been wondering about themselves for thousands of years, and their ideas have been many and varied. Among modern theories, the ones that are have traditionally been most generally accepted and widely used as a basis for human service practice are the *psychoanalytic theories,* the *learning theories,* and the *humanistic holistic theories.* More recently, *feminist theories* are being more commonly used as well. Each has influenced and been influenced by the others, and all are influencing those now engaged in ongoing thinking about this age-old enigma—the human being. Current practice models reflect these basic theories. Workers need to be knowledgeable about them and able to evaluate and make use of their constructs. Work with people will reflect the worker's conception of the nature of the personality, how it develops, and the impact of outside forces—individuals and groups—on that development. Out of such theories come processes for enabling desired change to take place. Workers use their concepts in understanding themselves as well as others and in working with others, again as individuals, in groups, or in larger societies.

Psychoanalytic Theory

Sigmund Freud (Table 3.2), the "father of psychoanalysis," was one of the giants who, in words supposedly first used to describe Charles Darwin, "saw what all men saw and thought what no man thought." Although Freud is now criticized for being too much of a determinist in his belief that all behavior is caused by instinctual drives of sex and aggression, for his sexist attitudes, and for using unscientific methods of gathering data, his impact on the development of personality theories has been tremendous.

His terminology—namely conscious, unconscious, id, superego, ego, defense mechanisms—are all part of modern language and are defined as follows (Walrond-Skinner, 1986):

Conscious: The part of the psyche that is open to immediate awareness.

Unconscious: That region of the mind that remains unavailable to a person until it emerges into consciousness through events such as dreams and free associations.

Id: The major portion of the unconscious; strives only to bring about the satisfaction of a person's instinctual needs.

Ego: A part of the personality whose task is to mediate the conflicting demands of the superego, the id, and external reality. The ego has a range of functions including observation, reality testing, rational thought, and perception.

Superego: The part of the unconscious that acts as a monitor and critic of the ego through conscious functions such as observation, evaluation, criticism, and conscience.

Defense Mechanisms: The unconscious means by which the ego protects itself from the instinctual demands of the id and the threats perceived in the external world. Defense mechanisms are employed as a normal part of functioning and serve to protect the individual from anxiety that he or she cannot handle. They include such things as regression, repression, rationalization, splitting, sublimation, denial, and intellectualization.

Schools of Psychoanalytic Theory.   Like all thinking, Freud's theories reflected the times and the culture in which they were developed. His disciples went in many directions, altering his original conceptions with their own ideas and directions. Freud

TABLE 3.2 Highlights of Psychoanalytic Theory and Psychoanalysis

Psychoanalytic Theory and Psychoanalysis
Sigmund Freud (1856–1939)

- Theory is based on the understanding that one's mental life is made up of both the conscious and unconscious.
- Belief in a threefold (id, ego, superego) mental apparatus that functions in close relationship to the physiological systems of the body.
- Concept of psychological adaptation whereby the mental apparatus attempts to produce a "steady state" and reduce conflict as much as possible.
- Psychoanalysis works to make unconscious material conscious through techniques such as analysis of dreams and free association.

focused on the internal life of the person, and his theories of change dealt with changing the person within. He saw the genetic background and the environment as important but secondary to the primary relationship of the client with the worker.

One of the more important uses of Freud's theories comes through the work of those who built on his ideas and changed their emphasis. Anna Freud, his daughter, Heinz Hartmann, and Erik Erikson have been instrumental in the development of what is known as Ego Psychology. This theory (Table 3.3) postulates that work must not be done only to resolve internal conflicts but also the demands of the environment. These adaptive functions are learned during maturation, and Erikson's work on development throughout the life cycle is particularly useful for workers who deal with social situations and their demands on people. Finally, another outgrowth of Freud's work was Analytical Psychology, developed by Carl Jung, a psychiatrist. Though he was greatly influenced by Freud, Jung's theory differed in many respects from psychoanalysis. For example, Jung believed that we are meant

TABLE 3.3 Highlights of Ego Psychology

Ego Psychology		
Anna Freud (1895–1982)	*Heinz Hartmann (1894–1970)*	*Erik Erickson (1902–1979)*

- Psychoanalytic theory that includes an emphasis on the autonomous functions of the ego, which are not viewed as only being influenced by unconscious drives including cognition, perception, and memory.
- The ego is primarily seen as enabling the regulation and adaptation of the personality to external reality.
- This concentration on ego strengths and the adaptive potential of the ego have provided the foundation for briefer treatments including crisis intervention.

to progress, to move in a positive direction, and not just to adapt, as the Freudians and behaviorists would have it. This perspective is invaluable for human service workers who strive to help clients, communities, and organizations reach their fullest potentials.

Feminist Theories

All theories are subject to critiques and reevaluation in the face of new ways of thinking. Such is the case regarding psychoanalytic and related theories. They were harshly criticized by feminist scholars who felt they addressed only the psychological experiences of men. Because of this, women's psychological development was often labeled as abnormal rather than different from men's—but legitimate in its own right (Table 3.4). Feminist theorists were also strongly influenced by the women's movement's emphasis on the deleterious effects of social and economic oppression on the psychological development of women and girls (Stout & McPhail, 1998; Unger & Crawford, 1992). Feminist theories continue to be revised as women scholars from diverse backgrounds critique and refine what has been done before.

Major contemporary feminist theorists include Nancy Chodorow, who postulates that masculine-feminine identities and roles are not biologically determined but are "reproduced" in every generation by social arrangements (Chodorow, 1999). Carol Gilligan contends, based upon her research that studied women's moral development, that men and women have different but equally valid approaches to moral issues: Men have a sense of morality based upon an ethic of rights while women have a sense of morality based upon an ethic of responsibility (Gilligan, 1993). Jean Baker Miller, a psychiatrist, and her colleagues presently work at the Jean Baker Miller Institute of the Stone Center at Wellesley College and examine the effects of power and social status on personality development. They propose that because women are a subordinate group in society, psychological characteristics, including passivity, docility, dependency, lack of initiative, and helplessness, emerge as a way to cope with this oppression (Miller, 1987). Sandra Bem, a psychologist and expert on gender roles, explores the ways that people organize, categorize, and use gender-related information as

TABLE 3.4   Highlights of Feminist Theories and Therapy

Feminist Theories and Therapy			
Nancy Chodorow *(1944–)*	*Carol Gilligan* *(1936–)*	*Jean Baker Miller Institute* *(est. 1995)*	*Sandra Bem* *(1944–)*

- An approach to psychotherapy and theory that has developed out of the philosophy of the women's movement.
- Reactions to the strong sexist bias that many women feel exists in the major personality theories.
- All feminist theories and therapeutic techniques share some common elements: debunking psychological concepts regarding sex differences (especially those found in psychoanalytic theory); a positive view of the female body; emphasis on the development of equal responsibility, talents, skills, and power in women; a fusion between personal and political goals regarding change; and an emphasis on the egalitarian nature of the therapeutic relationship.

they think about and solve problems. This can lead to stereotypes of how men and women should behave, think, and act (Bem, 1981; Unger & Crawford, 1992). These feminist theories clearly challenge human service workers to increase their self-awareness about gender stereotypes and how they hinder helping relationships with clients.

Learning Theory

It is generally accepted that learning theory (Table 3.5) began with the psychologist Ivan Pavlov's famous experiments in which dogs were conditioned to responses around eating. He has been followed by a long list of distinguished psychologists who first focused their attention on tests and measurements of human intelligence but more recently have turned to development of learning theories and therapy dealing with mental health problems. John B. Watson was the first of this group to emphasize strongly the importance of environment and the facts that all behavior is learned and that only observable and testable facts are significant.

Probably one of the best known behaviorists is B. F. Skinner, who developed the ideas of respondent behavior (that which is brought about by a specific stimulus and can be conditioned) and operant behavior (that which produces consequences that tend to be repeated when reinforced and discontinued when not reinforced). Many different practice models have developed from the theories of the behaviorists, who operate by setting up controlled situations in which behavior can be conditioned and reinforced. These models are widely used in teaching, in treating problems of human relationships, and in working with personal problems that lead to destructive behaviors. As behavior modification develops, certain features are assuming greater importance. One is the detailed specification of objectives with the possibility of subgoals that serve as steps on the way to the desired behavior. Another is the development of behavioral assessment techniques that permit specific definition of the problem and selection of the appropriate treatment, followed by assessment of the behavior change that results so that necessary alterations can be made in the treatment.

Presently, assessment procedures can be classified into three types: (1) self-report by the client; (2) direct observation of behavior by, for example, parents, siblings, institutional personnel, and so forth; and (3) physiological measures based on various tests. Work is in progress on various laboratory instruments to be used in assessment.

TABLE 3.5   Highlights of Learning Theories

Learning Theories		
Ivan Pavlov (1849–1936)	*John Watson (1878–1958)*	*B. F. Skinner (1904–1990)*

- Theories focused on external behavior that could be observed, not the inner mental life of the individual.
- Maladaptive behavior is viewed as either a deficiency of functional learning or as an acquisition of dysfunctional learning.
- Treatment approaches are geared toward eliminating or reducing the frequency or intensity of the problem behavior.

Humanistic Holistic Theories

The growth of knowledge never stands still and is never complete. For many, psychoanalytic theories were not subjected to sufficiently scientific testing or were too mechanistic, and learning theories, though perhaps more practical than psychoanalysis, were seen as too controlling, as negating the factor of individual choice, and as not allowing for the "humanity" of the person. The development of humanistic theory was a logical next step (Table 3.6). Abraham Maslow, Carl Rogers, and others began to develop ideas of "self-actualization," based on their view of people as essentially motivated toward growth and fulfillment, rather than beings who are controlled by instinctual drives of sex and aggression or who are objects to be manipulated into socially desirable learned behaviors. The focus of these theories is that the individual is constantly in a process of "being and becoming," basically motivated to live in such a way that the best within is realized. Through development of meaningful relationships with others, as in a group situation or with one other person, significant work can be done to achieve self-awareness or self-utilization. These theories are holistic, dealing with the totality of the individual and emphasizing flexibility, openness, and freedom from outside control.

Other Theories

In addition to these four basic personality theories (psychoanalytic, learning, humanistic holistic, feminist), there are at least four others whose influence on human service practice has been sufficiently significant to deserve mention. These are Albert Ellis's Rational-Emotive Theory (see following section on brief therapies), Fritz Perls's Gestalt Theory, Eric Berne's Transactional Analysis, and William Glasser's Reality Therapy.

Fritz Perls, a psychoanalyst, developed Gestalt Therapy, one of the forerunners of our modern emphasis on holism. It is based on the theory that people have an inherent drive toward growth, health, and self-actualization, which is achieved by a balanced wholeness. Perls emphasized acceptance of self in the present rather than dealing with the past and tended toward emphasis on individual right at the expense of social responsibility.

Eric Berne started out, too, as a psychoanalyst but separated himself from the classical movement and developed Transactional Analysis. This is based on the theory that human personality is divided into three separate ego states—the Parent, the Adult, and the Child—

TABLE 3.6   Highlights of Humanistic Holistic Theories

Humanistic Holistic Theories	
Carl Rogers (1902–1987)	*Abraham Maslow (1908–1970)*

- Emphasis on engaging the whole person and focusing on the future rather than the past.
- Attention is paid to the relationship between the therapist and the client with *both* seen as growing and changing from the therapeutic encounter.
- Important tasks of therapy include self-actualization, personal growth, and self-understanding.

and the basic human motivating force is the desire for recognition and that personal problems arise from within the personality. By recognizing and taking responsibility for these ego states, primarily through group interaction, they can be dealt with more constructively.

William Glasser, a psychologist trained in psychoanalysis, developed his Reality Therapy based on the premise that basically people need a distinct identity and tend to develop a "success" or "failure" identity, the former through secure love and feelings of worth, the latter through inadequate love and a feeling of worthlessness. Personal responsibility and actions to change such feelings are emphasized.

In addition to the so-called "scientific" theories that are based primarily on research and are all products of Western society, other cultures have differing theories about how people grow and develop to maturity. Many of these rest on faith in a set of religious beliefs that explain human functioning on the basis of particular dogma. It is essential not to overlook the fact that all theories are culture bound: They are postulated by people who are influenced by their own culture and by the times in which they live. "Nonscientific" theories must be respected and understood if we are to work successfully with people who believe in them.

Brief Therapies

This refers to a wide variety of therapies, all of which strive to help clients find satisfactory solutions to their problems using as few sessions as are needed (Table 3.7). Though all brief therapies have an overt focus on being time efficient, they draw on theories and techniques from earlier approaches, including psychoanalytic and learning theories (Cooper, 1995).

While many types of brief therapy are frequently used, there are several that have attained prominence in the human services. One is Rational-Emotive Therapy, developed by Albert Ellis, a psychologist. This therapy is based on a theory that postulates that causes of feelings and actions lie not in actual life experiences but in how we perceive such experiences (Ellis, 1996). He declared that by examination and rational thinking about these erroneous ideas we could change both them and subsequent behavior. In this therapy clients learn to think rationally about their problems.

Another relevant therapy is Cognitive Therapy, developed by Aaron Beck, that, like Ellis, draws upon learning theories. This approach emphasizes that cognitive processes

TABLE 3.7   Highlights of Brief Therapies

Brief Therapies
• There are many different types of brief therapies but all are derived from psychoanalytic, learning, and/or humanistic theories.
• Brief therapies all strive to be efficient and effective.
• Brief therapies have limited treatment goals with clear outcomes, an emphasis on intervening in the present, and an emphasis on client strengths.
• Brief therapists play an active role in keeping clients focused from session to session on what they are trying to accomplish.

affect behavior and that behavior can be changed through addressing a person's negative thoughts about his or her life, self, and experiences with the world.

Drawing upon learning theories and Freud's theory about the unconscious, the psychiatrist Milton Erickson developed the Utilization Model of Hypnotherapy. Erickson's approach is based on the assumption that people receive and process information outside of conscious awareness and that cognitive changes can occur without conscious awareness of the processes involved. Thus, during the hypnotic trance, the client is provided with indirect suggestions by the counselor about how to solve problems, thereby triggering the client to unconsciously solve the problem. This approach is ultimately based upon the belief that people can use their strengths to solve their problems (Nugent, 1996).

Finally, Solution-Focused Therapy draws upon the ideas of Milton Erickson and was developed by Insoo Kim Berg, Steve de Shazer, and others at the Brief Therapy Center in Milwaukee, Wisconsin. A major assumption of Solution-Focused Therapy is that focusing on the positive, the solution, and the future facilitates change in the desired direction. Therefore, the counselor and client focus on solution-oriented talk rather than on problem-oriented talk. There is an assumption that it is unnecessary to search the past to find solutions and that small changes in thinking and behavior can lead to significant life changes (Walter & Peller, 1992).

Managed care has greatly expanded the use of brief therapies, because limiting costs has often meant limiting the number of counseling sessions covered by insurance. It is therefore imperative that workers remain current about research regarding the effectiveness of brief (and all other) therapies and also to document the outcomes of their own interventions. These efforts will help ensure that clients receive the best care possible. Whatever the type of therapy used, it is also critical to have a counselor who is skilled in using that technique. These actions are ethical responsibilities as seen in the NASW Code of Ethics; social workers are mandated to practice within their areas of competence and develop and enhance their professional expertise through continually striving to increase their professional knowledge and skills (NASW, 1999).

"Personal" Personality Theory

None of these theories should be taken as an absolute. It is the responsibility of human service workers to study, to evaluate, and to take from them those ideas that are not mutually exclusive, seem by the best objective standards available to be well founded, and provide a basis from which workers can function effectively in a particular situation. (See Chapter 8, Developing an Eclectic Approach to Practice.) Of special importance is the work of Erikson, which is based on concepts from psychoanalysis. He extended these ideas with the teachings of Ego Psychology, the development of the healthy personality, and the importance of the stages of the total life cycle. He emphasized the dynamics of each stage as prescribed by the interplay of individual development and the social milieu in which the person exists.

In the hundred or so years since Freud pioneered this field, there have been major changes in our thinking about how best to understand and help people. We realize now that people do not need to be locked in by their childhood experiences but continue to grow and change throughout their lifetimes; that utilizing coping abilities and strengths rather than dwelling on pathology can produce better results; that the setting and the culture in which people exist contribute to problems and can be used to facilitate change; and that others are of great importance in helping people deal with the problems of living. Modern theories are the result of a building process and retain ideas from earlier theories that continue to be valid and useful. They are constantly being tested and revised insofar as is possible by the best scientific methods.

Social workers are fortunate in that this discipline originated in direct practice and with commitment to social change rather than with animal and laboratory research. Such a modern approach has always been implicit in social work, even during those years when the medical model was greatly stressed.

The foundations of this book come from multiple perspectives in psychoanalysis and psychology, we hope without the rigidity of Freud and Skinner; from the humanists, we hope without the naiveté and mysticism of Maslow and Rogers; from the biological theories of Hans Selye; and from the critical thinking skills found in the feminist theories of women's development. From psychoanalytic theory, the concepts that seem particularly meaningful are (1) the tripartite personality, (2) the defense mechanisms, (3) the developmental stages of life, and (4) the belief that the healthy person is one who can work and love. From learning theory, the significance of the environment in shaping human behavior and the use of structured learning situations to develop healthy and extinguish unhealthy behaviors seem to be essential ingredients of a well-rounded philosophy for working with people. From the humanists, emphasis on the total person endowed with a healthy and good drive toward maximum fulfillment and the importance in working toward fulfillment of relationships between individuals and within groups seem particularly important contributions. The importance of a sense of self-worth, the elements, often in conflict, of Adult, Parent, and Child within the person, responsibility for self, and the innate drive toward healthy growth and development are all concepts about human personality that foster better understanding. Finally, from the biologists, the concept of systems of internal balance and the concept of stress provide particularly useful tools for thinking about people. From the feminist theorists, we gain an awareness of how culture, race, class, gender, and sexual orientation bias theory, knowledge building, and the real-life practice of working with people.

Also, beginning in the 1940s, research in biology on brain chemistry has opened up a whole new way of understanding personality and behavior. Work in this field, which continues to develop rapidly, has determined areas of the brain and mechanisms that control specific mental states that are responsible for specific behaviors in individuals. Various mind-altering drugs have been developed and are widely used to control traits considered undesirable such as depression, anxiety, obsession, and so forth. There are those who think that the answers to all our problems in human functioning lie in chemical imbalance and accordingly can be controlled and eradicated.

While this is one of the most important developments in our lifelong effort to understand the human condition, there are many unanswered questions about its use. We have yet to determine the effect of artificial chemical changes in the brain over long periods of time; we do not understand all the side effects of drugs being used; we do not know how effective they are in altering already learned behavior or how they affect other desirable traits such as creativity. Finally, many are concerned about ethical questions involved in such alteration of human personality. Suffice it to say, however, that this is a major development about which those of us who work with people should be informed and open-minded.

The Concept of the Tripartite Personality

The tripartite personality affords one way of thinking about the existence of what may be a self-destructive part of the individual. Whether this owes to chemical imbalance, to the existence of the "lizard" brain, as some think, or, as Freud postulated, to the presence of primitive drives in what he designated the id (the seat of impulsive wishing and the pleasure principle associated with it), such aspects of the personality exist and are easily observable. Freud's concept of superego (forces controlling expression of these primitive drives and defining acceptable outlets for their energy) posits that the superego develops as the result of external social pressure. When it is too rigid, the superego can inhibit action and achievement; when too loose, it can allow the person to become subject to primitive impulses.

The ego is seen as the balance wheel between the individual and society. It is visualized as essentially the reality-oriented aspect that enables one to perceive one's environment realistically and achieve a balance between one's own personal needs and the demands and opportunities of the setting. There are four steps in the operation of this process: perception, integration, adaptation, and execution.

Perception

The initial step deals with how things are seen and understood. Reality can only be perceived through the eyes of the individual in terms of the self and its own needs. It can be truthfully said that everyone's reality is different—that even the psychotic's "unreal" reality is reality to the person who is perceiving it. This is graphically illustrated in the old story of the blind men and the elephant. None of these six men was completely right, none completely wrong, from an objective point of view. Each perceived by touch a part of the elephant and, hence, the whole in terms of his own frame of reference.

The task of workers in relation to perception is, first, to deal with and clear up their own myopia and then to try to understand what the client is seeing in the situation under consideration. One's perception of reality can be affected by lack of knowledge, by physical illness or handicap, by major or minor emotional disturbance, by previous experience, and by any of the social and personal pressures or inhibitions that predispose against clarity and realism. A good example of this is the attitude of some older Native Americans toward the involvement of their grandchildren in the Head Start programs. Their previous experience with children being taken away by force to white schools on the reservations had not been a good one, and they perceived the Head Start workers and buses as similarly destructive.

Integration

The second phase of the functioning of the ego is the integration (bringing together in an orderly fashion) not only of the perception of the reality in terms of what it means in relation to the individual, but also of what the adaptation requires in order for the individual to live with or to attempt to change the demands of this reality.

Adaptation and Execution

The process of adaptation constitutes the third phase. It is based on the previous two stages and the fourth stage of final execution or putting the adaptive mechanism into operation. After we have perceived the reality in terms of what it means for us, weighed the relative merits of various responses, and selected a response in terms of both thinking and feeling capacities and needs, we then adopt this as our own and act on it. Our adaptation may not appear to be the most reasonable or desirable one to the observer, but it is the logical one for us and the only one that we can make under the circumstances. For us to make a different adaptation, there must be new and different factors involved. It is imperative that human service workers keep this fact in mind because it explains "unreasonable" and "irrational" behavior that so often appears senseless and destructive to the observer.

There is much discussion as to whether this whole process of the functioning of the ego through perception, integration, adaptation, and execution is on a conscious or an unconscious level. Certainly, the unconscious carryover of previous feelings and experience, the all-powerful drive of the id impulses, and the heavy weight of the internalized superego are significant determinants of adaptive capacity and form. However, these do not represent the totality of the individual. We are also thinking and knowing beings, and this is an equally important aspect of self. In its broadest sense, the ego functions with both conscious and unconscious determinants that combine to determine adaptation and lifestyle.

Each aspect of functioning involves both a cognitive and an affective element. It is very difficult to separate the rational and the emotional contributions, but the worker must be sharply aware that both exist, are a part of all aspects of human functioning, and as such must be dealt with. The reaction of the Native American grandparents was based partly on feeling and partly on knowledge gained from previous experience with the early reservation schools. Only as they were able to deal with their fears and angers on an emotional level and to understand on an intellectual level that this was a new situation could they take advantage of the opportunity offered to their grandchildren.

The Concept of Defense Mechanisms

The defense mechanisms, as conceived by Freud, are unconscious distortions of reality to protect individuals from anxiety that they cannot handle. They include such things as regression, repression, rationalization, projection, denial, identification, and others. It is obvious that such mechanisms are used both consciously and unconsciously as ways of dealing with stressful situations. Though they can be maladaptive when rigidly fixed, they can be consciously used by self-aware individuals to good ends. The nature of life's demands is such that there are times when it is constructive to make temporary use of defense mechanisms to guard against anxiety and pain that would otherwise be overwhelming. Workers need to be able to recognize the presence of defense mechanisms both in themselves and in others, and they must make sound determinations of whether the defenses are constructive or destructive and consciously or unconsciously being used.

The Concept of Developmental Stages

The developmental stages of life were originally conceived by Freud and further developed by Anna Freud, Heinz Hartmann, and Erik Erikson. The individual is seen as moving in life through a series of developmental stages for which the overall pattern had been laid down at the time of conception. This is a holistic concept that involves the total person— biological, emotional, social, spiritual, and intellectual—and as such is an extremely useful way to think about human development (see Figure 3.2).

Progression through the developmental stages is not at a uniform rate within the person, nor is it uniform among individuals, but it is steady and continuous. We must be flex-

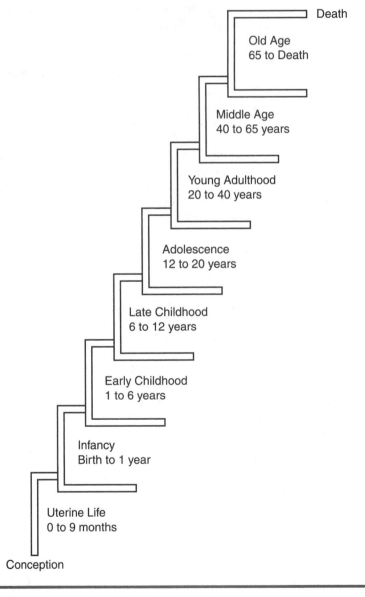

FIGURE 3.2   The ascending stages of life.

ible in considering a norm for development at any particular stage because norms vary greatly. We must consider what is normal for each particular individual in terms of that person's particular heredity and the particular environment at a specific time in the individual's development. Consideration of the marked degree of difference in physical, intellectual, and emotional maturity among any given group of 13-year-old girls will illustrate this point, and yet each of them will have her own norm and must be considered in light of it.

The stages in life are progressive, and each depends on those that have preceded it. Given a healthy environment, children who experience a healthy infancy in all respects should proceed normally and easily through the preschool years, the school years, and into adolescence. Children who have been unable to complete a developmental task satisfactorily in a given stage will move on to the next stage carrying with them unfinished business that will create difficulties when a situation arises that demands maturity in that particular aspect of living. This is particularly obvious during the years of adolescence, when earlier unsolved problems in family relationships may explode into furious conflict, destructive to both individual and group. In marriage, where the formation of a new family calls for extra capacity to achieve an adult level, early trauma may result in problems. The demands of the middle years and of aging, with their attendant losses and separations, call for a high degree of flexibility and capacity to tolerate change, the degree of which has been shaped by earlier living and growing. The pattern for adaptation to the problems of later years is set in the early years.

The concept of life stages, as with all knowledge, is dynamic—the concept itself is constantly in the process of changing. For example, we are beginning to see phases within the designated life stages that are predictable, and the better we understand these, the better we can ameliorate unhealthy development. Although there is no generally accepted legal or moral definition of the point at which human life begins, the nature of the interuterine experience has significance for future physical, mental, and social growth of the individual. Certain illnesses, injury, malnutrition, lack of prenatal care of mother, or use of drugs, alcohol, or nicotine by the mother can all affect the health of the developing fetus. Because of these profound effects, the prenatal experience is an important part of the life cycle.

The task of the infant is to establish the physical mechanisms that will sustain life—breathing, eating, defecating. Although relatively powerless to affect these, the infant must be able to make needs known and achieve a relationship with those around from whom come not only the physical care, but also the emotional trust that will sustain the child through the long period of dependency.

The tasks of childhood, both early and late, include learning to use language; establishing a place among family members; developing and learning to use physical, intellectual, emotional, and social skills; attaining emotional control based on understanding that he or she is not the center of the universe but a part of it; and learning to adapt to change.

The tasks of adolescence revolve around not only increasing maturation of abilities, but also sexual maturation and the need to achieve freedom from parental control and take charge of one's own life. Young adulthood presents the individual with the tasks of establishing an independent life, finding a spot in the workplace, making a sexual adjustment that may or may not involve marriage and children, creating a home, developing satisfactory social contacts, and making a place in society.

The tasks of middle age often require significant role change. Children leave home; aging parents need to receive rather than give care. Physiological changes take place that create awareness that life is not endless. Old age, too, requires further role change, often moving from independence to dependence. It is increasingly obvious, however, that "old age" is not a single condition, particularly if we define it as beginning at age 65. Rather, with increasing life expectancy, "old age" tends to fall into three phases: (1) the "young old," 65–75, when the individual often can still work and take care of him- or herself; (2) the "old," 75–85, when additional care is needed; and (3) the "old, old," 85+, for whom there is a range of needs from minimal assistance to total care. Again, we cannot stereotype people—not all 85- to 90-year-olds are unable to manage for themselves. Loss of friends and family and illness are major problems for many aged.

In utilizing the concept of life stages as a tool for working with people, workers must guard against considering them as rigid or as stopping points. They might visualize the development stages as plateaus that are so sloped upward that only by continuous movement can one's footing be retained. Once one begins to climb, there is no stopping until the end of life. We must remember that progression can be slowed or regression can take place because of the life experiences of the developing person in any phase of this climb. Disturbances may be manifested in all life areas when there are problems in any one area—for example, physical growth problems, behavioral difficulties, or social or intellectual abnormalities. Some of these problems are temporary; some become part of an ongoing pattern. Stresses of all kinds—accident, injury, illness, loss of or separation from family, overprotection, addiction, and abuse—can hinder normal growth.

The Concepts of Stress, Balance, and Coping Ability

In understanding the functioning of the individual, the concept of balance, or homeostasis, is important. Borrowed from physical medicine and widely adapted by various branches of the behavioral sciences, this concept posits a tendency toward a relatively stable state of equilibrium among the differing elements of an organism or system. Thus the individual can be regarded as possessing a strong drive toward living, growing, and surviving, which take place by continuous and ever-present processes of adaptation. Life presents the individual with a continuing series of problem situations, and the solution of one problem merely moves the person on to the next. The word "problem" is used here not in the narrow sense of something wrong that must be set right; rather, it means a situation demanding action or solution. This broad definition allows us to use the term in relation to the normal tasks of living as well as those abnormal, unexpected, or tragic events that occur in every person's life experience. As such, problems present challenge and opportunity, and they are the substance of which living is made.

Each of us, at birth, is immediately faced with a series of tasks or problems that we must solve to survive and grow. We must breathe, eat, eliminate, begin to relate to other people, and move toward an increasingly separate and independent existence. As we begin to perform these tasks, we learn how to deal with internal and external demands that are placed on us and to develop the ability to cope. As we successfully encounter the increasingly sophisticated and complicated demands of living and growing, our coping ability is strengthened. We find ways to meet the internal needs that are a part of our innate potential and to satisfy the external needs that are a part of our surroundings. We learn to deal with frustration and to develop mechanisms that allow for both growth and protection from pain and harm. By the very process of dealing with the problems that confront us, and to the extent that we deal well and adequately with the original demands, we develop increasing capacities to handle future, more complicated problems. Just as everyone has a different level of coping ability, so each person has a breaking point beyond which she or he cannot go. This point is determined by the many different factors that contribute to the life experience— one's constitutional endowment in dynamic interaction with one's surroundings.

Although at first glance it could be considered a contradiction in terms, it is helpful to think of this balance as a dynamic homeostasis. The nature of life is such that while balance is essential for functioning, it is constantly in a process of being upset, shifting and changing to adapt to the new input from experience and to the demands of maturation and development. The key here is that the organism or system that is thrown into imbalance will strive automatically to regain its steady state. Viewed from this frame of reference, people can be seen as having a drive toward remaining operational, even though this state may appear dysfunctional to the observer. The drive is significant and, combined with the equally strong tendency toward growth and development that is inherent in humans, gives human service workers a running start in their efforts to help clients achieve fulfillment in life.

Another equally important concept, also from physical medicine and closely related to that of homeostasis, is that of stress. Originally formulated by Hans Selye, a Swiss physician working in Canada, it postulates that the body makes a general adaptation to stress that involves certain overall processes, as well as specific adaptations to particular stresses. In making these adaptations, one gears oneself to either fight or run when one's balanced existence is threatened. This threat may be in any of the life areas—physical, intellectual, emotional, social, or spiritual—and in any combination of them.

A certain amount of stress is essential to maturation and development. Life poses the challenges, and one's built-in system for self-defense and growth mobilizes itself to deal with them. The healthful process of coping with these threats and challenges fosters growth and development. Unfortunately, there are increasingly frequent instances in modern life where one can neither fight nor run; rather, the person is trapped in situations where stress is continuous and unrelenting and healthy coping is impossible. The pollution of the planet—foul air, impure water, noise, and overcrowding—is one example of this. Another can be seen more and more in developing individuals whose maturational stage demands opportunity for meaningful occupation, but who are denied outlet for this need because of personal shortcomings or social conditions over which they have no control. The ongoing tension created by this inability to move must be dealt with; it may be turned inward against the self, resulting in physical or emotional illness or sickness of the spirit, or it may be expressed outwardly in antisocial behavior that is equally destructive to the individual and to others. Selye's concept is a basic one that has strongly affected our thinking in all areas of knowledge related to human nature, and we are studying and developing new understandings of what the concept means in living, in the aging process, and in death.

Life is never problem free. Each stage brings its challenges and its fulfillments but also its defeats. Each of us individually must face and respond to these in order to go on living.

Elisabeth Kübler-Ross, in her famous short book on dying and death (Kübler-Ross, 1997), postulated five stages in the process whereby an individual adapts to this ultimate crisis and reaches an acceptance of personal mortality. These stages equally describe the process by which many of us go about coping with lesser demands. These are:

1. Initial disbelief that the problem exists: "I just can't believe that this is happening to me."
2. Anger that this should happen to you while others go free: "I've always taken care of myself, eaten right, kept my weight down, never smoked—why do I have cancer?"
3. Bargaining: "Believe me, when I get through this I'm going to be a different person."
4. Depression that comes with the realization that the problem is real and will not go away: "I've been a bad parent—I've never given the children enough time."
5. Acceptance of the reality and readiness to face it: "We'll work out a plan—your Uncle Bob says he wants you to stay with him for a while."

The universality of these stages makes them useful both for worker and client in understanding the changing feelings and the process that is taking place in adaptation.

Summary

The development of an understanding of the human condition that is acceptable to and usable by an individual human service worker requires not only the acquisition of knowledge, but also the integration of many concepts into a meaningful whole. Openness to new ideas, objectivity, and flexibility are essential, because this endeavor is a never-finished task and there is no one complete answer.

SUGGESTED ASSIGNMENTS

1. Assign a major paper on a particular personality theory selected by students that will cover (a) origin, (b) principles, and (c) assessment of validity and utility. Also have students specifically address in which ways the culture, ethnicity, gender, and social status of the theorist influenced the theory. This paper should include some references to outside reading.

2. After completion of reading and discussion of chapter, assign students to outline a "personal" personality theory that for them best explains how we grow and develop and that fits in with their own experience and cultural background. Compare and contrast results in class.

3. Have students contact the National Association of Social Workers (1–800–638–8799 or at http://www.naswdc.org/) to obtain the most recent NASW Code of Ethics. Assign a short paper and class presentation on one of the six major principles therein, emphasizing its meaning, its significance, and its implications for practice. Require students to read and become familiar with the total code.

4. Have students select a type of therapy (i.e., psychoanalysis, behavior modification) and locate available research on its effectiveness. Have students describe and discuss these findings and also discuss how the parameters placed on mental health services by managed care might effect the use of this therapy.

5. After researching the type and availability of divorce support resources in their community, have students interview the leaders of divorce support groups to learn about how they help people cope with divorce and what strengths and problems they have seen in the divorced population.

6. Have students write a paper about their own spiritual beliefs and how these beliefs may influence their work with clients.

REFERENCES AND RELATED READINGS

Anastasia, A. (1996). *Psychological testing* (7th ed.). Upper Saddle River, NJ: Prentice Hall.

Belenky, M., Clincy, B., Goldberger, N., & Tarule, J. (1997). *Women's ways of knowing* (10th ed.). New York: Basic Books.

Bem, S. L. (1981). Gender schema theory: A cognitive account of sex typing. *Psychological Review, 88,* 354–364.

Berger, R., & Frederico, R. (1985). *Human behavior: A social work perspective* (2nd ed.). White Plains, NY: Longman.

Bryner, C. (2001). Children of divorce. *Journal of the American Board of Family Practice, 14*(3), 178–183.

Canda, E. R. (1980, Win.). Conceptualizing spirituality for social work: Insights from diverse perspectives. *Social Thought, 14,* 30.

Chodorow, N. (1999). *The reproduction of mothering.* Berkeley: University of California Press.

Cooper, J. (1995). *A primer on brief therapies.* New York: W. W. Norton & Company.

Corsini, R. E. (2000). *Current psychotherapies* (6th ed.). Belmont, CA: F.E. Peacock.

Ellis, A. (1996). *Reason and emotion in psychotherapy.* New York: Birch Lane Press.

Erikson, E. (1994). *Identity and the life cycle.* New York: W. W. Norton & Company.

—. (1998). *The life cycle completed.* New York: W. W. Norton & Company.

—. (1987). *A way of looking at things.* New York: W. W. Norton & Company.

Gilligan, C. (1993). *In a different voice—psychological theory and women's development.* Cambridge, MA: Harvard University Press.

GlenMaye, L. (1996) *Non-reporting of rape: A grounded theory approach.* Unpublished dissertation. Ann Arbor, MI: UMI Dissertation Services.

Greenspan, M. (1993). *A new approach to women and therapy* (2nd ed.). NewYork: Sulzberger & Graham.

Hetherington, E.M., & Stanley-Hagan, M. (1999) The adjustment of children with divorced parents: A risk and resiliency perspective. *Journal of Child Psychological Psychiatry, 40,* 129–40.

Kluckhorn, C. (1962). *Culture and behavior.* New York: Free Press.

Kübler-Ross, E. (1997). *On death and dying.* New York: Macmillan.

Mechanic, D. (1998). *Mental health and social policy: The emergence of managed care* (4th ed.). Boston: Allyn and Bacon.

Miller, J. B. (1987). *Toward a new psychology of women* (2nd ed.). Boston: Beacon Press.

National Association of Social Workers. *Code of ethics.* (1999). See: http://www.naswdc.org/code.htm.

Nugent, W. (1996). The use of hypnosis in social work practice. In F. Turner (Ed.), *Social work treatment* (4th ed.). New York: Free Press.

Reese, W. (1996) *The dictionary of philosophy and religion.* New York: Humanity Books.

Selye, H. (1978). *The stress of life* (2nd ed.). New York: McGraw Hill.

Slater, P. (1990). *The pursuit of loneliness.* Boston: Beacon Press.

Stout, K., & McPhail, B. (1998). *Confronting sexism and violence against women: A challenge for social work.* Harlow, Essex: Pearson Publishers.

Turner, F. (Ed.). (1996). *Social work treatment* (4th ed.). New York: Free Press.

Turner, F. (Ed.). (1999). *Adult psychopathology: A social work perspective* (2nd ed.). New York: Free Press.

Unger, R., & Crawford, M. (1992). *Woman and gender: A feminist psychology.* New York: McGraw-Hill.

Walrond-Skinner, S. (1986). *A dictionary of psychotherapy.* London: Routledge & Kegan Paul.

Walsh, M. (Ed.). (1987). *The psychology of women: Ongoing debates.* New Haven, CT: Yale University Press.

Walter, J., & Peller, J. (1992). *Becoming solution-focused in brief therapy.* New York: Garland Publishers.

Welfel, E. (2001). *Ethics in counseling and psychotherapy* (2nd ed.). Belmont, CA: Wadsworth Publishing.

Wernert, S. (Ed.). (1999). *Managed care in the human services.* Chicago: Lyceum Books.

SELECTED RELATED WEBSITES

Brief Therapy Center, Milwaukee, Wisconsin
http://www.brief-therapy.org/

Canadian Society for Spirtuality and Social Work
http://www.stthomasu.ca/academic/scwk/cass/

Data Sources and Research Centers on Children
www.princeton.edu/~children/data.htm

Divorce Magazine
www.divorcemag.com

Jean Baker Miller Training Institute
http://www.wellesley.edu/JBMTI/workingconnections.html

Social Work Access Network (SWAN)
http://www.sc.edu/swan/topics.html

Society for Spirituality and Social Work
http:// sehd.binghamton.edu/affprograms/sssw/

World Wide Web Resources for Social Workers
http://www.nyu.edu

Working with Ethnic Diversity in a Pluralistic Society

What is a pluralistic society, and what are its advantages, disadvantages, and major problems?

What groups do we presently define as "ethnic," and how is this definition determined by their history and their position in society?

How can human services become more aware of the diversity that exists within the ethnic populations who call the United States home?

How can human service workers use the concepts of systems theory in understanding and working with the concerns of members of ethnic groups within a pluralistic society?

Human diversity is a significant factor in working with all people. It is not only a determinant of individual and social functioning; it also affects every aspect of practice in human service. Only as workers are sensitive to differences among people, knowledgeable about their causes and effects, and skillful in recognizing and working with them will practice be effective. Although dealing with diversity has always been a part of education for practice, its importance has become increasingly obvious in the last half century. This increased awareness has been sparked by major historical changes.

The civil rights movement of the 1960s forced into the forefront of U.S. consciousness awareness of the existence of groups of people within the society who, because of their differences, were denied access to many of its benefits and were subject to personal and institutional discrimination. Changes that came as a result of this movement are reflected in laws and institutions, and minority people themselves have learned that as groups they possess strength, can effect social change, and can demand their rights to full participation in society.

A second factor is what has been called the "new immigration" of people fleeing from economic and ecological disaster, civil unrest, wars, starvation, lack of opportunity, violence, and oppression. Previous immigration had, for the most part, been invited and welcomed when the country was young and needed settlers and workers. However, the country is growing older and this is no longer true, except in those instances where immigrants can be exploited, as in migrant farm or household workers.

In spite of its affluence, the United States faces major problems—unemployment, poverty, crime, violence, drugs, homelessness. Such problems most strongly affect those without a stable place in the social structure, and newcomers are particularly vulnerable. Because of the destructive experiences they have undergone, they may also bring physical and emotional problems, a history of malnutrition, and lack or loss of schooling.

We seem to be moving toward a more pluralistic society wherein sharply different ethnic groups exist side by side, sharing in its benefits and enriching it by their diversity. Such changes do not come easily, and there will always be conflict where there are different interest groups and varying loyalties. However, the inherent strength of a democracy lies in its ability to reconcile them. People carry with them down through the generations vestiges of their original ethnicity, but as they are exposed to different cultures adaptation takes place, and all of the people and institutions involved are changed by the process. History indicates that this adaptation can be successful until and unless population diversity is used by unscrupulous, power-hungry leaders who emphasize differences and exploit them for their own ends.

In such a volatile situation, human service workers, who carry with them their own ethnic backgrounds, are faced with the challenge of practicing effectively. The process by which they enable people to use personal and institutional resources to live better and to work for the creation of more adequate ones is the same, but the pitfalls are many. The great advantage is that all people possess a common humanness, all have the same basic needs, and all live out the same life cycle. While there are some genetic differences, these are minor compared with the overall similarities. Each individual utilizes genetic differences and life experiences in a different manner.

The major task is to recognize that human diversity exists, that some people and groups are different from other people and groups by virtue of their history and their life experiences, that these differences can be expressed in ways unique to a particular group, and that this expression often constitutes great strength and must be understood and considered objectively.

The Language of Ethnic Diversity

In preparing to deal with ethnic diversity, it is important to become conversant with the language and concepts relating to it and their meanings. Some of the most significant are:

Ethnicity: Ethnic characteristics of people that distinguish them from others. In this country those whose ethnicity singles them out include Native Americans, African Americans, Hispanic Americans, and Asian Americans.

Color: Pigmentation of the skin that, along with physical features, is characteristic of a particular ethnic group.

Race: The stock or common ancestry of a particular ethnic group.

Racism: The belief that race determines human traits and capabilities and that particular races are superior to others.

Assimilation: The process by which an individual, group, or entire people merges and becomes indistinguishable as a result of prolonged contact; the basis of the melting pot theory.

Culture: The life patterns, language, and beliefs of a group of people.

Subculture: A group within a larger group of people with which it shares some common characteristics; it also possesses some unique ones.

Multicultural: Relating to or made up of several different cultures.

Pluralistic society: A society made up of diverse ethnic groups that retain vestiges of their own cultures but whose primary loyalty is to the society itself.

Minority status: A group set apart within another group, usually numerically smaller but not always—as with women.

Discrimination: Unequal or preferential treatment, injustice toward particular individuals, groups, or peoples; may be personal (expressed by individuals) or institutional (expressed in policies and laws).

Integration: Incorporation as equals into a society or an organization of individuals of different groups or races.

Segregation: Separation or isolation of a race, class, or ethnic group by discriminatory means.

Social class: The level occupied in the social order, with the differences based on wealth and group identification. Generally, societies have been considered as divided into upper, middle, and lower classes with some subgroups, but recently the category of underclass has been used to identify those people from a broad range of backgrounds who are outside of organized society and do not share in its benefits.

Ethnic Diversity: Population Highlights about Our Pluralistic Society

We are, in this country, a nation of ethnics. This is clearly shown by information about our society which was collected in the 2000 Census. Each ethnic group has its own strengths and weaknesses, but from this diversity can come the greatest strength and richness of life for all. The challenge is to create the kind of open society where that richness can exist.

Currently, the U.S. population stands at about 275 million, with approximately 82 percent of people listed as white (Population Estimates Program, 2000). However, clumping white U.S. society into a single category is as misleading as not understanding the important cultural differences between people of color. After the Civil War, vast numbers of immigrants began to arrive from southern and central Europe. They were not Protestant, not Anglo-Saxon, and had different languages and cultures from those who preceded them. Because of this, it is difficult to describe a white American, since about 200 million people can trace some of their ancestry back to the following groups (in descending size order):

English, German, Irish, French, Italian, Scottish, Polish, Dutch, Swedish, Norwegian, Russian, Czech, Slovakian, Hungarian, Welsh, Danish, and Portuguese. In addition, there are many white Americans of Hispanic background (Karger & Stoez, 2001).

African Americans were brought to this country unwillingly as slaves and kept as such for more than 200 years. Legally freed as an expedient in fighting a war, they have had to struggle for the last hundred years to get the benefits of education, access to economic power, and legal protection against exploitation. As with the Emancipation Proclamation, the legislation that followed the civil rights movement of the 1960s has not been definitive in assuring these rights, and the efforts to assure them continue. For example, in the past few years there have been controversial affirmative action decisions including California's Proposition 209, which ended affirmative action in hiring and admissions. In Texas there was the 1996 Hopwood decision, which ended the use of racial preferences in college and university admissions. These decisions have raised concerns about putting schools in California and Texas at a disadvantage in recruiting qualified minority students (DiNitto, 2000).

African Americans are strongly represented in our country; in 1999 there were about 35 million, almost 13 percent of the total population. This population continues to grow in size, and since 1990 it increased by 4.4 million people or 14 percent; meanwhile, the total U.S. population grew by 10 percent. It is projected that the African American population may increase to 59 million by 2050, a 70 percent rise (U.S. Census Bureau Facts for Features, 2000). As well, over one-third of the black population is under 18; however, there are fewer elderly African Americans than elderly whites. This reflects the fact that overall African Americans have shorter life expectancies than do whites, and from this we can see the toll taken by the ravages of poverty, oppression, and lack of access to basic services such as healthcare.

Clearly, racism and oppression still make it extremely difficult for African Americans to enter the mainstream. For example, the unemployment rate for blacks is still more than twice that of whites. Yet, African Americans exhibit great adaptive strengths because of their strong kinship bonds; flexibility of family roles; and the high value placed on religion, education, and work (Hines & Boyd-Franklin, 1996). These strengths helped African Americans in 1999 to have the lowest rate of poverty for their people since the Census Bureau began collecting data in 1959. However, this does not change the fact that far too many—about 9 million African Americans—still live in poverty (Karger & Stoez, 2001).

Asian Americans were originally represented by the Chinese, who were brought in a hundred years ago to build the railroads and do the menial tasks involved in extending white settlement westward. They originally came, intending to return, to provide money for families at home—there were provisions limiting their ability to become citizens—but many remained.

There is tremendous diversity in the Asian population, who have origins in the Far East, Southeast Asia, or the Indian subcontinent including Cambodia, China, India, Japan, Korea, Malaysia, Pakistan, the Philippine Islands, Thailand, and Vietnam. The five largest Asian population groups in the United States are Chinese (1.6 million), Filipino (1.4 million), Japanese (850,000), Asian Indian (815,000), and Korean (800,000). Pacific Islanders, a related group, have origins in any of the original peoples of Hawaii, Guam, Samoa, and other Pacific Island groups. Clearly, the Asian and Pacific Islander population is not homogenous but comprises many groups who differ in customs, language, and length of residence in the United States. In 1999, there were almost 11 million Asian and Pacific Islanders in this country. It is projected that by 2080 Asians will constitute 12 percent of the U.S. population (Humes & McKinnon, 2000).

While the social and economic data on Asians is mixed, perhaps the most striking feature is that they had the highest median family income in 1995. Economic and social data also point to a population that has made great strides, especially in the educational area. For example, in 1998, 26.5 percent of all males had completed college. Of that number, 27.3 percent were white, 13.9 percent black, 11.1 percent Hispanics, and 46.4 percent Asian (U.S. Bureau of the Census, 1999; Statistical Abstract of the United States, 1998).

It helps to look at subgroups in order to better understand the diversity of experiences of members of the larger group. This is certainly true in the case of Asian and Pacific Islanders. For example, while Chinese and Japanese Americans have achieved economic success, Southeast Asians are at higher risk of poverty than whites. Also concealed in economic statistics is the problem of many recent low-wage immigrants who work in sweatshops in "Chinatowns." It is important to be aware that Asian poverty levels range from less than 5 percent for Japanese Americans to 35 percent for newly arrived Southeast Asian immigrants (Karger & Stoez, 2001).

Hispanic Americans occupied parts of the Southwest when the eastern seacoast was first colonized. In subsequent wars and smaller military actions, they were driven off the lands they held. There is also a rich diversity within the Hispanic American population, who have origins in twenty-two different countries including Mexico, Puerto Rico, Cuba and other Caribbean islands, the Dominican Republic, and other countries in Central and South America (Ramirez, 1999).

The present influx of both legal and illegal immigrants fleeing the pressures of population and poverty in their native countries makes it difficult to accurately estimate their numbers. The 1999 census estimated the Hispanic population in the United States at about 32 million, or 11.7 percent of the total population. By the year 2005, Hispanics will comprise the largest minority group. By comparison, the non-Hispanic white population now makes up about 72 percent of the total population—by 2050 it will represent just 53 percent (Ramirez, 1999).

The numerous and diverse Hispanic populations have different cultures and customs as well as different levels of economic success once in the United States. Of those living below the poverty line in 1996, nearly 28 percent were Mexican American, 33 percent were Puerto Ricans living on the U.S. mainland, 12.5 percent were Cuban Americans, and 19 percent were from Central and South America. This compares to just 6.5 percent of whites and 26 percent of African Americans who lived below the poverty line. The poverty status of many Hispanics has worsened in the last two decades in relation to other groups, including African Americans. At present, there are somewhat more Hispanics in poverty than there are African Americans (Karger & Stoez, 2001; U.S. Bureau of the Census, Poverty 1998).

Native Americans were in the unfortunate position of being residents of this country when colonization took place and the newcomers undertook to exterminate the original occupants of the land. In addition to being victims of genocide, Native Americans were considered less than human, and it took a court decision to recognize them as people.

Reservations, the Bureau of Indian Affairs, and the setting aside of "Half Breed Tracts" were meant to provide for remaining segments of the population, but the long history of broken treaties, exploitation, and the retaking of reservation lands when they proved to have desirable resources belied these efforts.

Native Americans comprise slightly less than 1 percent of the total U.S. population, but there is great diversity within the Native American community, which has more than 550 federally recognized tribes. Yet, many other groups of Native Americans do not have this recognition and are unable to receive the social welfare benefits that the government is required to provide to tribes. Native Americans continue to struggle with the lowest income, the worst health, and the lowest social indices of social problems in the United States (DiNitto, 2000).

Yet, despite much adversity, it is important to remember that over the last thirty years these groups have made substantial gains in becoming a significant part of the larger society and getting access to its benefits, and in so doing they have changed that society. Discouraged that the process has not been faster and more complete, some groups evidence a growing tendency toward segregation and polarization. This varies according to the group and the situation and among individuals, and it is a changing phenomenon of which workers must be aware. In addition, as ethnic groups have become stronger, more vocal, and numerically greater, and more aggressive in reaching out to be included in the benefits of society, resistance to them and their demands has developed in the larger society. This takes the form of efforts to restrict immigration; to circumscribe the sharing of health, welfare, and educational services; and to limit employment. The climate toward members of ethnic groups is often hostile.

Expressions of Ethnicity

Ethnicity finds expression in every aspect of individual, family, and group life. It affects personal appearance, family and group structures, processes, and relationships. It defines the roles and assignment of tasks; it determines who makes the decisions; who spends the money; who is responsible for care of the children, handicapped, and aged; the relationship with extended family members; and the use of community resources.

Ethnicity is expressed in the ways people regard and deal with the crises of life—the developmental ones that mark progression from conception to death; those brought on by role change such as marriage and parenthood; those accidental events such as loss of a home, loss of a job, or death or disabling of a breadwinner.

Ethnicity is expressed in customs, in attitudes and behaviors with regard to such things as pain, violence, what can be verbalized and what cannot, dependence and independence, and in the ability to accept help. Such customs—ways of behaving—are internalized and become emotion laden, resulting in the feeling that this is the way things are supposed to be done, and so changes can be difficult and disturbing. Such expressions are matters of concern for human service workers who must have a working knowledge of them if possible and certainly have respect for their existence. While there is some advantage for the worker who is a member of the specific ethnic group being dealt with, there are also disadvantages—there may be variations within the ethnic group, and the worker's understanding may be limited to his or her own unique section of that group. In addition, variation in social class between worker and client can be a problem, as can the worker's attitudes toward members of the shared ethnic group who are poor, unable to cope with the problems of living, or not moving toward adaptation with the larger group with the same speed—particularly if workers feel that they have "made it" and others should also be able to do so.

Preparation of Workers

Preparation for work with varying ethnic groups includes the same as preparation for human service in general, but there are some special aspects that need to be stressed.

1. Workers must be sensitive to differences, aware of what they bring in personal attitudes, biases, beliefs, and knowledge about their ethnically different clients that can affect their ability to consider problems objectively, define them accurately, make valid assessments, and present acceptable solutions. When they lack understanding, they must be able to recognize it, to be nondefensive and able to engage clients in helping them comprehend meanings. They must be particularly aware of the ever-present danger of stereotyping and generalizing as explanations of behavior.

2. Workers must be equipped with knowledge of the past history of the particular ethnic group, which may not only be a major factor in their ability to trust, but also a source of resentment and anger toward workers for what they represent. Workers must be prepared to recognize and deal with such feelings if they exist, but they also must recall that people vary widely and be knowledgeable about the specific situation and individuals at hand.

3. Workers must be knowledgeable about and sensitive to the meaning of the present status and situation of the ethnic group and the individuals with whom they are working. In many ways this is more important than past history. We now have laws guaranteeing the civil rights of all people—we need to know whether and how they are being enforced on the federal, state, and local levels. Workers need to know if education, jobs, housing, and healthcare are available equally to all; whether there is a climate that encourages opening the benefits of society to all, forbids discrimination, and frowns on personal racism. It is particularly important that workers know the situation in the local community—which may be lagging behind in recognition of rights of ethnic groups, and attitudes toward them in provision of opportunities.

4. Workers must be aware of the policies and practices of the agency they represent, in terms of both how relevant they are to the needs of ethnic people and how relevant they are perceived as being. Perceptions as well as realities can constitute barriers that workers must cross to be effective. Often policies are set and practices developed that do not change easily as reality changes—workers must be cognizant of this and be prepared to work for a more realistic service plan.

5. Workers must be conversant with the impact of the often conflicting demands that weigh on people of one culture who are trying to adapt to life in another culture. The varying systems of which they are a part and to which they have loyalties are complex, both in themselves and in how they relate to one another. Workers must differentiate between customs and behaviors that must be altered if the client is going to survive personally and socially and those that can and should be retained.

6. Workers must have sensitivity, an almost intuitive awareness of sore spots and barriers to communication and open relationships. With some this seems to be an innate personality characteristic; with some it must be consciously cultivated. Experience and knowledge contribute to its development—particularly important in working with people whose reality is different from that of the worker. This ability to "read" the situation and the people therein will often be the determining factor in effective practice.

7. Workers must be aware that ethnic groups are not monolithic. Both individuals who are a part of them and the groups themselves can vary widely in the rate and extent of change that is taking place. When two cultural groups exist together, they and the individuals that comprise them are constantly in the process of being affected by each other and changing. Those most in contact with each other will change most rapidly. In addition, assimilation is not a one-way street—we need only look at the changes in art, literature, music, language, dress, and food, for example, that are taking place as a result of the presence of ethnic groups in modern society. Workers need to be aware of the changes in both individuals and groups, for these can be a source of conflict among those who would retain the status quo and those who would change.

The Use of Systems Theory

Pluralistic societies tend to be extremely complex, particularly when the groups that make them up are in the process of redefining their relationships. There is a tendency, when the stresses that accompany this process are greatest, for the groups to become polarized and to attack each other. The challenge is for workers to understand this process and the pressures it exerts on both individuals and groups and to avoid becoming a part of it. What is needed is a basic theory that is useful in thinking about such situations, and social systems theory can serve that purpose. Human service workers have been cognizant of the usefulness of systems theory in understanding and working with people and their social groups. It is particularly applicable to those who are a part of ethnic groups and striving to remain a part of their own systems but also becoming a part of the larger one.

Originating in biology many years ago, systems theory has gradually been adopted for use in other areas of study. It attempts to define the relationships among the parts of a whole. A system is defined simply as a whole made up of interrelated and interdependent parts (Figure 4.1). The parts exist in a state of balance, and when change takes place within one, there is compensatory change within the others. Systems become more complex and effective by constant exchange of both energy and information with their environment. When this exchange does not take place, systems tend to become ineffectual. A system is not only made up of interrelated parts, but is itself an interrelated part of a larger system.

The utility of this concept as a way of thinking about a human being as a totality is evident. It provides us with a dynamic point of view that stresses changing relationships and interrelationships rather than the static moment-in-time statement of classic diagnosis. The dynamic element in people creates a major problem in working with them and their groups. Because they are constantly changing, a static description or prescription is often out of date before it is even completed.

In addition to its dynamic nature, systems theory provides a yardstick that can be applied broadly to the person as an individual, to the person as a member of a family, to the

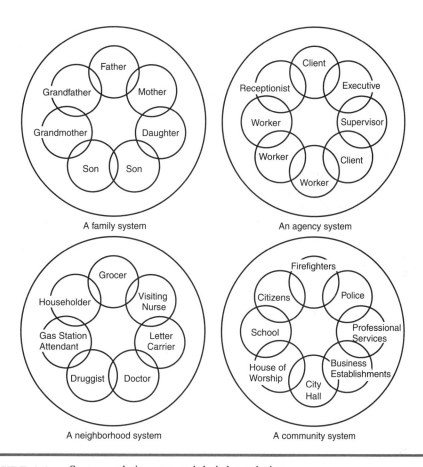

A family system · An agency system · A neighborhood system · A community system

FIGURE 4.1   Systems, their parts, and their boundaries.

person as part of a small group, to groups in relationship to each other, and so on, up to the most complicated social systems. This yardstick can be used (1) to assure a unified view of the interlocking components, (2) to assess the relationships within the system and to speculate as to how they will be affected by change within any part of the whole, (3) to pinpoint the crucial point where attack is most likely to bring about desired change, (4) to determine the type and mode of intervention to be utilized, and (5) to anticipate probable results of intervention on each level.

Systems theory also tends to remove the onus of responsibility for all change from the individual by recognizing the importance of the situation in creating and maintaining problems in functioning that are often beyond the power of the individual as a part of the system to change. It removes human service workers from the central position as changers and emphasizes their role as enablers. This coincides with the basic principle that fundamental change comes from within the individual or the system; it cannot be imposed from without, although an outsider can facilitate that change. It emphasizes the role of the natural mechanisms of adaptation. When changes are made in the system—as by rational agreement, legislation, program, disaster, and so on—people are faced with the necessity of adapting. We learn to live with the changes that occur in our surroundings, often slowly, but we have no other choice.

In looking at the nature of systems (wholes made up of interrelated and interdependent parts), it is obvious that there are elements that strive to maintain the status quo as well as those that are oriented toward activity and change. These divergent tendencies are related to the two basic functions of a system: (1) its internal task to maintain the balanced relationship among the parts of which it is composed, and (2) its external task to perform the function for which it was devised and to relate to its environment. In addition, a system tends to move toward old age and death, particularly if it is closed and lacks the input of new energy. If too much energy is devoted to maintaining relationships that have become rigid, the system can accommodate little input and expends its whole energy in maintaining itself. It cannot perform the task for which it was devised, and the system malfunctions.

Applying Concepts from Systems Theory to Working with People

What implications does all this have for workers whose task it is to improve the functioning of clients, to increase the effectiveness with which clients can perform various social roles? For those workers whose focus is trying to facilitate change on a larger scale—in institutions or social systems? How can workers make practical use of systems theory in their jobs?

They may well begin by asking themselves three questions: (1) What are the boundaries of the system or systems with which they are dealing? (2) What are the patterns and channels of communication both within the individual system under consideration and among the related external systems? (3) What are the explicit and implicit rules that govern the relationship among the parts, both internally and externally, particularly with respect to input (openness to new ideas or material), processing (working with these materials), and output (feedback or results of this work)?

Workers first define the boundaries of the particular system with which they need to work. These will be determined by the focus needed by the worker to deal most effectively with a particular area of malfunctioning. System boundaries may encompass a tiny area or be almost infinitely extended. For example, in considering the problems of an individual, workers can choose differing frames of reference and define several different boundaries. These might encompass a neighborhood, a state, or a nation, depending on the level on which it is necessary to operate. As an example, we can take the specialized functioning of the physician. Using one frame of reference, he sees his young patient with a venereal disease as a biological system composed of a series of specialized systems, each of which affects the other. He will intervene in the biological system with medication. He will function in another system on another level by reporting the disease to the health department, which will then attempt to reach everyone with whom the patient has had contact. On a third level, he will intervene by participating in health education programs in the local high school. In so doing, he is working with three different service systems: (1) doctor, patient, clinic, paramedical personnel; (2) doctor, patient, paramedical personnel, health department people, patient's contacts; and (3) doctor, school personnel, community planners, lay people.

It is obvious in looking at systems that the concept of balance among parts is a particularly important one, and it is vital to remember that when a change is made in one part of the system there must be a compensatory change in the others. It is equally obvious that there is a factor of inertia to be considered, a push toward retention of the status quo balanced by a push toward change. This delicate balance, this dynamic interrelationship, is a vital element in any system. Workers thinking in systems terms enable themselves to see the total picture, the relationship between the parts involved, and the type of change that is necessary to achieve a healthier balance. It is hoped that they can select the level and mode of intervention that will be most effective and that they may work on several levels at once.

Systems change becomes increasingly complicated as we deal with larger, more diverse, and older social systems where the relationships, roles, and overall tasks of the system have become sharply defined and rigid. The worker who attempts to help change the system of a hospital unit, a school classroom, a neighborhood, or a community to help it function more effectively may find the task one that can only be achieved by pressure or policy and administrative change at a very high level.

Workers are as much a part of many social systems as are their clients, and as much subject to their controls and pressures. Unfortunately, the systems responsible for human services have in many instances become rigid and inflexible, bureaucratized to the point where they are not adequately meeting human need. This becomes particularly significant and poses problems involving loyalties and basic responsibilities when the roles of workers require that they challenge and change the system of which they are a part and represent. The challenges themselves are an encouraging indication of vitality, and though they are also a source of endless anxiety, frustration, anger, and fear, conflict in some form is essential to growth, and we should welcome it for the opportunity it presents.

Families as Systems

Systems theory has played an important role in the field of family therapy. This is because families are also systems—ones that are characterized by intimate and specialized relationships. More than the sum of its parts (the individual members), family systems are the parts plus the way they function together. Within the family system there are three subsystems: parents, parent-child, and siblings (also see Chapter 10). Families are also part of even larger systems, communities, culture, and political systems.

Virginia Satir, a social worker and one of the pioneers of family therapy, used the analogy of a mobile to illustrate how the family members are interrelated. In making a family mobile, all members of the family must be taken into consideration and arranged accordingly in order to balance the mobile. "All families are in balance. The question is: What is the cost to each family member to maintain that balance?" (Satir, 1988).

Each traditional model of family therapy—communications, Bowenian, strategic, and structural—bases its thinking on some version of systems thinking (Table 4.1). The idea that families are systems and it is the interaction (communication) between the parts that brings the system to life came out of research in the 1950s on families with a member who had schizophrenia. While many of the assumptions about a family's role in schizophrenia later turned out to be incorrect, this work did result in many concepts that do help explain communication in all types of family systems (Nichols & Schwartz, 2001).

TABLE 4.1   Traditional Models of Family Therapy Using Systems Theory

---

Communications Model of Family Therapy

I. Gregory Bateson   Donald Jackson   John Weakland   William Fry   Jay Haley

- Known as the Palo Alto Group, at the Mental Training Institute, their research on communication to explain the development of schizophrenic behavior within the familial environment was a springboard for the developing field of family therapy.
- In 1956, Bateson and his colleagues introduced the concept of the double bind.

II. Virginia Satir

- Theorized that there is a direct connection in families between communication and self-esteem; the outcome of effective communication is increased awareness, empathy, and new perspectives.
- This model focuses on family dynamics; emphasizes nurturance to build family self-worth; and uses dramatic interventions, metaphors, sculpture, stories, and scripts acted out by the family about scenes in their life.

Bowenian Model of Family Therapy

Murray Bowen

- Also called the Intergenerational or Systems Model of family therapy, this was one of the forerunners of the family therapy movement.
- Family patterns are seen to develop over time and are often transmitted from generation to generation. Such patterns can be seen in a family genogram.
- Key theoretical concepts include: the differentiation of self, the ability of the child to become separate from the parental unit, and triangles, which occur when two-person relationships are faced with high levels of anxiety and they pull in a third party to defuse the intensity with increasing anxiety; the triangle cannot contain the tension, and an interlocking web of triangles is formed.

Strategic Model of Family Therapy

Jay Haley   Milton Erickson   Don Jackson   Cloe Madanes

- The theory of strategic therapy states that the patient's symptoms are a result of attempts by family members to correct what they consider "problem" behavior.
- Focuses on short-term, targeted efforts to solve a specific problem.
- The goal of strategic family therapy is to replace dysfunctional patterns for successful ones.
- Key concepts include: The presenting problem serves a function in the family that is not recognized, symptoms occur to maintain the family functioning, and change occurs through behavior; insight is not important.

Structural Model of Family Therapy

Salvador Minuchin

- The basic tenet is that there is an underlying structure that guides families; dysfunction occurs when the structure is disrupted.
- The central point of this therapy is reinforcing the original family structure through key interventions. The therapist's role is very directive in the course of structural family therapy.

Adapted from: SWORL: Social Workers Link to Children and Family Resources. Available online:
http://members.nbci.com/_XMCM/jennmurphy/index.htm

One of the most important concepts was called double bind communication—this is communication that transmits contradictory messages between people who are in a close relationship, such as parent and child. For example, a parent may sabotage his child's meaningful relationships outside of the family yet say to the child, "Do not see me as making demands on you; I only want what you want." The child is then placed in a no-win situation because regardless of what she does—seek out relationships or not seek out relationships—she cannot please her parent and will be punished (Walrond-Skinner, 1986). Although many controversies have arisen over the years about how double bind communication effects families, there are two things about this idea that have greatly influenced family therapy: There are multiple levels of communication, and the destructive patterns of relationship are maintained by self-regulating interactions of the family group (Nichols & Schwartz, 2001).

Usually the crisis that precipitates the need for help comes as a problem of an individual family member, such as a child failing in school or involved in delinquent behavior, a father who cannot hold a job, a mother who drinks heavily, an interfering grandparent, or a marriage that is unhappy and deteriorating. The balance within this malfunctioning family is based on the behavior of the troubled family member, and the system will tend to pressure this member to continue in that role. Any change within the member apart from the system is extremely difficult to maintain. While the worker may help family members on an individual basis, focus should be on work with the family as a whole to change the family system and give the individual a fighting chance for healthy behavior.

Important concepts from systems theory that have been applied to work with families include the following (Nichols & Schwartz, 2001; Walrond-Skinner, 1986):

Families: Rule-governed systems with a tendency toward stability or homeostasis.

Subsystems: Individual family members and subgroupings such as the marital dyad and the sibling group.

Supra-system: The family's physical, economic, and interpersonal environment.

Boundaries: The "invisible membranes" surrounding each set of relationships (or subsystems) within a family. Within the family boundary are its members and their roles, norms, values, traditions, and goals, plus other elements that distinguish one family from another and the social environment. Healthy boundaries are not too open or too closed; weak boundaries make it difficult for each person to differentiate his or her feelings from others in the family; boundaries that are too rigid result in psychological isolation.

Feedback: The process through which families regulate the system's behavior. Feedback can be positive, leading to change and variation, or negative, leading to stability and homeostasis. A balance between the two types of feedback is necessary for the optimal functioning of the family system.

Homeostasis: A balance that is maintained by each family member: Behaviors are reinforced, even if they are dysfunctional. While homeostasis is important in keeping family members together, it can also be an active agent in keeping families from making needed changes.

Hierarchy: The relationships of individuals or subsystems in a family with each other.

Families also play a major role in transmitting the shared ancestry, values, and customs that define ethnicity (McGoldrick, Giordano, & Pierce, 1996). The complex series of systems of which any individual consists becomes even more complicated when the factor of ethnicity is considered. People are subject in all aspects of their lives not only to the pressures of their ethnic group to conform to its expectations, not only to the demands of their personal ethnic loyalty, but also to pressure of the larger society to conform to its requirements. Therefore, when workers define the boundaries of the systems with which they must work, when they assess the patterns and channels of communication and the explicit and implicit rules that govern these relationships, they must always take into consideration the factor of ethnicity.

Putting It All Together: Using a Systems Perspective with an Ethnic-Sensitive Focus

The following examples illustrate workers applying a systems perspective with an ethnic-sensitive focus (Table 4.2).

Yolanda Martinez

Yolanda Martinez is a 13-year-old Mexican American. Her family moved from an urban southwestern city, which had been their home since migrating from Mexico ten years earlier, to a midwestern town so that her father could work in a meat packing plant. The family had left behind in the Southwest a large, supportive, ex-

TABLE 4.2   Guidelines for an Ethnic Assessment

- Assess the importance of ethnicity to families and clients.
- Validate and strengthen the family's and client's support system.
- Be aware of, use, and strengthen the family's and client's support system.
- Help the family and clients identify and resolve value conflicts.
- Be aware of families and clients who use cultural stereotypes as ways to justify irresponsible behavior or resistance to change.
- Know there are advantages and disadvantages in being of the same ethnic group as the families you serve.
- Be aware of your own limitations and ignorance about other ethnic group as the families you serve.
- Be aware of your own limitations and ignorance about other ethnic groups—be open to mutual learning with and from your clients about ethnicity.

Adapted from: Monica McGoldrick, Joe Giordano, and John Pearce, *Ethnicity and Family Therapy,* The Guilford Press, 1996.

tended family network. Since the move, Yolanda had become withdrawn and was getting poor grades in school. In addition to the tensions of early adolescence, her situation was compounded by social isolation both in school and in the community; by lack of understanding from her family (both parents worked outside the home, and her brother, an athlete, was accepted and lionized); by pressure from her grandmother, who lived in the home and did not speak English, to retain her language and native customs. Yolanda's mother, Maria, initiated the referral to the town's Family Service Agency and identified Yolanda as the problem. The worker, however, requested the entire family come to the agency for an evaluation.

The worker was not Mexican and honestly reflected upon her lack of knowledge regarding their customs and ways. She then began to educate herself through reading and discussions with a Mexican American colleague. She learned many things; Mexican families typically rely upon a large, extended family for emotional support especially during times of transition and change; family collectivism, inclusiveness, and interdependence—*familismo*—make it difficult for many Mexicans to ask for help outside of the family; and that parents and grandparents were given the highest status and utmost respect by the younger people in the family (Falicov, 1996).

Being open to the cultural and ethnic differences resulted in the worker's conveying a sincere interest to the Martinez family about learning more from them and also to conducting a systemic, ethnic-sensitive assessment focusing on (1) Yolanda as an individual; (2) her family, including extended family in their former hometown; (3) the school, which was only beginning to learn how to deal with students from different cultural backgrounds; and (4) the community, where there was a tendency to stereotype the incoming Mexican Americans.

The worker also expanded the boundaries of her assessment to gather information from the Martinez family about their migration history, their views about acculturation to their new homeland, what support systems had helped the family cope with the migration, what values they felt were different in the United States from those in Mexico, what strains the family experienced from any differences in values, and the degree to which each family member identified with traditional Mexican values and those of contemporary United States society (Falicov, 1996).

Son Nguyen

Son Nguyen, a refugee from Vietnam, was sponsored by a church to come to the United States. His problems were practical and immediate—finding a home and furniture, learning to use community resources, learning the language, getting a job, and finding a place for himself socially, as he was without family and one of the first of his ethnic group to come to this community.

The worker was familiar with the struggles experienced by Vietnamese living in the United States. One of biggest changes was the loss of the extended family structure. In Vietnam, Son would be living among a network of family and relatives and would resolve his problems within the family circle (Leung & Boehnlein, 1996). In order to provide Son with a new network, the worker made use of a small, informal group of Asian Americans who were helpful, even though many of them were of a different cultural orientation. Volunteers from the church and the community at large were marshaled to find the essential furniture, provide transportation, and help Son in learning his way around the community. Classes in the English language were available at a local community college, and a volunteer provided one-to-one additional teaching.

John and Margaret Iron Bull

Margaret and John live on the reservation and are foster parents for two lively grandsons whose father was killed in a car accident and whose mother is an alcoholic. They are concerned about the negative aspects of life on the reservation, where there is poverty, alcoholism, drug addiction, and poor schooling with a high rate of dropouts, and what effect these will have on the boys. The close family ties of Native Americans stand them in good stead. Although John is unable to work because of emphysema, he has the help of relatives.

The foster care worker operates with several related systems—acting as a liaison with the school, both creating and helping the family make use of resources, such as food stamps, the local hospital, and a recreation center for the boys, and working with the tribal council that is attempting to get small industries and possibly casino gambling on the reservation as a source of jobs and money. Much of the work is directly with the grandparents, who in the Native American family structure are the caregivers and providers of training and discipline (Sutton & Broken Nose, 1996). This pivotal role in their extended family makes it even harder for them to accept the changing world in which the boys are growing up.

Matilda Robinson

Matilda Robinson, an African American widow, lives alone in a housing project where conditions are extremely dangerous, where drugs, gangs, drive-by shootings, and poor living conditions abound. A virtual prisoner in her apartment, she lives in fear of violence, of someone stealing her small Social Security check, of her increasing infirmity (she is 85), and of her need for healthcare. The worker has her picked up once a week for a day at the Senior Center, where she has her meals and socializes. She is taken grocery shopping and to the clinic as needed, and a visiting nurse will stop in as necessary. The worker is also involved with the tenants group that is trying to get the city housing authorities to take care of essential maintenance of the apartments, get the police department to provide better protection, and help the outreach workers who are trying to cope with the growing gang membership and the drug dealing.

This worker is also African American and knows of her people's historical tradition of a strong spiritual orientation going back to their roots in Africa, continuing through the era of slavery, and into the present time (Hines & Boyd-Franklin, 1996). However, the worker did not want to stereotype Mrs. Robinson based upon her own experience as an African American. When meeting with Mrs. Robinson, the worker did not just assume Mrs. Robinson was religious, rather she inquired about this aspect of her life. Mrs. Robinson did indeed have strong religious beliefs and was involved with a local Baptist church. The worker was then able to use this strong support system to further help Mrs. Robinson. The pastor, who as a member of the community was quite aware of the dangerous environment in which Mrs. Robinson lived, made sure to have members of the congregation escort her to and from church services and social functions. Church members also provided friendly visits, which helped decrease her loneliness as a result of being trapped in her apartment due to the rampant crime in her neighborhood.

The Worker's Social Responsibility

Although individuals, families, and groups are, in the final analysis, responsible for their adjustments to a different culture and while many of the workers' tasks will lie in facilitating this, there is also a larger responsibility. Personal and institutional racism, social pressures, and policies affecting different ethnic groups can destroy people in spite of their best individual efforts. Because of their professional relationships, workers are often in the position to know best how destructive such things can be, and they have a professional responsibility to become involved in trying to change them.

This begins with the worker's personal life and extends to the agency the worker represents, to other institutions and bureaucracies, to local, state, and federal government, and to the media that are so important in setting attitudes and behaviors.

Each worker must decide, on the basis of personal abilities and time available, the extent and manner in which he or she will be involved in attempting to change such destructive social factors or to marshal the necessary resources to do so. Such change tends to come slowly, and often the only recourse available to workers and clients is to face the unpleasant reality and work around it. In the long run, however, the survival of a democracy rests on its recognition of the value and worth of all individuals and of their diversity.

The increasing number and variety of ethnic groups in our society make it essential for human service workers to prepare themselves for what is known as "ethnic-sensitive practice." This includes knowledge of and sensitivity to not only historical and cultural differences, but also changing social situations and the attitudes and behaviors of those belonging to the larger group and of members of the ethnic group.

The single most important factor in working with ethnic diversity does not lie, however, in the knowledge and skill areas but in values. The worker who is honestly accepting of differences, sensitive to their meaning, and secure enough to recognize and acknowledge the need to take time to learn and to promote understanding will be able to work with many different kinds of people.

Summary

Modern human service workers have a special need for understanding ethnic diversity and a pluralistic society because of the virtual abandonment of the old melting pot theory and the emergence of strong ethnic groups. Such groups function as social systems in defining the cultural roles of individuals within them and the relationship of the group to other such groups in the society. The cultural differences affect every aspect of the workers' practice and require special knowledge and skill.

SUGGESTED ASSIGNMENTS

1. Assign each student to select a particular ethnic minority (different from the one of which he or she is a member) and write a major paper dealing with the past and present history of this group and the tasks facing its members in the process of adaptation to life in this country. Include consideration of ways in which this ethnic group has contributed to life here. Students selecting the same group could plan a joint class preparation and could invite members of that group to talk about their experiences.

2. Using information in this chapter about the demographics of ethnic diversity, and also from other sources (e.g., the U.S. Census website), facilitate a classroom discussion about the many implications for human service workers, relevant organizations, and the diverse clients they serve.

3. Have each student prepare a short paper to share in class on his or her personal ethnic background, the history of his or her people, their life in this country, and how the student sees this as a factor in effectiveness as a human service practitioner.

4. Assign students to prepare a basic systems analysis for working with a particular problem. If they are in field work, they can select one from there, otherwise one from their personal experience. Duplicate these and distribute them to the class as a basis for discussion of the use of systems theory in practice.

5. Have students select a family case from their work or field placement and choose a model of family therapy based on systems theory to develop an assessment. Discuss in class the different perspectives each model provides.

6. Using the examples illustrating workers' application of a systems perspective with an ethnic-sensitive focus, have students enact each example as a role-play. Have students take turns playing the worker and various family members. Encourage students to discuss the different perspectives each role gives them and relate this to their self-awareness about ethnic-sensitive practice.

REFERENCES AND RELATED READINGS

Anderson, R., & Carter, I. (1990, 1999). *Human behavior in the social environment: A social systems approach* (5th ed.). Hawthorne, NY: Aldine.

Bradshaw, J. (1988). *Bradshaw on the family—A revolutionary way of self-discovery.* Deerfield Beach, FL: Health Communications.

Davis, L. (Ed.). (1999). *Working with African American males: A guide to practice.* Thousand Oaks, CA: Sage Publications.

Devore, W., & Schlesinger, E. (1998). *Ethnic sensitive social work practice* (5th ed.). Upper Saddle River, Cambridge, UK: Pearson Allyn and Bacon.

DiNitto, D. (2000, 2003). *Social welfare: Politics and public policy* (6th ed.). Boston: Allyn and Bacon.

Ewalt, P., Freeman, E., Kirk, S., & Poole, D. (Eds.). (1996). *Multicultural issues in social work.* Silver Spring, MD: National Association of Social Workers Press.

Falicov, C. (1996). Mexican families. In M. McGoldrick, J. Giordano, & J. Pearce (Eds.), *Ethnicity and family therapy* (2nd ed.). New York: Guilford Press.

Grey, W., Duhl, F., & Drizzo, N. (1982). *General systems theory and the psychological sciences.* Chicago, IL: Intersystems Publishers.

Hines, P., & Boyd-Franklin, N. (1996). African American families. In M. McGoldrick, J. Giordano, & J. Pearce (Eds.), *Ethnicity and family therapy* (2nd ed.). New York: Guilford Press.

Humes, K., & McKinnon, J. (2000). *The Asian and Pacific Islander population in the United States: March 1999.* U.S. Census Bureau, Current Population Reports, Series pp. 20–529. Washington, DC: U.S. Government Printing Office.

Karger, H., & Stoez, D. (2001). *American social welfare policy: A pluralist approach* (4th ed.). Boston: Allyn and Bacon.

Katz, W. (1993). *A history of multicultural America: Minorities today.* Boston: Steck-Vaughn.

Leung, P., & Boehnlein, J. (1996). Vietnamese families. In M. McGoldrick, J. Giordano, & J. Pearce (Eds.), *Ethnicity and family therapy* (2nd ed.). New York: Guilford Press.

McGoldrick, M., Giordano, J., & Pearce, J. (1996). *Ethnicity and family therapy* (2nd ed.). New York: Guilford Press.

Nichols, M., & Schwartz, R. (2001). *Family therapy: Concepts and methods.* Boston: Allyn and Bacon.

Population Estimates Program, Population Division, U.S. Census Bureau, Washington, DC (2000). Available online: http://www.census.gov/population/estimates/nation/intfile3–1.txt.

Ramirez, R. (1999). *The Hispanic population in the United States: March, 1999.* U.S. Census Bureau, Current Population Reports, Poverty Series pp. 20–527. Washington, DC: U.S. Government Printing Office.

U.S. Census Bureau Facts for Features. (2000). http://www.census.gov.

Satir, V. (1988). *The new people making.* Mountain View, CA: Science and Behavior Books.

Sutton, C., & Broken Nose, M. A. (1996). American Indian families: An overview. In M. McGoldrick, J. Giordano, & J. Pearce (Eds.), *Ethnicity and family therapy* (2nd ed.). Guilford Press.

Tidwell, B. (1987). Racial discrimination and inequality. In *Encyclopedia of Social Work* (18th ed.). Silver Spring, MD: National Association of Social Workers Press.

Walrond-Skinner, S. (1986). *A dictionary of psychotherapy.* New York: Routledge & Kegan Paul.

SELECTED RELATED WEBSITES

American Association of Marriage and Family Therapy
http://www.aamft.org

Amnesty International
http://www.amnesty.org/

The Mental Research Institute—Palo Alto, California
http://www.mri.org

Race and Ethnicity Resources on the American Studies Web
http://www.georgetown.edu/crossroads/asw

Simon Wiesenthal Museum of Tolerance
http://motlc.wiesenthal.com/

U.S. Census Bureau Home Page
http://www.census.gov/

Developing and Maintaining Communication with People

What is the process by which meanings are transferred?

How do verbal and nonverbal communications differ, and how do they supplement and complement each other?

In what ways do perception, context, and culture affect communication?

What are the elements of the diffusion process, and how are they used in communication?

How has the Internet changed the way people communicate?

When two or more people interact, communication takes place. It would be impossible to avoid unless all of the senses were destroyed. Basically, we communicate what we are. Webster's dictionary defines communication as "sharing that which is common, or participation." The concept is a dynamic one, implying activity on the part of all persons involved. There is no communication without a receiver as well as a sender. One could, as poets do, communicate with the wind or the waves, but it would be a one-way street with a lone person sending and receiving.

The initial task of human service workers is to develop and maintain communication with their clients, their colleagues, and other significant people within the community. To do this they express themselves through verbal and nonverbal channels as well as through symbols, such as the sharing of food or drink, that have a commonly understood meaning. In addition, they must be receptive to expression from others. Inability to establish communication and breakdown of ongoing communication are major problems in our complex, variegated society—a source of difficulty in families, groups, and institutions and in society as a whole. The basic difficulty seems to lie in the fact that we communicate our selves, and our selves differ markedly; we communicate meanings, and meanings not only vary as to implication, but how they are phrased may distort the intended message as well.

How are meanings transferred, and how do we arrive at that commonness of understanding and participation that is communication? The process itself is clear and sounds simple. A sender, who wishes to establish communication, evaluates the potential receiver, and, being unable to transfer ideas, attitudes, and feelings per se, encodes them in a manner that allows for transmission. The receiver perceives the coded message and translates or decodes it into an understandable and usable form. The receiver in turn encodes a response and starts it back to the original sender.

The back-and-forth channels may become clogged by interference or "noise," which so disturbs and distorts the intended message that it does not convey what the sender intended. This interference may range widely from attitudes and feelings, to group pressures, to reality situations. Here is an example: An African American student came to see his adviser, a white, middle-aged, female professor. Observing that he was ill at ease, she commented as she searched the files for his records, "Are you a local boy?" He replied, with considerable dignity, "I resent that." What happened in this communication? The faculty member, a parent with boys the age of the student, evaluated him in terms of her own experience, rather than in relation to his specific reality in a specific social situation. This created interference in both the encoding and the decoding, and the communication became to the receiver a racial slur rather than the intended supportive interest.

Basics for Clear Communication

1. Attitudes and feelings of both receiver and sender are vitally important. They affect all communication and can so distort sending and receiving that breakdown occurs.

Wanda was an involuntary client, a 14-year-old runaway picked up by the police for soliciting and brought to the shelter. Anger, fear, and rage at her parents focused on the worker, whom she identified with them. Her distrust made effective communication almost impossible—she could not hear the concern, acceptance, and desire to help. In the initial interview the worker merely explained the arrangements under which Wanda would be living, expressed her own wish to help, and set a time to see her in the morning.

2. An understanding of the similarities and differences between the people involved will determine the extent to which a common understanding and acceptance of modes of communication can be relied on. Differences in age, sex, cultural identification, social position, and ethnic background all affect the ability to communicate with each other. Awareness of and sensitivity to the meaning of these differences is the first essential for opening communication channels.

The new foster care worker assigned to Mrs. Navarone, who had undertaken to care for her grandchildren when their alcoholic mother was killed in an accident, was appalled both at the poverty of the home and the serious problems the children showed—stuttering, bedwetting, rage. Knowing that talking about such problems would not be easy for Mrs. Navarone, particularly with a virtual stranger, a non–Native American, she communicated her concerned interest by discussing first reality needs—beds, clothing, dishes—and then provided them. First things first.

3. The capacities of the client to use both verbal and nonverbal communication media and interpret the symbols should be understood. Clients can be people who are illiterate and semiliterate, hearing impaired; people who have speech problems, different educational levels; and people who lack the ability to verbalize.

Andrew Nowicki had gone through eight grades of school without learning to read. When times were good, he worked construction and made a living for himself and his family. His literate wife helped him socially, but when an injury caused him to be laid off and he went to apply for welfare, he was handed a form to fill out—simple, but too difficult for him to read. The worker's task was to communicate acceptance and respect for Mr. Nowicki as a person to enable him to accept help in interpreting the document and then assess the usefulness of the form itself.

4. Workers should be able to use a variety of means of communication to meet the needs and capacities of their clients. These can be both verbal and nonverbal.

With Mrs. Atkins, a bedridden, terminally ill woman, the worker shared tea and cookies, held her hand, and stroked her hair as they talked. Much of the discussion was of the past, of the small difficulties in the home, and of the future of her handicapped son after her death.

With Mr. Brown, an angry, potentially violent, long-unemployed man, the worker structured interviews in her office and, while empathetic, was never a part of his anger and fear, although recognizing it with him.

With Billy Markwitz, a rebellious, constantly testing, but unsure teenager, the worker gave credence to his feelings but focused on the reality with which he must deal. Honesty and openness were the keynotes, as was a refusal to be manipulated.

5. Workers should be able to evaluate the need for repetition and emphasis, and then ensure feedback to test comprehension. One of the best ways to do this is to repeat the client's statements as a question: "You understand the Center is open only from 5:30 to 9:00 at night?"

When Sarah Loomis decided it would be unsafe to take her children home, where her husband, who had a history of physical violence, was drinking heavily, the worker gave her both verbal and written directions to the shelter after calling in her presence to be sure that there was space and that she would be expected. When Mrs. Loomis, although usually a fairly competent person, seemed unable to grasp this, the worker arranged transportation by a volunteer.

6. Workers should use "loaded" words, gestures, and symbols only as their meaning is commonly understood and accepted. Humor is a particularly risky tool—only as workers know this fact well can they use humor differentially.

Mrs. Carstens, who had lived a long life of poverty and struggle, used the strong humor of the dispossessed of the world and would croak happily with the worker over Murphy's Law—"Anything that can go wrong will!"—as she faced the latest disaster of a grandchild picked up on a drug charge. The worker might respond "Sometimes it sure seems that way—you've had a lot to deal with," thereby recognizing her feeling, the reality of her life, and her way of dealing with it.

7. The tempo of communications should be geared to the client's level. Too much information, too many and too complex ideas given too quickly, or too much elaboration can be bewildering, causing lack of comprehension, withdrawal, and even anger. Equally, too simplistic communication can cause resentment in those capable of quicker and more comprehensive understanding. Intense emotion can affect the ability to "hear" communications.

"He's a nice boy" (the worker was 55), Mrs. Higgins (age 82) confided to her cronies in the home, "but he talks so fast I can't keep up with him."

"He must think I'm dumb!" Bill Woods growled resentfully. "Like he had to explain everything twice."

"The thing I like about Mr. Williams is that he always makes sure I understand. He says, 'Now you're clear about that,' and he writes things down so I can go over them later," contributed Mrs. Swanson.

8. Workers should be aware of ways to eliminate interference both in their own communications and in those of their clients. Interference can be anything from the noise of a TV program, to the presence of another person, to strong feelings. Sometimes it requires all the worker's dexterity to remove unwanted persons.

The Travers were anxious, overprotective parents, appalled by their 15-year-old daughter's pregnancy. They did all the talking, and she sulked. The worker said directly, "I need to talk alone with Sarah for a little time. There's coffee in the waiting room. Why not go have a cup, and we will get together again later." She rose as she said this and opened her office door.

Nonverbal Communication

Nonverbal communication (communication without the use of words) is the basic, primitive form of conveying information from one person to another. It has been estimated that in normal communications between two people, only one-third of the meaning is transmitted verbally and nearly two-thirds is transmitted nonverbally. Nonverbal communication is used when individuals do not possess command of a language. The channels through which it operates are fundamentally affective rather than cognitive, although a cognitive element is clearly involved. Nonverbal communication takes place universally when two individuals meet for the first time, size each other up, and develop ideas about the kind of person with whom they are dealing—whether the other is hostile or friendly, weak or strong, concerned or indifferent.

Infants cry wordlessly, wave their arms, and pucker up their faces to communicate feelings of discomfort. The response of the parents to these early attempts of their infant to say how it feels—and how it feels is usually in relation to how they feel—will determine the infant's formulation of concepts related to these actions. The parents' response will also determine the infant's development of ways to communicate feelings of hunger, happiness, anger, and so on. Only later will come the words that will embody these feelings.

Nonverbal communication is continuous, with or without verbal accompaniment. It is the principal means by which attitudes and feelings are conveyed, particularly in the initial stages of a relationship, but it goes on throughout any continuing contact between people. Because nonverbal communication never ceases, there is great danger that a worker may be communicating contradictory messages. One may say verbally, "I'm so glad that you stopped by," while at the same time conveying nonverbally, "I'm tired and harassed, it's late on a Friday afternoon, and I'll be glad to see the last of you."

This kind of communication is confusing at best and can be extremely destructive to vulnerable people. We see this with children caught in a situation where there is basic rejection of the child's needs and demands, and where the anger and frustration about this are communicated constantly by nonverbal means, while the parents verbally profess love and concern. Such children are confused because they do not know which communication is valid.

Sensitive workers, who are aware of their own feelings and recognize the impact expression through nonverbal channels has on the people with whom they are working, will attempt to deal with their own feelings in constructive ways. They can ventilate feelings of frustration with a fellow worker, hopefully one who will be healthy and knowledgeable enough to encourage ventilation rather than to reinforce the negative feeling. Or workers can use a good supervisor whose responsibility it is to help deal with these feelings. They can also in some instances acknowledge the existence of the feelings with the person to whom they are talking, try to understand their source, and decide whether it is possible to change the situation that provokes them. This can be done in a way that enhances healthy communication.

In some instances workers can face and verbalize their own conflicting feelings with both individuals and groups to good effect. The worker who can say directly to a client, "I don't feel well prepared for our session today, but I think we can make it meaningful," acknowledges a reality of which the client is doubtless aware and sets up a situation in which both can then deal with it.

Over the years, our particular culture has tended to view expression of feeling as a sign of weakness or "femininity" so that very often deep and significant feelings can only be expressed nonverbally or symbolically. Even then, the expression may be so disguised that it requires knowledgeable interpretation. If there is feeling—and there always is—it will frequently be expressed by nonverbal messages. We are not always aware of nonverbal communications, but they can be potent influences in determining decisions and judgments.

Nonverbal messages are conveyed through the person and the setting. Age, gender, race, speech, personal appearance—physique, posture, body odor, dress, tension, facial expression, behavior, silence or speech, tone of voice, gestures or movements, eye contact, touch, body sounds—all convey messages to the receiver, as does the physical setting—its appearance, aesthetic quality, comfort and privacy (or lack of them), and general climate. The ways in which we convey nonverbal messages about ourselves are endless. Once workers know where to look and what to listen for and to sense in both self and client, their sensitivity and ability to understand will increase. Let us look more closely at some examples of these nonverbal media.

Tone of Voice

Tone of voice is a frequent form of nonverbal communication. From the carefully noncommittal tone designed to conceal to the uncensored exclamation of pain, joy, anger, fear, or grief, it is a revealing part of the whole process of conveying messages. The meaning of words can vary greatly according to the tone of voice in which they are spoken. The worker who wishes to test this need only select a simple phrase such as "I understand" and experiment with the many different meanings one can convey by altering one's intonation. It is important that the worker's interpretation of nonverbal communication is accurate. This can be checked by a comment such as "You sound like you're really angry" or "That sounds like it's pretty painful for you," which will open the way for verbal expression.

Facial Expression

Facial expression is another important mode of conveying messages. To an extent, faces tend to become "set" by the life patterns of the individual in expressions of apprehension, happiness, anger, passivity, friendliness, aggressiveness, and so on. Upon this lifetime foundation, response to the immediate situation will be superimposed. For example, the "poker face," a person who traditionally plays it cool, is much less likely to express through his or her countenance the transitory feelings that are affecting him or her. However, the face that strives for bland concealment or negation of feeling—the mask face—conveys a meaning to the knowledgeable observer that is as significant as free change of expression.

Silence

Silence is a potent form of nonverbal communication that can express many different things, according to the context in which it is used. It may be a companionable sharing, an expression of anger or despair, or recognition of an impasse. Its use is influenced strongly by the cultural background of the individual; its meaning varies according to behavior patterns of the group. Silence can create great anxiety and be interpreted as an expression of hostility—thus, workers must be particularly aware of and knowledgeable about the needs of their clients if they choose to employ it as a means of communication or as a technique.

Gestures and Movements

Gestures and movements are time-honored methods of conveying attitudes and ideas. Relaxation or tension of the body, restless movement, biting the nails, shifting the feet, clenching or wringing the hands, drumming on the table—the list can go on ad infinitum. One of the most frequently stressed indices of communication in this mode is use of the eyes. Eye contact can be a significant factor in assessing the state of mind or feeling of the person with whom the worker is communicating. Here again, culture must be considered along with individual patterns of behavior. The old beliefs about "the evil eye" are still prevalent among many people. Looking directly at a person or not meeting the gaze directly may be considered rude or taboo in a particular culture or family group. The eyes, "the windows of the soul" as they have been rhapsodically called, have special significance in relationships among people.

Physical Appearance

Physical appearance communicates definite messages about one's state of mind and feeling, as well as about one's ideas and general personality. Extremes say something about the impression one is striving to create and one's feelings about oneself. Conformity or nonconformity with the generally accepted patterns of appearance carries a message. Cleanliness or lack of it can be significant. Physical appearance may also bring responses determined by previous experiences or biases. The worker who is an older white woman or a member of an ethnic group may be seen as a stereotype of what is considered undesirable in that group.

Body Sounds

Body sounds such as belching, sighing, cracking the knuckles, whistling, humming, eating noisily or quietly—all are ways individuals convey messages about themselves.

Demeanor

Overall demeanor or bearing—the way one sits, stands, or lies down—says many things to the observer. Individuals who are stooped and tired, slumping in pain or defeat, or carrying their shoulders straight and head high reveal something about themselves.

Touch

Physical touch is a particularly potent form of nonverbal communication. From earliest childhood, the presence or absence and the kinds of physical contact are important factors in the emotional life of the individual. For infants, touch is a well-demonstrated necessity. Constructively used, it has a tremendous potential for strength and support, but it can also be destructive, as illustrated by the battered child, whose parents, by their actions, are certainly communicating something about themselves. Touch as used by workers with clients needs to be given careful consideration in light of modern conditions. With increasing concern about child abuse and harassment in all forms, touch can be misinterpreted—attitudes can vary widely. One must consider the situation, the context, and the nature of the relationship between client and worker.

Environment

The environment in which communication takes place can convey a meaning or may contradict the words used. Are clients kept carefully at a distance? Are workers prompt, considerate of clients' schedules, careful to explain changes, and reliable—and vice versa? The client who keeps the television going when talking with the worker, the worker who allows frequent phone interruptions, and the last-minute call or no call at all about previous arrangements—all communicate meanings as effectively as if they were words. Nonverbal communications tend to be strongly culture bound. Their use and significance are determined by the culture in which they originate. This poses for workers the dual task of being aware that their own nonverbal communications might be saying something quite different than intended and that, in interpreting such communications from others, they must be aware of cultural differences.

Verbal Communication

Development and use of first a spoken and then a written language are closely associated with the evolution of the human brain. As both the language and the brain have matured, we have become able to transmit not only simple factual data but also ideas and highly complex concepts, to store and retain exact knowledge, and to pass it on intact from one generation to another. Our present civilization rests on our ability to use language.

On the surface, once a language has developed and its meanings have been agreed on, verbal communication would seem to be a simple, straightforward, and satisfactory process. Not so! The possibilities are infinite. Not only are we a Tower of Babel in the many differing languages that exist on earth, but within given languages we have many different dialects, and words have various meanings. Economic, social, professional, and work groups develop their own vocabularies. It has been estimated that the medical student must learn 6,000 new words in order to communicate with mentors and colleagues and make use of the literature in the field. Meanings of words can change as, for example, the word "gay," which once meant cheerful or happy now is almost always used to mean homosexual.

In addition to these purely mechanistic problems, there are problems related to the user of the words, who can make language a dividing element rather than one that pulls people together. Words and phrases may be so much a part of the individual using them that the speaker is unaware of what is being said and its probable impact on the hearer. For example:

A white worker was involved in marriage counseling with an African American couple. The husband was employed as the token black in an otherwise all-white company. In talking with the wife about a quarrel they had on the way home from a company party, the worker asked, "Did you feel uncomfortable being the only black woman with all those white ladies?" The worker was surprised and chagrined when what he was actually saying was pointed out to him.

When people find it difficult to express an idea or feeling in words for any reason—because they fear the reaction of the hearer, because they cannot accept what is struggling to find expression—they may disguise what they are saying in such a way that the true meaning is present but hidden. If what needs expression is too painful or threatening, they may overreact and say the opposite of the real meaning.

> Margaret was sent to work in a housing project where the tenants were predominantly welfare clients. Because she lacked adequate supervision, her increasing concern and anxiety went unnoticed. At the end of six months, she left school. At her final interview with her faculty adviser, she reiterated that she "loved her neighbor," although it was obvious that she disliked and feared the welfare clients. She was unable to accept reassurance that she did not have to love everyone, and she returned to the protected culture that had made this an absolute for her.

The worker who is faced with the need to interpret and understand disguised messages in truth needs the "third ear," described by Theodor Reik in *Listening with the Third Ear.* One should be cautious, aware of the high possibility of error, and schooled to attempt to validate one's interpretations through correlation with other behavioral clues the client is presenting.

The effectiveness of efforts to speak honestly and clearly depends on selection of words, perceived and understood meanings, the context in which words are used, and the specific meaning ascribed to them by the culture of both sender and receiver. In addition, verbal communication requires agreement on the various forms of language. Storytelling, humor, the double entendre—all can be extremely useful forms of communication but are rife with opportunities for misunderstanding. While they lend richness to discussion and often allow for expression of subtle feelings and ideas that otherwise would be difficult to convey, these types of verbal communication must be used carefully and only when accompanied by real sensitivity to reactions of the participants in the communication experience.

Electronic Communication

Over the past decade, human service providers, agencies, and hospitals have steadily increased their use of computer and other electronic technologies. Human service providers have expanded their repertoire to include email, listservs, and the Internet. Many of these technologies can make personal information accessible beyond the confined parameters of an individual computer or a single organization. Many hospitals now use the Internet to communicate patient information, medical techniques, and other information both within and outside the hospital. As discussed earlier (see Chapter 1), managed care has greatly encouraged the use of electronic communication because it is the fastest way to communicate information needed to approve and pay for patient care.

The Internet and related electronic technologies have also ushered in an era of creative and innovate ways to deliver human services. A primary example is *telehealth,* the use of electronic technologies to deliver health-related services, including counseling and psychological services. Through web pages, email, chat rooms, video conferencing, telephony (real-time audio over the Internet), electronic forums, and/or electronic forms, it is possible to provide anywhere and any time assessment, diagnosis, intervention, consultation, education, research, and surveys. Distance is irrelevant since telehealth transcends state, national, and international boundaries. Telehealth services have become quite useful in rural areas, which often suffer from a dearth of physicians and other professionals. Telehealth facilitates immediate consultation without having to be physically present. Telehealth services are also used in institutions (e.g., prisons) and for supportive services to homebound and disabled clients who are physically unable to get to agencies. Clearly, telehealth services meet many needs (Levine, 2000).

Increasingly, the Internet has been used to communicate for the purposes of advocacy and activism by a wide range of people and organizations including politicians and nonprofit community agencies (see Chapter 9). Money can be raised, issues debated, and people from all over can connect electronically to work together. The Internet can provide a low-cost and far-reaching way to communicate with many people all over the world. Use of the Internet for advocacy and activism is fairly new for human service workers. Trial and error has shown the importance of thoughtfully developing a strategy for using this technology that reflects the mission, goals, and resources of the people or organizations. Otherwise, confusion, misuse, and frustration can derail the best intended efforts to support a worthwhile cause, organization, or person seeking political office (see Table 5.1).

This use of electronic communications also forces human service workers to examine the risks and benefits. Novel situations can also arise: For example, how would a worker counseling a client over the Internet handle a suicide attempt when the client lives in another state or country? How do state licensing laws apply in the borderless world of the Internet? Codes of ethics and/or position statements by professional organizations for three major mental healthcare providers—social workers, psychologists, and psychiatrists—reveal similar themes around the use of electronic communications technology in clinical practice. These themes include requiring the practitioner to inform clients of the limitations, risks, and need to take precautions (e.g., not using identifying information and using pass-

TABLE 5.1   Categories for Developing an Internet Strategy for Activism and Advocacy

- Clarify the organization's mission, goals, and capabilities.
- Identify the current capabilities created by the Internet: e.g., chat rooms, listservs, websites, networking, email, rapid outreach, access to data, fund raising.
- Identify the needs of the organization to be served in the online activism: e.g., mobilization of support, fund raising, action alert/updates, notice of demonstrations, newsletter, transborder exposure, informal networking.
- Understand and identify the dangers created by the Internet: e.g., security breaches, overreliance on remote communication, SPAM/overload, and diversion from real work.
- Understand and identify the difficulties in using the Internet: e.g., cost and expertise in maintaining website, viruses, hackers, website quality issues.

Adapted from: Barnhizer (2002).

words and encryption) to maintain the confidentiality of electronically transmitted client information (Beel, 1999; Levine, 2000; Welfel, 1998).

Finally, using electronic communication to provide human services means that workers and clients will not be in the same physical space and usually not face to face. The vast majority of electronic communication will be through written communications. Workers place great emphasis on establishing a human connection with clients—the foundation of a helping relationship. Helping clients through electronic means forces human service workers to revisit ways through which they will facilitate establishment of this critical connection—after all, so much is conveyed through verbal and nonverbal communications. Thus, a critical question arises: "When using electronic communications in human services, how can we best convey empathy and understanding?"

Communication by Symbols

Symbols are objects used to stand for something else or to represent abstract ideas. While their meaning may be generally accepted throughout a given culture, how they are used and interpreted can vary widely. A nonverbal medium, they can be selected consciously or unconsciously and designed to appeal to the senses, the intellect, attitudes and biases, fears and frustrations, as well as to strengths and hopes. Symbols can serve a multiplicity of purposes—as attention-getters, as creators of an atmosphere conducive to communication on another level, as a medium for expression of ideas or feelings whose sophistication or subtlety makes expression and comprehension difficult. We all employ symbols much of the time, but when using them consciously for a particular purpose or drawing conclusions from their use, it is important to remember that they are culture bound and subject to different interpretations by different people.

Interpreting Communications

Regardless of the medium of communication used, the receiver interprets or decodes the meaning of the message. These decodings do not always result in comprehension of the intended meanings that, it must be remembered, have been encoded by the sender. Such encodings and decodings are made in light of three factors—perception, context, and culture. These elements are always present and may vary widely among individuals and groups.

Perception

Perception involves how the communication is interpreted by the senses, how it is understood, and what it actually means to the person who receives it. Because we perceive from our own frames of reference, we can both frame our communications and receive them in ways that distort the intended message. For example, what could be perceived as a threatening glare might be merely the anxious grimace of a person unsure of the situation.

Perception of a communication may be distorted by the context in which it occurs. This context involves the entire temporal and spatial situation in which the communication takes place. A message that may seem inappropriate in a specific frame of reference may be entirely understandable in a different one. For example, every classroom teacher is familiar with the child who slams into the room in the morning, making the maximum amount of noise and disturbance in direct contradiction to established ways of behaving. The teacher knows that the child may be reacting to something that happened before entering the classroom and is sending out messages about it, just as another child, who may have left a similar family crisis at the breakfast table, slips silently to the seat and sits huddled in misery. Both communications are understandable when considered in light of the total situation in which they take place. Similarly, the grimace of anxiety might say something quite different in the shelter of an office setting as opposed to a dark, lonely alley.

Perception is affected by the expectations and biases of the perceiver. In a research project, a group of school principals was shown two films of a small girl throwing rocks at some other children. In the first film, the rock thrower was blonde, blue-eyed, and neatly and demurely dressed. In the second, she was dirty, tousled, dark-haired, and wearing a torn pair of jeans and a shirt that was too small. The first child was adjudged the victim, probably driven to actions by the other children. The second was considered the aggressor, who should be disciplined for her behavior.

Context

Context (the time, place, and situation in which a communication takes place) not only affects perception, but also does much to determine the content of messages sent and received. Context involves the number of people concerned and the relationships among them. Communications in both natural and formed groups are affected by the group structure. There are not only "station-to-station" messages (those that lack in feeling and relate only to working roles), there are also "person-to-person" ones (in which work roles are less important and emotion is more significant). These are not always congruent. The speech of people in groups tends to reflect the roles they play in the group and what they think their roles require. Those with power and status tend to transmit this fact, whereas those with lesser positions transmit their lack of power and status. As power speaks to power, so lack of power speaks to lack of power, and thus subgroups are developed and reinforced.

Who speaks, when, how, to what purpose, and to what effect are determined by the way the group is structured. Sometimes this structure is imposed by rigid rules and protocol, sometimes by an unspoken but equally rigid framework of accepted customs and group norms. In some families, for example, children are literally not allowed to express an opinion; in some medical teams, the MDs do all the talking; in some corporate boards, only the top management personnel are allowed to speak. The group communicates differently as its makeup varies. An adolescent boy will usually communicate quite differently when his mother is part of a group versus when she is absent. The entrance of a supervisor into a coffee group often changes the kind and content of communication taking place.

It is the worker's responsibility to create an atmosphere in which open communication can safely occur, to develop skills in the use of feedback, to check validity of communication, and to assess where people are coming from in their words and actions. The past as well as the present affects the ability of a person to "talk" to others.

Eric Berne's formulation, developed as a part of his model of Transactional Analysis, is useful in visualizing this. He sees all of us as having three levels of organization from which we send and through which we receive messages—the Adult, the Child, and the Parent within the self. When communications are received on the same level from which they are sent, the channel operates effectively and common understanding is achieved. When communications are perceived and responded to on a different level, there is breakdown in communication.

Mrs. Winter, at 60 an obese, hypertensive, neurotic person, was advised by her physician to give up coffee. She responded indignantly, "You drink all the coffee you want—why shouldn't I?" The physician sent his message on an adult level, directed to an adult. She received the message and responded as a child. There was no real communication, and the purpose of the exchange was defeated.

Culture

Another aspect of past and present that is paramount in determining validity of communication is culture. Culture is defined in Webster's as "the totality of man's learned, accumulated experience." Experiences determine our language, values, attitudes, and behaviors, and they set down patterns of living and relating to others that are "right" in that particular culture. As we develop within a culture, we internalize the "right" ways, and, as an intrinsic part of us, they can act as barriers between people. Ruth Benedict (1948), one of the great pioneer anthropologists, wrote, "The life history of the individual is first and foremost an accommodation to the patterns and standards traditionally handed down in his community." To paraphrase George Orwell (1953), "All people are different, but some are more different than others."

There are differences in lifestyle, such as those between old and young, between welfare recipients and United States senators, between those who dwell in New York City and in Cutbank, Montana, which markedly affect communications patterns. Differences in educational level, particularly in the use of language and symbols, can cause breakdowns in the transfer of meanings. Differences that cause great difficulty are the cultural gaps between members of minority groups and representatives of the predominant culture, which may involve not only language, religion, patterns of living, accepted values and ways of behaving, and expectations, but also ways of communicating.

The most important factors in the establishment of effective cross-cultural communication are the worker's commitment to the welfare of the client and knowledge and skill in using a transactional process. Understanding and empathy need to be based on a genuine respect for differences, on awareness that people in every culture (including ourselves) think that theirs is superior to all others, on a knowledge of past and present relationships between the different cultures, and on willingness to go slowly and be open to learning. As workers become familiar with a different culture, they can find ways of communicating effectively both verbally and nonverbally. They need to recognize that they, too, are culture bound in their selection and use of ways of communicating. The most important single factor in effective cross-cultural communication is the worker's commitment to the welfare of the client and the knowledge of and skill in use of transactional processes.

Communication of Ideas

Human service workers are increasingly in the position of needing to communicate with highly specialized groups such as legislators, councils, and committees, as well as with the general public, in order to change values, introduce new ideas, and secure support for different ways of doing things. Examples of this can be seen in the efforts of the Planned Parenthood program to ensure that children are born only to families capable of caring for them and wanting them, and in the work of the expanded nutrition programs throughout the country toward improving public nutrition habits, particularly in families where there are growing children. In both of these instances, the underlying values that support current customs and behaviors are strongly entrenched. These values have deep cultural roots relating to the sacredness of the family, the right to have children, and the right to be free from outside interference in one's personal life.

Workers who undertake to change these attitudes not only need to be aware of the many factors that support prevailing modes of behavior, they also must have knowledge of ways to bring about acceptance and implementation of change. It is simply not true that if you invent a better mousetrap the world will beat a path to your door. You must know how to reach people, how to persuade them that the old mousetrap is not all that good, and how to encourage them to adopt new ways of thinking and behaving that will enable them to use the better mousetrap. Such changes must occur at both the individual and the social systems level. Obviously, the two are so closely related that they are constantly mutually affecting each other. A special type of communication, labeled *diffusion,* has developed in order to facilitate such change. It is defined as "the process by which innovations spread to the members of a social system."

Diffusion

The process of diffusion involves five elements. First is the source of the new ideas—the theoreticians, the inventors, and the researchers who develop new ways of approaching problems but all too often are unable to sell their knowledge to the people who need it. The specialized knowledge, skill, and language of the originators of new ideas need translation into terms that outsiders can understand and relate to.

Second is the message, encoded and sent out by those who wish to make this new knowledge available to and used by the people who can benefit from it. This message is articulated in a way that potential users can perceive accurately; it is designed to point out advantages of a different way of doing things and the rewards that can be expected to compensate for the pains of change.

Third are the channels through which these messages flow. Channels include the mass media and interpersonal communication or, most probably, a combination of both. Each medium has advantages and disadvantages. When faced with a new idea presented through mass media such as television, newspapers, workshops, or the Internet, most people tend to try it out with their families and friends, who can either reinforce or extinguish the idea by their responses. There is a real advantage in having a respected teacher, leader, or professional sponsor an idea so that when a worker introduces it on an interpersonal basis, it will have some established credibility.

Fourth is the receiver of the new ideas, the potential customer of new ways of thinking and behaving, the member of the social system who is being influenced. It is particularly important that the innovator have accurate knowledge of the culture, the value system, and the norms that support the attitudes and behavior that need to be changed in the receiver. Messages that are not based on this knowledge will not be relevant to the receiver's experience and will probably go unheard.

Fifth and last are the effects of the innovation, the consequences over time. These are as follows: changes in knowledge, changes in attitude, and changes in behavior. Time is of special significance when working with innovation. People who want to bring about change are often impatient and tend to forget that individuals and social systems change slowly. The worker is always dealing with three aspects: the past, the present, and the future. Even in revolutionary change this is true. The burned-out hulks of buildings in Los Angeles bear mute testimony to this fact in what they have been, in what they are, and in what they can be.

Everett Rogers (1983) visualizes diffusion and acceptance of innovation as a four-step process: (1) knowledge, which involves awareness of the idea and some understanding of what it means; (2) persuasion, which involves the development of an attitude of acceptance or rejection of the new idea; (3) decision, which involves adoption or rejection of the idea; and (4) confirmation, which involves seeking out support or rebuttal of the new idea. Once an idea has been accepted through this process, an underlying value system develops that will support and institutionalize it. The rapid development of complex innovations that characterizes our technological society requires that the human service worker, in order to be effective, be able to use diffusion theory.

In summary, we are only beginning to analyze scientifically and to understand the barriers to communication. The struggle for competence in this area, for clarity and honesty, is lifelong. Workers who never develop or who lose the capacity to "hear" accurately what they are "saying" through all media handicap themselves unnecessarily.

Communication in Interview and Discussion

The development of language for communication of meanings and for the creation, storage, and retrieval of knowledge is considered by scientists as the major factor in moving people forward in their long march toward civilization. Skill in the use of language and the ability to use it flexibly are essential for people who work in a helping capacity with other people. Interview and discussion—the two essential modes of language use in human service—differ in structure and process but are similar in many aspects:

1. Both involve two or more people.
2. Both are transactional in nature, involving give and take between and among the participants.
3. Both are verbal forms, but communication within them is also nonverbal and symbolic.
4. Both have as their purpose the reaching of some kind of understanding or decision.
5. Both may be formal or informal, planned or spontaneous.
6. Both may have immediate and/or long-term goals.

Interviews

Interviews are usually considered to be face-to-face meetings between two or more people, although purists would argue that when two or more people are present, the meeting automatically becomes a discussion. The purposes of an interview are many and varied—information getting or giving, therapy, resolution of a disagreement, consideration of a joint undertaking, and so on. As usual, the roles of the worker and client differ, with the worker carrying the major responsibility for establishing communication and for seeing, hearing, and being sensitive to the client and the client's needs. The worker's activity or passivity will be dictated by the practice theory he or she adopts and by the needs of the client.

Although maximum privacy, comfort, and lack of interruption are eminently desirable elements in some situations, significant interviews can be conducted in a crowded hospital ward, in a kitchen overrun with children and dogs, and even in a noisy subway. The interruptions of television, demanding children, other workers, phone calls, and so on can be more disturbing for the worker than the client, whose natural lifestyle may include them. The worker can be free to capitalize on both informal and formal opportunities by utilizing these criteria: What can both participants be comfortable with? Where can there be the most open and honest thinking and communication? What is necessary to achieve the purpose of the interview?

Interviews that occur within the framework of a purposeful helping relationship are a part of the process of realizing its purpose, and obviously there should be both a general and a specific goal for each interview. In evaluating the interview, the worker must consider how it moved the relationship toward the ultimate goal, as well as how it met the immediate one. An interview should have its own structure—a beginning, a middle, and an end. It should begin with the establishment of common understanding and, in an ongoing contact, be related to what has happened before; it should continue through the work of weighing and considering feelings, behavior, and events; it should conclude with a summing up of what has taken place, with agreement on what the subsequent activity will be. In a series of interviews, this structure helps to provide continuity.

In talking with people, there are ways of putting words together that tend to bring about desired results. In general, the worker will find that judgmental attitudes will inhibit honest communication. The worker's role is not to impute blame; rather, it is to observe the nonverbal cues, to listen to the verbal cues, and to relate speech and action to what is being seen, heard, and sensed. Workers can question and respond in ways that help clients to express and understand feelings and attitudes:

1. By seeing and putting into words both sides of an ambivalent reaction. ("You are both pleased and displeased with your boy's independence?")
2. By taking the client's own words and phrasing a question around them. ("You say you feel funny about adopting a child?")
3. By identifying the attitude or emotion and then taking time to talk about it. ("It sounds to me as if you are frightened. Why does this behavior scare you?")
4. By commenting about what the client is saying and something that has been said or done before. ("And you felt the same way about your first husband?")

5. By accepting silence, encouraging gesture, movement, or murmur. Workers can question and respond in ways that encourage the client to think about and try to understand the situation:

   a. By repeating the client's words in the form of a question. ("You never did get along with any teacher?")

   b. By asking for further clarification of a statement. ("Did you mean . . . ?" or "I don't quite understand what you mean.")

   c. By restating the main point the client is making. ("You think that the work of the committee is a failure?")

   d. By directly inviting the client to express an opinion or a feeling about the subject under discussion. ("What do you think is causing the increase in drug use among the young people around here?")

Workers can question, comment, and respond in such a way that the interview becomes a structured learning situation on ways to look at and deal with problems:

   a. By selecting and commenting on the area of greatest concern to encourage the client to focus on it. ("You're most uncomfortable right now about Rick's being so unhappy in school.")

   b. By questioning about and commenting on ways in which the client has attempted to deal with the situation and the results of these efforts. ("You mentioned that your talk with Rick's teacher wasn't very successful—what actually happened?")

   c. By picking up alternatives that the client has suggested or by suggesting new ones. ("You had considered asking for a conference with both the teacher and the guidance counselor?")

   d. By involving the client in future planning and assigning homework. ("Before we talk on the 20th, would you like to try setting a regular time for talking with Rick, and we can then see how it worked?")

Direct questions that call for specific answers are useful as a kind of shorthand, although they do not tend generally to lead to maximum participation. If the relationship is good, clients will usually answer truthfully to the best of their ability, if they are certain that it is safe to do so and feel that the question is relevant and appropriate.

There are so many different kinds of interviews that it is difficult to select any one that is illustrative of the total process. Workers' roles will vary according to the practice theory they adopt and the mode of interviewing it dictates, the needs of the clients and the way in which they respond to the workers' efforts, the purpose and goal of the interview, and, to some extent, the setting in which it occurs. The interview that follows is an excerpt from a simple, purposeful conversation that begins between two people in the presence of a third and ends as a discussion among three people.

 William Bingham, minister of the Glenview Church, had been asked by Mr. and Mrs. Woodford to persuade her parents to move into a retirement community. Mr. and Mrs. Anderson were both in their 80s. While Mrs. Anderson was still able to putter around and do a few things in the house, Mr. Anderson was totally deaf, and a recent stroke had left him incontinent, with the use of only one arm, and requiring a walker. With the various programs for the aged for which the couple were eligible and the proceeds that could be realized from the sale of their house, they could manage to pay for their care. Mrs. Anderson would not go unless her husband was willing, and Mr. Anderson clung with stubborn and desperate fear to his home and the last vestiges of independence available to him. Reverend Bingham agreed to talk with them when, in the course of his pastoral duties, he made a call at the home. Mrs. Anderson met Reverend Bingham at the door and invited him in.

"Here's Reverend Bingham, Dad," she called to her husband, who was sitting huddled in a chair before the fire.

Mr. Anderson responded minimally and then withdrew into silence, while the minister and Mrs. Anderson talked about the weather, her health, what was happening in the church, and so on. Finally, Reverend Bingham brought the conversation around to the business of the interview.

REV. BINGHAM: I had a purpose for coming today, Sallie. Mary asked me to talk with you about your plans. She's worried about you and her Dad.

MRS. ANDERSON: I know. She told me you were coming. (Tears welled in her eyes.) We've got to do something. We just can't do the work any more.

Rev. Bingham: I know—you've done the best you can, and it hasn't been easy.

MRS. ANDERSON: Doctor Rogers wants him to go to Elm Hill, but he won't consider it. He's mad now because Mary told him she asked you to see us.

REV. BINGHAM: Maybe I better tackle him directly then. (He turned to the silent figure in the chair.) How are you feeling today, Paul?

MR. ANDERSON: What'd you say?

MRS. ANDERSON: He doesn't have his hearing aid on. Want your hearing aid, Dad?

REV. BINGHAM: How do you feel?

MR. ANDERSON: Feel all right.

REV. BINGHAM: Good! Mary asked me to talk with you.

MR. ANDERSON: No use in it. I'm not going.

REV. BINGHAM: Not going where?

MR. ANDERSON: What?

REV. BINGHAM: Where are you not going?

MR. ANDERSON: (Angrily) I can't hear a word you're saying. Get my hearing aid, Sallie. (The hearing aid was produced and adjusted with considerable normal bickering, which, however, held an edge of anxiety and fear.)

MR. ANDERSON: Now, what did you say?

REV. BINGHAM: I asked where you weren't going.

MR. ANDERSON: I'm not going to Elm Hill. I don't need a nursing home.

REV. BINGHAM: (Gently) I didn't come to try to force you to go to Elm Hill, if that's what you're worried about, Mr. Anderson. You have to make your own decision.

MR. ANDERSON: (Fiercely) What did you come for then?

REV. BINGHAM: I came because I'm your minister and Mary's and Alton's. I came because they are worried about both of you, and because I know you're having a hard time. You're at the place where you have to make some decisions that are really important, and I thought perhaps I could help.

MR. ANDERSON: I've already made up my mind what I'm going to do. I'm going to stay right here.

REV. BINGHAM: I know that's what you'd like to do, and I can sure understand it, but for how long?

MR. ANDERSON: As long as I can.

REV. BINGHAM: But the time is very close when you can't. All I'm asking you to do is to think about that and start planning for it so you can make a decision without being forced to do it hastily without proper consideration of everything involved. Dr. Rogers says. . . .

MR. ANDERSON: Dr. Rogers is a young fool!

REV. BINGHAM: (Grinning) Depends on where you sit. To me, if he's a fool, he's an old one.

MR. ANDERSON: (Smiling in spite of himself) I guess that's true. He must be about 55.

REV. BINGHAM: Young or old, he knows his medicine. You couldn't have a better doctor, and he says you need special care. He says this whole thing is too much for Sallie at her age and with her high blood pressure.

MR. ANDERSON: (Turning to his wife) Can't you get that woman to help you again?

MRS. ANDERSON: There just isn't anybody any more, period! Mary keeps coming over, and with the baby she shouldn't be doing anything extra. She's too thin.

MR. ANDERSON: You don't have very much to do. Just keep the house and take care of me.

MRS. ANDERSON: I'm 84 years old, Paul, and I'm tired. I can't cook and clean and shop and take care of you at night. This house is too big, and we can't do the yard any more. Alton doesn't complain, but they've got their own home to take care of.

MR. ANDERSON: They're just putting me out to die like an old horse.

REV. BINGHAM: I think all older people feel that way sometimes, but it just isn't true with you. Everybody has to accept inevitables, and age is one of them. No matter how old we are, however, our choices are limited.

MR. ANDERSON: It's easy for you to sit there and say that.

REV. BINGHAM: I know, but not completely easy. It's ahead of me, too.

MRS. ANDERSON: (Desperately) Paul, we just have to do something.

MR. ANDERSON: All right, go ahead, take me out and put me away.

REV. BINGHAM: Retirement homes aren't putting people away. They're especially designed to meet the needs of many different kinds of people. Have you ever seen Elm Hill?

> MR. ANDERSON: No, and I don't want to.
>
> REV. BINGHAM: There are others besides Elm Hill. The only thing is that it's close to Alton and Mary, and in good weather you could probably even walk down to their place. There's Rest Haven out on Cortland Road, which is close to the reservoir, and lots of people from there go fishing. Both of these have the three different facilities—apartments, rooms, and hospital beds—and all three offer the care you both need. I think you can take some of your own furniture with you so you can still have your own bed, which is real important.
>
> MRS. ANDERSON: I'd like to be close to Mary and the children.
>
> MR. ANDERSON: (Defiantly) And I'd rather have the fishing!
>
> REV. BINGHAM: Why don't you look at both of them—and any of the others you'd like—and see what alternatives are open to you.

This interview, although only a skirmish in the total campaign, was successful in that it moved Mr. Anderson from an immovable position to the point where he was thinking about alternatives. Reverend Bingham used support, confrontation, universalization, and presentation of alternatives in a manner characterized by empathy and compassion, but with understanding and acceptance of reality. His use of humor to relieve the tension was deliberate and in keeping with his character, and it struck a responsive chord in a frightened, sick old man. The lines of communication were initially between two individuals, but at the close of this interview had to encompass communication among the three.

In the final moments, this meeting became a discussion.

Discussion

Discussion is a type of verbal interaction, "informed" conversation among a group of people. Ideally, it is a democratic pattern of communication in which each contributes thinking and participates in the decision making, which is arrived at through consensus.

Increasingly, life in modern society demands group membership and group participation, although valid concern is being voiced that in the process the individual may become lost. Groups come in almost every combination and size, are formal and informal, and exist for almost every purpose—learning, therapy, socialization, problem solving, recreation. They are characterized by a development process—formation to maturity to discontinuation—that can be conceptualized as proceeding by stages, much as does individual development.

Group discussion has numerous advantages: It provides opportunity for contributions from participants with differing points of view; it gives members of the group a chance to participate in decision making and hence greater motivation for accepting and translating decisions into action; it allows for the development of creative potential of group members, for learning, for growth, and for change. Its disadvantages arise from the fact that groups tend to repeat the social conditions in which they exist and to develop norms for behavior, power constellations, and pressures toward conformity that can be destructive. They can be and often are nondemocratic. The isolate outside the group is often the isolate within.

In discussions, channels of communication are multiplied in direct proportion to the amount of interchange taking place among the discussants as well as to the number of discussants. For example, a classroom situation where the channels are limited to those between the teacher and the students can hardly be called a discussion in the true sense of the word. If, however, the discussion is enlarged so that communication channels open back and forth among the students and the teacher, it can become a true discussion with each contributing to, thinking about, and analyzing the contributions of others. What starts as an interview between a worker and two people often ends as a discussion among three people, particularly if the worker is skillful. The basic patterns of communication will alter to encompass all the people present. The larger the group, the greater the possibility of the loss of universal expression. The most significant interchange usually takes place in small groups.

The following excerpts are from the meetings of a club group of a dozen boys between the ages of 12 and 14. They took place in a settlement house in the Family Center of a midwestern city. The boys were from the three major racial groups in the area—African American, Hispanic American, and white. The group was formed by the Family Center to provide recreation and a growth experience in group interaction. Harry, the leader, was a staff group worker. At the first meeting, the boys and the worker talked about what the group's function should be. At this point they seemed mainly interested in the worker and his role, finally deciding that he would be a group member and adviser. They decided to select a project later, to concentrate on getting an organization underway, and to discuss structure at the next meeting.

At the second meeting, the decision was made that the group should have a president, vice president, secretary, treasurer, and sergeant at arms. Once this was agreed on, the group considered the business of voting. It was decided that nominees could not vote and that in case of a tie, there would be a new vote until one candidate received a majority. Sam was elected president; Angel, vice president; Mike, treasurer; Bill, secretary; and Leon, sergeant at arms. During the election, interest and participation were high, and at several points the worker intervened when the boys attempted to coerce each other, by reminding them they had decided to use parliamentary procedure, consisting of nomination, discussion, question, and vote. They responded to this control and finished the business at hand. After his election, Sam took over the meeting and the boys decided to spend their next meeting planning an overnight camp-in in the center's gym and to have refreshments at this meeting. Mike volunteered to bring doughnuts, Angel and Leon to make punch.

The worker began the next meeting with a game designed to afford expression for some of the accumulated energy the boys brought from school and to provide an opportunity for interaction before the meeting was called to order by Sam. This was no mean feat, as the boys tended to run around or converse loudly, and Sam sometimes forgot the purpose of the group. Discussion centered on the camp-in. Bill, the secretary, suggested he use the blackboard to write down details. This was agreed on, and he recorded the items discussed. The first order of business was to determine a date. Angel suggested the same week, but Harry pointed out that this would not allow enough time to make all the necessary plans. The worker requested that it be on a weekend because of his own schedule. After much debate, Friday, April 10 was selected. Sam suggested that he be the one to confirm the date with the director, Ms. Marcusson, and was excused to do so. The group decided that the camp-in should extend from 7 PM Friday to 10 AM Saturday. Food, the next item on the agenda, was discussed enthusiastically by all the boys. There was quick agreement about the eggs and sausage, strong difference over pop or juice and toast or pancakes. Pancakes and juice won by vote. Agreement was unanimous on one dollar per person for food, and Mike suggested that any leftover money be given to the worker, who thanked him but suggested that any leftovers be returned to the treasury or divided among the members. The decision was that it go to the treasury.

The next two meetings were devoted to planning details of the camp-in. During this time, structure was emerging; the boys assumed responsibility for planning the games that had become the opening part of each session and for accepting the discipline of discussion. A combination of play and work emerged, and the chaos that so often seemed about to take over never really materialized. Three boys, Sam, Mike, and Max, all 14-year-olds, were vying for the position of leader, but there was little real animosity among them. The younger boys formed their own subgroup, but they accepted any of the three leaders, probably because there was good acceptance and interaction among the older and younger members. Sometimes tension arose when a proposal was modified or defeated by vote, but it apparently was resolved as further business took place.

At the fourth meeting these decisions were made: who would cook and clean up (nomination and vote); who would buy the food (the worker, by unanimous vote, as it was agreed he would know where to get the best buys); who was eligible to attend the camp-in (all who had attended at least two planning meetings, paid their dollars, and gotten a permission slip); and what would be acceptable behavior. It was agreed that open quarrelling and fighting would not be tolerated. The general behavioral mode was to be "civilized" behavior. If anyone started fighting or was uncooperative, he would have to go through a paddling line. The worker asked for an example of just what kind of paddling would be administered. After discussion it was agreed that this should be paddling the hand on the rump. This seemed reasonable and acceptable to all.

Eight members of the group attended the camp-in, which was voted an unqualified success. Al was late, Max was forbidden to attend by his parents because he had been caught shoplifting earlier in the week, Miguel was attending his sister's wedding, and Danny had an infected ear. After an evening of games, movies, and snacks, gym mats were unrolled on the floor, and everyone got into pajamas. Spiders ran out of the mats and boys pretended fear, but they enjoyed chasing and squashing them. There was an ongoing exchange of jibes, but they seemed well tolerated and there seemed no concentrated scapegoating. The boys, exhausted, fell asleep around three o'clock, were up at seven, cooked breakfast, and cleaned up to the satisfaction of Ms. Marcusson. This experience in group interaction was judged to be a constructive one by both the boys and the worker.

The club continued and was a meaningful part of their lives during the year. In analyzing the group, the worker thought the original goals were achieved through the following developments: (1) The boys learned to talk and work together, to develop and enjoy a give-and-take relationship with others, and to draw strength from the bond that developed from shared experiences and feelings; (2) they created and worked within a structure of their own making, participated in the decision-making process, and learned the satisfactions and difficulties of creating and carrying through a project; (3) they experienced the strength of the group that grew from use of the capacities of the individuals and the solidarity of the whole; (4) they learned to deal with their own feelings toward both themselves and others in a group situation. The worker's role here demanded that he facilitate the development of these experiences.

A major tool was discussion, which the boys had to learn to use in order to compromise, to arrive at decisions, and to abide by the decisions of the majority. A good example of this occurred in dealing with the touchy subject of discipline during the camp-in. Ms. Marcusson was a strong executive who ruled with an iron hand, but she was respected by the neighborhood kids, and so the rules laid down by the center for use of its facilities were accepted fairly readily. The form of discipline that the boys had to choose was that relating to their own individual and group behavior within these rules. The worker brought up the subject, pointing out that it was helpful to agree in advance on what would be expected behavior and how it would be enforced.

SAM: (Self-righteously) No fighting, no swearing, no goofing off . . .

MIKE: (Quickly) No ripping off . . .

ALLEN: (One of the younger boys, bravely) . . . and we'll kick out anybody who does!

MAX: (Defensively) Nah, that's no good . . . (Chaos of voices agreeing, protesting, offering other suggestions)

SAM: (Yelling) Shut up, you guys. We ain't gettin' anyplace, and I gotta go deliver my papers.

WORKER: The idea's to have fun, so we don't want to make it too strict. You've all been coming to the center long enough to know what's expected here, and we get along pretty well with each other.

LEON: Yeah—let's just say civilized behavior like at the meetings, and Harry will make like the fuzz. (Chorus of protests, including one from Harry)

ALLEN: Why can't we kick anybody out?

WORKER: In the middle of the night and your parents expecting you to stay here? Isn't it better to work things out among ourselves anyway?

RALPH: We could paddle anybody who got out of line.

MIKE: (With relish) Yeah, I'll bring the paddle.

SAM: (Sensing a threat to his leadership) That's no good. How about just a slap on the rump by hand? (This brought a chorus of agreement from the subgroup of younger boys—Bobbie, Leon, Bill, Ralph, and Eddie.)

> **ALLEN:**   (A younger boy who saw the way the wind was blowing and changed sides quickly) I move we say civilized behavior and anybody who gets out of line gets a swat on the rump.
>
> Sam quickly called for a second and a vote, and the motion carried.

Summary

Communication on many different levels is an essential ingredient to all human relationships, including those designed to provide needed services for people. The possibilities for misunderstanding are infinite. It is the responsibility of human service workers to be aware of the dynamics of communication, to be sensitive to the possibility of error, and to be both motivated and competent to ensure that communications within helping relationships are valid and complete. Once established, communication channels do not necessarily remain open. It is often necessary to rework them, being sensitive to problems, evaluating their causes, and taking steps to deal with them. The diffusion of electronic information technologies into the human services has expanded the possibilities for communication yet also introduced novel situations for both clients and workers. In addition, particularly in the course of a professional relationship, manner and intensity of communication can change. In the midst of a crisis, for example, clients may need and use communication in a way that is out of the ordinary and then, when the crisis is over, retreat to more normal patterns. Workers need to know what is needed and what is appropriate.

SUGGESTED ASSIGNMENTS

1. Have students prepare a paper on one of the three major factors—perception, context, and culture—affecting coding and decoding of messages in communication, using an interview in which they took part as an illustration.

2. For an in-class exercise, have students attempt to convey different meanings nonverbally, such as by tone of voice, demeanor, gestures, and movements. If facilities for videotaping of such exercises are available, they can be useful by letting students see themselves in action. As part of the exercise, emphasize that we communicate ourselves first and foremost—age, race, sex, and social class are immediately obvious and hold different meanings for different people.

3. Using diffusion theory, assign students to plan in writing a campaign designed to enable a particular group of people to become familiar with and begin to accept a new idea. The instructor may either specify a single group and idea for the total class or allow students to select their own. Students should present their plans to the class for discussion.

4. Have students contact professional associations (e.g., National Association of Social Workers, American Psychological Association) to research their position regarding use

of the Internet to provide mental health services. Students should include the following points in their research:

- Guidelines in the relevant code of ethics regarding use of the Internet.
- Does the professional association have a formal position on how to handle situations that arise when their members are licensed to practice in one state, yet if they provide health services online they may provide services in states or countries where they are not licensed?
- What are the risks and benefits, to both clients and professionals, of providing services online?

5. Have students work with a community organization to develop a strategy for using the Internet to promote their cause.

REFERENCES AND RELATED READINGS

Barnhizer, D. (2002). Environmental activism on the Internet. In S. Hick & J. McNutt (Eds.), *Advocacy, activism, and the internet: Community organization and social policy.* Chicago: Lyceum Books.

Beel, N. (1999). *Ethical issues for counseling over the Internet: An examination of the risks and benefits.* Available online: http://geocities.com/Athens/Olympus/4609/ethics.html

Benedict, R. (1948). *Patterns of culture* (4th printing). New York: Mariner Books.

Benjamin, A. (1989). *The helping interview* (3rd ed.). Boston: Houghton Mifflin.

Berne, E. (1964). *Games people play.* New York: Ballantine Books.

Epstein, L. (1992). *The task centered interview* (3rd ed.). New York: Macmillan.

Fast, J. (1970). *Body language.* Chicago: Evans.

Freudenheim, M. (1998, August 12). Privacy a concern as medical industry turns to Internet. Available online: http://www.nytimes.com/library/tech/98/08/biztech/articles/12healthcare-internet.html

Garrett, A. (1989). *Interviewing: The principles and methods* (2nd ed.). New York: Family Service.

Grohol, J. (1999). *Best practices in e-therapy: Confidentiality & privacy.* Available online: http://www. ismho.org/issues/9901.htm

Kadushin, A. (1993). *The social work interview: A guide for human service professionals* (3rd ed.). Needham Heights, MA: Longman.

Karger, H., & Levine, J. (1999). *The Internet and technology for the human services.* White Plains, NY: Addison Wesley Longman.

Levine, J., (2000). INTERNET: A framework for ethical analysis in the human services. In J. Finn & G. Holden (Eds.), *Human services online: A new arena for service delivery* (pp. 173–192). Binghamton, NY: Haworth Press.

Orwell, G. (1953). *1984.* New York: Signet.

Reik, T. (1969). *Voices from the invisible: The patient speaks.* New York: Farrar and Strauss.

Rogers, E. (1983). *Diffusion of innovations* (3rd ed.). New York: Macmillan.

Welfel, E. (1998). *Ethics in counseling and psychotherapy.* Pacific Grove, CA: Brooks/Cole.

SELECTED RELATED WEBSITES

American Psychiatric Association's Statement on the Practice of Telepsychiatry
http://www.psych.org/pract_of_psych/telepsych.cfm

Gestures and Body Language
www.webofculture.com

Office for the Advancement of Telehealth
http://telehealth.hrsa.gov/

Psychology of Language
http://www.psyc.memphis.edu/POL/POL.htm

Establishing and Using Helping Relationships

What are the characteristics of helping relationships, and how do they differ from other relationships?

How can helping relationships be visualized as having three phases, and what are the significant aspects of each?

What is the meaning of "implicit promises" in helping relationships, and how can they be avoided?

The need to relate meaningfully with other people is basic in human existence. It is inherent in people; one of the first tasks of the newborn is to reach out to those around on whom physical as well as emotional survival depend and relate to them. The infant is said to be "bonded" to this first person or people in a deep and lasting relationship, the nature of which will not only affect future personal development, but also the ability to relate to others. This capacity is subject to individual differences, but its development and use will depend largely on the person's life experience. The child who is met with hostility, indifference, or misunderstanding is likely to develop a reservoir of mistrust that will serve poorly in later life, creating attitudes that inhibit others from approaching and/or prevent acceptance of proffered overtures.

Meaningful relationships are probably the most important source of satisfaction and fulfillment in the total life experience, but they can also be destructive and a source of unhappiness and frustration. It is well substantiated by studies that people lacking in these relationships generally function poorly and their death rate is higher than that of the total population.

Relationships grow out of shared experiences. In the course of an ordinary lifetime, an individual experiences many different kinds of relationships—parent–child, teacher––student, spouse–spouse, employer–employee, and so on. The one that concerns us here is the "helping relationship." It differs somewhat from other relationships but shares with them the common characteristic of being a dynamic interaction between two or more individuals. This interaction begins when communication first takes place and is a continuous

117

process throughout the lifetime of the relationship. It is a reciprocal process, cumulative in nature, in which, once initiated, each successive response tends to be made in terms of those which have preceded it.

Helping relationships are not personal and they are not friendships, although friendships may grow out of them and may even be a part of them. When the latter is the case, the worker has a dual role, for the professional relationship is a disciplined one in which the self must be consciously used in order to be of help to the client. This does not mean that professional relationships are constrained or formal—the best ones are warm and safe, although not always comfortable.

Good helping relationships are transactional in nature and are based on mutual trust and respect. Participants must have the ability to be interdependent without anxiety; they must be able to communicate not only on thinking but also on feeling levels; they must be able to be honest and to disagree or express differing opinions without being destructive; they must be able to let go.

Good helping relationships do not just happen. The worker makes conscious use of self in establishing a specialized kind of goal-directed connection with another person. While workers make use of what comes naturally, they also can learn and develop generalized skills in relating to people and then apply these skills to specialized situations and persons. As workers do this, they develop increased ability to empathize with clients, to perceive accurately, and to understand the clients' perception of self and situation. E. R. Carkhuff (1987) visualized this as a three-stage process of attending, responding, and personalizing.

In attending, the worker conveys intent and beginning understanding by use of self and the physical environment, by use of listening, and by use of observation. In responding, the worker expresses warmth, empathy, and genuine concern. In personalizing, the worker helps clients relate to their own particular situations and to the worker involved. Like any other dynamic process, relationships will often need to be reworked to maintain maximum effectiveness, but the three skills that Carkhuff visualizes are basic at any point during the process.

Characteristics of Helping Relationships

Accepting

The basis of any relationship is acceptance of the individual's right to existence, importance, and value. Indifference or lack of concern can completely inhibit the development of any meaningful interchange and can be more destructive than actual dislike. Like and dislike are dynamic states, usually precursors of action, but indifference is a static condition from which nothing grows. The violent racial confrontations, the marches and demonstrations of the 1960s, may have created a focal point of anger, but they also served to lessen indifference and to create a potential for action. Out of acceptance should come freedom to be oneself—to express one's fears, angers, joy, rage, to grow, develop, and change—without concern that doing so will jeopardize the relationship.

Acceptance also involves recognition of the uniqueness of individuals as people who possess the need and right to participate in making decisions about matters relating to their own welfare. The extent to which a person can exercise this need varies among individuals, but the need is there. It is a vital part of the total growth process in life. One purpose and a significant feature of the helping relationship is the process of enabling clients to exercise and increase their ability to participate in this decision making. The individual's right to and need for self-determination are areas in which we often get confused because of the social implications. When one person's exercise of self-determination adversely affects another, the necessity for some limitation becomes obvious. However, this necessity does not negate the existence of the need as a part of the relationship.

One of the major problems with the concept of acceptance is the fact that people tend to confuse it with "liking" the total individual and "approving" of that person's behavior. Thus the student who says "I can accept anyone except the child rapist" has lost sight of the concept itself and is judging the behavior. We accept the reality of the individual's existence and place in the total scheme of things.

The genuineness of acceptance of and concern for the client is a vital ingredient in the development of a meaningful relationship. Initially, it is a regard for "people," but it should be quickly developed into a regard for "this person."

Acceptance involves expectation. We not only accept people for what they are, we accept them for what they are capable of being, and this reality-based expectation assumes great significance in a helping relationship. The worker's expectation of the client's potential will influence the worker's attitudes and behavior and will have a bearing on the outcome of their joint endeavors. It cannot be too strongly emphasized, however, that this expectation must be based on reality and arrived at without the influence of bias or stereotype.

It is not hard for human service workers to play a caring role in relationships. People who want to believe that someone honestly accepts them as they are and cares what happens to them are both easily deceived and subject to deceiving themselves—particularly in the initial stages of the relationship and particularly if they are children. Such dishonesty is a time bomb with potential for reciprocal dishonesty and for the development of an inability to trust and to relate meaningfully in future contacts.

Dynamic

The dynamic character of relationship demands that both or all of the significant individuals participate actively in the process. A one-sided reaching-out effort does not constitute a relationship. The capacity to invest oneself in other people must exist within all participants, although the extent of this capacity may and does vary in degree among individuals.

This give and take, the transactional element in relationship, constitutes a kind of interdependence that some workers find intolerable, particularly if they cannot accept the worth of the people with whom they are working or if they carry with them vestiges of past personal conflicts. A good example of this is the worker in a welfare program who commented that he would not have a relationship with "those people." He had "pulled himself up by the bootstraps from the coal mines of Pennsylvania" and "they could do so too if they were worth anything."

A relationship is dynamic not only in terms of the activity of the people within it, but also in that it is constantly changing as an overall entity. Neither the individuals involved nor the relationship itself exists in a vacuum. People change and grow; new feelings and attitudes are constantly being integrated and fed into vital relationships, which must in turn be able to encompass these changes if they are to continue to exist. Social change, such as the entire women's movement, which has resulted in changes in sex roles, has put a strain on family and personal relationships that leads to their breakdown in a significant number of cases. A helping relationship must be able to accommodate change, often the purpose for which it was formed initially. Workers need to recognize and accommodate these developments and work to facilitate them.

Emotional

The essence of relationship is emotional rather than intellectual. Primarily, it is the give and take of attitudes and feelings that build a relationship and provide the channel through which ideas are imparted and decisions reached. When a relationship is faced with feelings or attitudes that it does not recognize or cannot or will not deal with, the channel becomes clogged and no longer serves its dual function of (1) being an end in itself by meeting the emotional needs of the client and (2) serving as the channel through which rational endeavor can be made.

It is obvious that the importance of nonverbal communication in relationships can hardly be overstressed, particularly in the early stages. It is through this medium that emotional interchange most frequently takes place. Later, as words are added when necessary to describe feelings, it is equally important that the two levels of communication tell the same story—that one does not belie the other.

A good example of the kind of communication that is not geared to the emotional needs of individual clients is seen in the attempt to reach the instant intimacy characteristic of modern society by calling people in nursing homes by their first names. Frequently, this is perceived as denigrating, putting the elderly person in the position of a child—the ability to recognize the status inherent in the more formal title is often all these people have to hang onto.

Purposeful, Time-Limited, and Unequal

By definition, a helping relationship is purposeful and goal-directed; otherwise, there is no reason for its existence. It is directed toward enabling one of the participants—the client—to achieve a more satisfactory degree of functioning. As such, it is time-limited. When the purpose is served, the goal achieved, then the specific relationship is terminated. It is also an unequal relationship in which the participants have differing roles and responsibilities, one to give and one to receive help. It is directed to meet the needs of one participant through provision of the needed help by the other.

In considering these three aspects of the relationship, it is well to remember that they are not absolutes. While workers may hold as an overall goal the client's becoming self-sufficient, self-starting, self-determining, and independent of outside assistance, this, again, is a matter of degree. No one is ever totally self-sufficient. The very nature of life itself makes the concept of absolute cure fallacious. Degree of functioning must be weighed in light of inherent individual potential and externally determined social possibility.

The time limitation is subject to measurement by the same criteria. Because life experience is characterized by continuous demand for adaptation or problem solving, it is impossible to name a date and say that from this time on no further help will be needed. However, an unnecessarily prolonged relationship tends to become sterile and meaningless, and it can create dependency. The worker's role demands teaching clients how to use help, how to use their own capabilities, and where to turn when future assistance is needed. A major task with many clients is to help them deal with a value system that implies that asking for help is a sign of weakness and inadequacy. In some instances this may be true, but frequently such a request is an indication of adequacy and strength.

Because workers regularly encounter new clients, new relationships must be formed frequently. Here again, the worker's role demands striving to help clients achieve greater flexibility and understanding of people and a broader capacity to relate so that these clients can adapt to the different people with whom they must work in the future.

It is a basic fact that a helping relationship is geared to meet the needs of clients and not those of workers, and yet if certain needs of workers are not being met, these workers probably will be very poor at their jobs. In their work they should be satisfying their need to be successful; they should be meeting the need to implement the basic philosophical conviction that the individual has worth, that the good of the society and of the individual are inseparable, that individuals have the capacity for growth and realization of their potential, and that although basic change comes from within, an outsider can provide help. Beyond this, workers' personal needs should not be involved.

Frequently, a helping relationship is confused with a friendship. While friendships differ from each other in purpose and time duration, the question of whose need is being met constitutes the major discrepancy between them and helping relationships. A friendship develops to meet the needs of both participants equally, although perhaps in different ways. Workers who find themselves meeting their own personal needs in relationships with clients would do well to scrutinize themselves and their role very carefully. Some elements of friendship may be appropriate, but only as the worker is aware of them and of the purpose they are serving. From a helping relationship a friendship may grow, but this is separate from the purposeful, goal-directed, working interaction.

In addition to confusing the helping relationship with friendship, workers frequently think that a relationship must be formal and structured. Actually, the structure may only serve the purpose of bolstering up a shaky worker who is fearful of free-and-easy contacts with clients. There are definite uses for structure and form, but the basic relationship should not hang on these; it should exist and be usable in a crowded swimming pool, a hospital bed, or the privacy of a quiet garden or office.

Honest, Realistic, Responsible, and Safe

Ultimately, to be effective and ethical, a helping relationship must be honest, realistic, responsible, and safe. Honesty between and among people is so difficult to attain that many of us never experience such a relationship. Often we do not intend to be dishonest, hypocritical, or deceiving, but our defenses are such that we can only perceive ourselves as quite different from what we actually are. We all are familiar with parents, teachers, or social workers who conceive of themselves as good in their roles—as warm, loving, giving people—but who are actually cold, rejecting, and often destructive. For this reason, it is essential that workers strive to know themselves as they really are, with their own unique combination of strengths and weaknesses. They must also perceive reality as it is in terms of both people and situations. They must be aware of and deal with the distortion created by their own needs and desires, as well as their tendencies to see things as they would like them to be or to sit in judgment based on their own personal value systems, which may create a blindness all its own.

Any significant relationship contains elements of what psychoanalysts label transference and countertransference. People tend to relate in terms of how they have related to significant others in their past experience. In transference a client might see her domineering father in a domineering employer and react with the same helpless anger and frustration that she felt as a child. When the transference reaction is carried to an extreme, the reality of the current relationship is lost.

The tendency to transfer feelings is not limited to clients; workers also experience it and have difficulty in controlling it. This is called countertransference. The manipulating parent who outwits the teacher in a conference may arouse the same murderous rage in the teacher as did her childhood friend under similar circumstances. We transfer not only feelings, but also ways of responding to these feelings, and when we utilize these responses without awareness of their true origin and meaning, they are often self-defeating. Workers must recognize the reality of the current situation, be aware of the potential for transference, and be capable of both controlling it in themselves and utilizing it in clients to advance the therapeutic goals of the relationship.

One of the best tools for dealing with transference reactions is to keep the reality of current situations in view. When the client remarked to her worker, "I can talk with you just like I did with my mother," he replied gently, "But I'm not your mother." This opened the door to consideration of how this relationship differed from the previous one and how things had changed from the past.

In no sense should the concept of helping relationships be limited to one-on-one situations—one individual relating to one other individual. Relationship is a basic factor in work with people in groups as well as on an individual basis. The intensity is generally diluted by the group situation, although it is the rare group worker who does not have individual contacts with clients outside the group.

There is no theory of working with people, no method of practice, that does not contain within it consideration of basic human relationships. In most theories the investment of the worker's self in the process is the essential and common ingredient. The extent of investment—the degree of intimacy and objectivity—varies according to the demands of the particular mode of practice.

Only as workers are responsible to the commitments of a helping relationship will their clients also be able to exercise the needed responsibility within that relationship. Only as clients feel it is safe to reveal themselves without fear of being harmed or judged in a destructive fashion will they be able to make use of this relationship.

There is a narrow line that honest workers must tread in exercising judgment as opposed to being judgmental. Their role will call for their making and using judgments, but these must be based on something more objective than their own personal value system, unless that value system has been subjected to the most searching scrutiny and constitutes a valid standard by which to judge. This standard should be based on reality, a reality that is two-sided. In order to comprehend both sides, the worker must be able to see two views of the client and the situation. For convenience, we will call these the small and the large view.

The small view is the narrow one that enables workers to see and understand because of their capacity to empathize with the client, to participate in the client's feelings and ideas without being a part of them, and to understand how the client perceives self and situation and how the client thinks and feels about both. In short, workers must be able to hear that "sound of a different drummer" to which a client steps. This small view is essential, for part of the worker's task is to understand and to reconcile similarities and discrepancies between the large and small views.

On the other hand, workers must also be able to perceive the larger view in all its ramifications. They must understand the client and the client's behavior within the context and interrelationships of the total situation. How wide an area this view must encompass will depend on the situation the worker must comprehend and deal with in order to assist the client.

Judgments arrived at on the basis of the correlation of these two frames of reference are much more likely to possess the objectivity that is essential to avoid the judgmental and condemning activities that tend to inhibit the formation of effective relationships. The two sides of reality—the reality as it is and the reality as the client sees it—must be fully comprehended before the worker can make a valid judgment.

Judging is so confused with the assigning of blame that workers traditionally have been hesitant to make valid and appropriate estimations or form opinions about right and wrong, good and bad. It is, however, an essential part of the worker's responsibility, and to be effective, it must be done objectively and soundly, based on acceptance of the person.

In considering the uses and abuses of relationships, the worker must guard against implicit promises, which often are not consciously dishonest but are nonetheless unrealistic. These involve:

- Implicitly promising more than can be delivered (trust me, reveal yourself to me, and all will be well).

- Attempting to pretend a false acceptance that may or may not deceive but in either event is destructive to the client's capacity to be honest and to trust.

- Implying that the relationship is permanent when in reality the client's worker may change many times in the course of a helping endeavor.

Overall, workers must be responsible in a helping relationship for being worthy of the trust that clients place in them due to the nature of the workers' role. While they are accountable to their clients, their superiors, and society as a whole, workers must be accountable primarily to themselves because only they can be aware of what they invest in their helping relationships. While their own humanity and fallibility make it highly probable that they will err at times in this respect, workers should develop sufficient self-awareness to know when they have done so, to resist the temptation to rationalize their own behavior, and to avoid its repetition.

Authoritative

By definition, a helping relationship is an authoritative one. Workers often have trouble in accepting and using this aspect of the relationship because they do not know how to do so. They may retain personal conflicts about authoritative persons and situations with which they have been involved, they may lack commitment to the use of authority, or they may lack the understanding that authority does not necessarily involve violation of another's rights and freedoms.

Two kinds of authority are appropriate in helping relationships:

1. **The authority of knowledge.** Workers who do not possess more and better knowledge about how to deal with the concerns of their clients than do either the clients or the general public have no right to intervene in people's lives. Teachers must know their subjects and know how to teach; doctors must know medicine and have skill in using this knowledge; social workers must know people and society and be able to use self in working with both; lawyers must know the law and be able to use it, and so forth.
2. **The authority of social sanction.** In discharging its responsibility to provide maximum opportunities for its members to lead healthful lives in the broadest sense, society sanctions human service workers and charges them with the task of carrying out its mandates. This sanction requires that workers use authority to enable, to direct, and to limit their clients in making use of the resources of society.

In reality, clients soon become cognizant of workers' competence in this area. As one client remarked, "I know what's wrong—I need her to tell me what to do and how to do it." With the vast majority of clients, use of authority is a problem only if the worker makes it so. With those few who cannot accept any exercise of authority in relation to themselves, special practice skills are needed.

The Phases of a Helping Relationship

A helping relationship, like any time-limited operation, can be visualized as having phases: Phase 1—the beginning; Phase 2—the middle; Phase 3—the termination.

Phase 1: The Beginning

Phase 1 is marked by uncertainty and exploration—a tentative feeling out, an attempt to evaluate the other person and determine what may be involved in this new situation. How trustworthy is this person? Will he or she harm me, or can I let down my defenses? Will he or she like me if he or she knows what kind of person I really am? Will he or she lead me on and then kick me in the teeth like other people do? Can I safely push him or her around, or is he or she likely to push me? Does he or she really know anything that will help me?

This is a sizing-up and testing-out period and should be accepted and acknowledged as such by the participants. Not all relationships flower or become significant. It is at this point, when meaningful communication is beginning to be established, when roles are defined, when needs are being expressed, acknowledged, and responded to, that workers must be extremely sensitive to both verbal and nonverbal communication of feelings—fear, anger, uncertainty, lack of trust. They must be aware of feelings that inhibit development and use of the relationship, always remaining cognizant that this involves a judgment that may often be little more than an educated guess at this point in the relationship. Workers must convey acceptance to the client and the desire to understand what is actually being expressed.

The outcome of this testing-out period should be an agreement—usually unspoken—between the worker and the client. In essence, the terms are simple:

1. This is how we see each other.
2. This is the process through which we operate in this give-and-take situation.
3. This is the framework in which we will operate.
4. The first three terms are subject to change.

This agreement may vary, depending on the needs of the client and the capacities of the worker. With a person who has been severely traumatized by previous human relationships and cannot trust or reach out to anyone, the agreement would involve much more support and structure by the worker, with repeated demonstrations of the capacity to be understanding, helping, nonpunitive, and nonthreatening. With the client who can only be dishonest and manipulating, the worker may relate on the basis of "Okay, this is the way you want to play, but I'm not fooled." With yet another kind of person, the agreement may be for a good fighting relationship characterized by aggressive confrontation and conflict. Phase 1 is the period during which definition of relationship, the client's need, and the type of relationship necessary in the initial stages are agreed on, but always with the understanding that this is a dynamic process.

One of the conditions on which Mary could remain in school was that she accept counseling. Testing had revealed that she was able to do the work, but her behavior in class was so disruptive that it could not be tolerated. The school social worker recognized that much depended on the initial interview, and when Mary slouched in late and sullen and banged her books down, she faced it directly.

"Looks like you're not happy to be here."

"What can you do about it?"

"That's up to you. I don't think you'd have come here at all if you didn't want to stay in school, and right now I'm your best bet for doing that. I'd like to help."

"Why?"

"Well, for one thing, it's my job, but I wouldn't have taken it if I didn't care what happened to people. It looks like you could use some help, and if you want it, I'm here to provide it."

"Big deal!"

"Why are you so angry with me?"

Mary couldn't resist the chance to tell an adult off, and so they started.

Phase 2: The Middle

Phase 2 is the working period of a relationship, although in the strictest sense Phase 1 is also a working period. The initial testing and questioning are completed, an agreement has been reached, and the business for which the relationship was established can take place. This should be a comfortable phase in that each participant has an adequate understanding of where each stands with the other and what to expect.

There is no justification for the establishment of a helping relationship unless there is business to be conducted. The fact that a relationship is in operation does not automatically deal with the problem at hand. It is necessary to stress this because of the current emphasis on feeling as being all-important. This exchange of feelings and attitudes must serve two purposes: It must meet the need of the client, and it must provide a channel through which the work can take place. In the first phase, it may be a part of the work, but only a part.

The middle phase, which begins when the initial agreement has been reached, is a dynamic one in which changes should be taking place, both in the feeling balance between worker and client and in the reality situations with which they are dealing. Thus the relationship is a constant process of adaptation and readaptation to changes, but the underlying characteristics of acceptance and honesty must always be present. In a sense, meaningful relationships are constantly in the process of being redefined, but these new definitions are not the same as in Phase 1. They are made against the background of knowledge of the self and the other and of shared feeling, thinking, and experience.

The middle phase of each relationship will differ because the individuals involved differ, as do the problems, but it should:

1. Be characterized by acceptance and honesty.
2. Be goal oriented.
3. Keep moving and changing.

After several interviews in which Mary repeatedly tested the worker's concern by tardiness, failure to carry through with agreed-upon tasks, and silent expressions of distrust, they reached a point where the worker suggested a group experience with other students. As usual, Mary reacted negatively but finally came around to discuss the idea.

"What can a bunch of crazy kids do for me?"

"It helps to know you're not alone—"

"I know that."

"—and some of them might have some insights and ways of dealing with similar problems that you might try."

"Hunh!"

"—and your ideas and experiences might help some of them."

Mary decided to try—the latter appealed to her—but she also wanted to hang onto the worker.

Phase 3: The Termination

Phase 3 involves the process of termination. When we consider a helping relationship as being time-limited, we do not define the length of time involved. With some clients it may be a lifetime. There is nothing wrong with this, as long as the worker is cognizant of the reasons and they are valid ones, is aware of the process involved, and is conscious of the roles being played by the participants. Because the ending of any meaningful relationship has emotional significance for the participants, even though they have been aware of its limited nature since its inception, the worker must be aware of and, if necessary, prepared to deal with this aspect.

In recognition of this, society has set up certain rituals of farewell such as celebrations, sharing of food, and giving of gifts, which are ways of saying, "Remember me." The process of termination should be such that the client is able to (1) utilize the total helping relationship experience as a constructive part of a lifetime of experiences and (2) learn from its ending how to deal more effectively with inevitable terminations yet to come.

The depth of personal investment in a relationship is the most important factor in determining the degree of pain and anxiety at termination. Superficial relationships in day-to-day experience are terminated lightly and easily. Our extremely mobile society tends to create immense numbers of these relationships, quickly developed and easily ended. It is a source of concern that the multiplicity of such experiences may limit the capacity for deep personal investment of oneself in others. Yet each of us has a great need for relationships in which we are known as we are and accepted for ourselves. In this type of experience, we tend to invest ourselves, often much more deeply than the busy worker realizes, particularly when the worker's investment is necessarily of such a different nature. With this in mind, the worker's role in termination is to provide an experience that will be constructive and pave the way for participation in and use of future satisfying relationships by the client, in both personal and outside life.

Termination should accomplish three things:

1. Deal with unfinished business.
2. Deal with feelings about termination.
3. Provide direction for the future.

The school year was coming to an end. Mary had decided on summer school to make up deficiencies and a part-time job, but the worker would not be there. They had talked about this and spent some time dealing with current concerns, deciding what remained to be done, and talking about the future. The worker was going to study.

"What will you be taking?"

"Two courses—one on drugs in high schools—"

"There's plenty of that!"

"—one on children and divorce."

"There's plenty of that."

"Yeah—things change."

"What do you get out of this?"

"Lots of satisfaction—you've come a long way."

"Maybe—we'll see."

"I'll be here next year if you need me. In any event, stop in and let me know how things are going."

Summary

It is not hard for warm, outgoing, friendly people to establish relationships, particularly with needy clients, but a relationship in and of itself is not enough. The worker must be competent to use the relationship effectively and provide the needed services. Without this, the relationship can become a source of frustration to clients saddled with workers they personally like and enjoy but who cannot give clients the help they need. The relationship's justification is that it is of service to the client. The relationship is important but is only one aspect of the totality. It is the worker's responsibility to ensure this.

SUGGESTED ASSIGNMENTS

1. Assign a short paper dealing with the characteristics of helping relationships that the student least understands and about which he or she has the most concern. Use these papers as a basis for class discussion.

2. Assign students to role-play dealing with relationship problems such as:
   a. Anger—expressed verbally or nonverbally
   b. Transference
   c. Dishonesty (of either worker or client)
   d. Dependency
   e. Others as desired

   One student will assume the worker's role, one the client's. Discussion can center around (1) manner of expression of feeling, (2) techniques for dealing with feeling, and (3) ways to avoid development of such problems.

3. Divide students into small groups, where each will present a relationship in which they were involved as helper or helpee, stressing techniques either used or observed in the beginning and termination phases. The group will then evaluate these as to effectiveness and report back to class with any questions that concern them.

REFERENCES AND RELATED READINGS

Biestek, F. (1957). *The casework relationships.* Chicago: Loyola University Press.

Brems, C. (2000). *Basic skills in psychotherapy and counseling.* Belmont, CA: Wadsworth.

Carkhuff, E. R. (1987). *The art of problem solving.* Amherst, MA: Human Resources Development Press.

Combs, A., & Gonzales, D. M. (1993). *Helping relationships: Basic concepts for the helping professions* (4th ed.). Harlow, Essex: Pearson Education.

Ivey, A., Pederson, P., & Ivey, M. (1994). *Intentional interviewing and counseling: Facilitating client development in a multicultural society* (5th ed.). Pacific Grove, CA: Brooks Cole.

Rogers, C. (1961). *On becoming a person.* Boston: Houghton Mifflin.

7

Using the Basic Problem-Solving Process

How can people be helped to change destructive patterns of living?

How are the steps in the problem-solving process as used in human service related to the classic scientific method?

What do we mean by outreach in human services, and how can concepts from marketing theory be useful in this?

No aspect of life is static. Evolutionary change comes so slowly that it may appear static, yet the process is continuous. Throughout a single lifetime, adaptations are, of necessity, made more swiftly. The individual, as well as the species, is involved in a constant process of change and adaptation, both to the requirements of normal growth and developmental patterns and to the demands of the environment.

People may be born with handicaps—physical, intellectual, or emotional—that tend to lead to the development of destructive patterns of living. Pressures of the environment and the social situation can cause people to adapt in ways that are equally destructive, although these may be the only adaptations possible to ensure survival in a particular situation. The task of human service workers is to improve the functioning of both individuals and society. Workers thus are concerned with enabling people to alter patterns of behavior that are destructive and also with changing the unhealthy social situations that lead to their formation.

Why and How People Change

We must consider how and why individuals and social systems change, apart from natural development and maturational change, and how this change can be facilitated:

- People change as a result of rational decision in order to provide greater self-fulfillment and to avoid pain and discomfort.

- People change when they learn, through facing and accepting the logical and inevitable consequences of their own behavior, that what they are doing is not really meeting their needs in a satisfactory and constructive way or contributing to their happiness and well-being.

- People change through the development of relationships in which emotional needs are more adequately met and defenses accordingly need not be so rigid and constraining.
- People change when, as a result of learning different ways of behaving, they provoke different responses from other people, which in turn push them to respond differently.
- People change when they are required to adapt to changing demands of the social systems of which they are a part.
- People change when they have hope of reward for the risk they are taking in upsetting the status quo.
- Systems change when there is change within the parts that comprise them and when provision is made for the utilization of new input.

Rarely do these conditions of change occur singly; frequently they are seen in various combinations. Together they encompass the rational characteristics of people as well as their psychological, physical, social, and spiritual components.

One of the basic philosophical tenets of human services is that fundamental change must come from within, although an outside force can help to facilitate it. This is true of systems on all levels, from individuals to the most complex social group. Basically, they all must be responsible for changing themselves.

Workers act as catalysts, setting into operation the conditions and forces that lead to change. To do so, they operate from another basic philosophical belief: that people can be understood by utilization of the scientific method of study. This method provides a disciplined, orderly framework for workers' thinking and an overall pattern that can be learned and used to deal with the problems of life.

The classical scientific method involves recognition and systematic formulation of a problem, collection of data through observation and experiment, and the formulation and testing of hypotheses (tentative explanations of the problem). The researcher hopes that a valid theory or law emerges from this process. The orderly framework for working with people is an adaptation of this scientific method. It becomes a constant and ongoing process from the point at which the worker becomes involved in a situation until termination. Though the words we use to describe the process are different, the process is basically the same.

Structure of the Helping Process

The structure of the worker's activities is as follows:

1. Engagement: Involving oneself in the situation, establishing communication, and formulating preliminary hypotheses for understanding and dealing with the problem.
2. Assessment: Appraising the situation on the basis of data (facts, feelings, people, circumstances, and systems) involved.
3. Definition of the problem: Formulating the need.
4. Setting of goals: The end toward which the effort is to be directed.

5. Selection of alternative methods and an initial mode of intervention: Looking at all the possible ways of tackling the problem and selecting the most propitious one.
6. Establishment of a contract: Agreeing on a definition of the roles and responsibilities of the participants.
7. Action leading toward the desired goal: The work that is necessary.
8. Evaluation: Weighing the outcome of action in terms of success or failure.
9. Continuation of working plan, abandonment of unsuccessful intervention and selection of a different approach, or termination: Both continuation and selection of a different interventive strategy are based on a repetition of this basic problem-solving process.

In light of our basic belief that people have a need and right to be involved in decision making in matters that concern them, we must ask: What is the role and responsibility of the client in this whole process? First, we must remember that this process is a description of the activity of workers—this is their working structure. Second, clients must always be involved in each step to the extent that they are capable of participating. This involvement is part of the total process, and workers who shortcut or evade, probably using the justification that it is a time-saving device, are contributing to failure, creating dependency, and making more work for themselves. This way of working should be a growth experience for clients; only as they are involved in it will they grow. This process is valid no matter what the level of intervention. It is applicable with individuals, groups, and communities. It is an orderly way of thinking and planning and an actual process that takes place. It is also descriptive of successful coping behavior that people have always used to survive, and it is a continuous and adaptive process (see Figure 7.1).

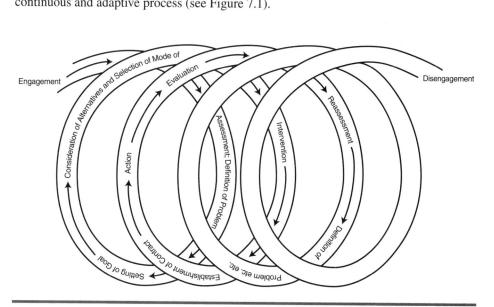

FIGURE 7.1   The ongoing process of working with people.

Engagement

Engagement is that period in which workers begin to orient themselves to the task at hand. The initial involvement in a situation for which a worker has responsibility may come about in different ways.

Voluntary Application for Help.   These clients are usually conscious that they have a problem; they have probably considered and perhaps tried various ways of dealing with it that have been unsuccessful, and they are sufficiently aware of their need for help to request it. They may or may not know what the real problem is, but they know that something is hurting, and they want relief from this pain and concern. They may or may not be prepared to do what is necessary to get this relief—as do most people, they probably want an easy, quick, permanent, and all-encompassing solution with little or no additional pain or effort on their part and probably as little real change in their life pattern as possible. Crises, with the resultant fear, anger, and feeling of helplessness, are potent forces in bringing individuals, groups, and communities to seek help. On occasion, workers may either precipitate a crisis or allow one to happen in order to bring a person or a group to the realization of the need to go outside themselves for help.

Involuntary Application.   Circumstances force some clients to secure help against their own wishes. These are critical situations that leave no alternative, such as extreme poverty, incapacitation, disasters, or social pressures from significant individuals and institutions (wife, husband, parent, employer, schools, military, legal, or correctional services) that enforce compliance with referral. Although there is usually an element of reluctance in all requests for help, clients who feel that they have been forced into participating present an additional hurdle for workers, whose initial task is to recognize and deal with this reluctance.

Reaching-out Effort by Workers.   By the nature of their responsibility, workers will often be required to reach out to involve themselves with people who are not actively seeking or being referred for help. These people may or may not be conscious of their need, and they may be unwilling, unmotivated, or unable to do anything about it, but the risks to them and to society require that action be taken.

The tasks of workers in the engagement period are (1) to involve themselves in the situation, (2) to establish communication with everyone concerned, (3) to begin to define the parameters within which the worker and the client(s) will work, and (4) to create an initial working structure. Beginnings are important. While it is always possible to go back and start over, the initial fresh impetus is gone forever. A second start involves reworking what has happened in the first. Beginnings in human services may be as simple as walking into a crowded waiting room or receiving a letter, a card, or a phone call, or as complicated as attending a board meeting involving differences about a major company decision or going into a neighborhood that is in a state of crisis over some loaded issue such as school busing.

While not essential, it is helpful if the client can have direct contact with the worker during the engagement period. So much nonverbal communication takes place under such circumstances and so many feelings can be expressed and worked out that, whenever possible, an effort should be made to ensure this type of interaction. Direct contact also gives the worker an opportunity to observe the client, and much can be learned from such observation.

Throughout the relationship and particularly the assessment stage, workers continually evaluate behavior, carefully bearing in mind that interpretation of such observation is based on judgment and that such judgments can be erroneous. For example, people often use humor or attempts at humor to deal with anxiety, and the worker, instead of considering this inappropriate behavior, must realize what it actually is. Often behavior does not jibe with what the client presents orally. For example, one who presents himself as a reasonable, considerate person may actually be aggressive or attacking.

The worker needs to be a keen observer, noting the actions, determining causation as far as it is possible, and often, when it is appropriate, pointing out any discrepancy between the reality of the situation and the behavioral response to it. Such recognition of this discrepancy may be a relief for the client, particularly if the decision to behave in a certain way is conscious, or on occasion, it may provoke anger and denial.

In this initial step, workers can only proceed from their general knowledge of people and social situations and their awareness of themselves, with knowledge that the clients involved will be judging them and what they represent at the same time that workers are evaluating their clients. Preconceived opinions about a worker's clients and their situations, their problems, and their solutions, as well as emotional biases, prejudiced attitudes, anxiety, fear, and hostility on the part of both the worker and client, can operate to make honesty in engagement difficult. An essential part of workers' equipment is objectivity, open-mindedness, and capacity to be aware of and to control these reactions in themselves. An equally important skill is the ability to discern the existence of these attitudes in clients and to deal with them either directly or indirectly. Workers may do this by encouraging open expression of and discussion about them and by demonstrating through the shared working experience that they need not be the determinants of outcome.

In modern parlance, engagement involves a "selling" job. In a sense, workers are selling themselves and their services, and the task is much easier when their position and status are clearly defined for the client. Today, when values are changing, when the human services are obviously not meeting many of the needs for which they were designed, and when challenge and questioning of the status quo are the rule rather than the exception, workers who represent established social institutions may find themselves meeting with widely varied expectations and attitudes. Even teachers, physicians, and lawyers—members of the long-established and high-status helping professions—are subject to questions concerning their motivation, their knowledge, their skill, and their attitudes toward their clients.

The prevalence of such attitudes makes the task of starting where the client is and presenting self and service in a manner that is relevant to the client's need a little more difficult. While it is the responsibility of clients—insofar as they are able—to make themselves and their needs understood, workers carry the greater share of the responsibility for enabling them to do so. Engagement can be achieved only in terms of the concern of the people involved. When the worker is sensitive to what this concern is and can communicate this sensitivity, engagement can begin on the basis of the worker's service being relevant to the client's need. The engagement process should provide opportunity for the client to express expectations of the worker and the institution that the worker represents. People see helping individuals and services differently and often will withdraw when they are disappointed.

The results of the engagement process should be these: (1) The worker is part of the situation; (2) initial communication channels have been opened; (3) the worker and the client stand together in an approach to a common concern, with some definition of the role of each based on expression and clarification of the client's expectations and what the worker has to offer; and (4) there is agreement on the next step in the process.

Assessment

Assessment is the appraisal of a situation and the people involved in it. This process of assessment has two purposes: It leads to a definition of the problem, and it begins to indicate resources for dealing with the problem. Workers move from operating on the basis of general knowledge to operating on the basis of specific knowledge of a specific set of circumstances and people. They collect pertinent data, test and analyze these data, and arrive at conclusions.

Factual material (and we must always be aware that feelings are facts) about any one individual or social situation is limitless. Therefore, it is essential to apply the "principle of parsimony": The worker must collect only that information that has relevance to the situation at hand and is essential to the formulation of valid working judgments. But even in the provision of specialized services, the totality of the individual must be considered, although emphasis will be on the particular aspect of individual functioning for which the service is designed. If, for example, the problem is a physical handicap, the worker will concentrate on this, but she or he will also determine the cause-and-effect relationship between this difficulty and the other aspects of the client's self. A physical handicap has a marked effect on a person's self-image, and this will affect that person's capacity to relate to other people, perhaps his or her capacity to learn and the ability to utilize his or her potential for happiness and achievement. Effective service must take all of these relevant aspects into consideration.

Sources of data are many. The primary one is the client. What clients are and how they feel and behave should be given first consideration. After all, it is their needs about which we are concerned, regardless of whether the client is an individual or a total community. Historically, workers have moved from a stance that demands checking of the client's statements and observations with a variety of outside sources, to one that considered the client's view to be the only information necessary, to the present attitude, which considers the client's view to be of major importance but only one aspect of the matter. Above all, workers must be realists, and reality presents different faces to different people. These differences constitute a significant part of assessment. Clients know how they feel (but often not why), what they are concerned about, what they have done to try to alleviate the situation, and the results of these efforts. They know that they want relief from discomfort and, much of the time, how they would like to go about getting it. Checking of outside resources should be done with the client's knowledge and permission.

The significant people in a client's life experience constitute a secondary source of information. These include both people with whom they have personal relationships, such as family and friends, and people within the more extended systems of which they are a part, such as church, job, and so on. In considering whether and how to use other people as sources of data for assessment, the ideas, feelings, wishes, and capacities of the client are of primary importance. The client has both a need and a right to know who is being involved and to participate in getting the necessary information.

The final sources of data are records, test reports, studies, and evaluations of various kinds. In utilizing this material, the worker must keep in mind that its reliability is based on the validity of the testing instruments used, on the competence of the people who did the testing and prepared the reports and studies, and on the capacity for objective judgment by the person or people through whom the results were filtered.

Though the collection, testing, and analysis of pertinent data are listed here as separate steps in a process, they usually occur simultaneously. In talking with the client and others, in reading reports, and in studying tests, workers are constantly assessing what they are learning and observing. They look for assets and liabilities within the individuals, the situations, and the relationships; they observe and weigh the important feelings and attitudes of the people involved; they contemplate the causes of the current situation and look at how such problems have developed and been dealt with in the past; they consider the availability of resources both real and potential within the client and the community that will meet the evident needs. This assessment is done in terms of the various systems involved, the relationships that exist within them, and their relationship with each other. It is particularly important to look for the places where pressure is likely to be exerted to retain the status quo within the system as well as where effective intervention should take place.

Definition of the Problem

Definition of the problem can in no sense be considered a simple process. It has been compared to peeling an onion in its multilayered composition and its effect on the participants, but its complexity must be understood if defining a problem is to be dealt with effectively. Any problem can be considered conceptually, both horizontally in terms of its ramifications in the present and vertically in light of past, present, and future etiology.

It is currently fashionable to decry the significance of causation, particularly in work with crisis and in encounter groups. It is considered a cop-out, an excuse, a refusal to face the reality of the here and now. Consideration of causation can certainly be misused as a substitute for responsible action, but this does not justify ignoring it. Workers who do so are failing in a basic aspect of their role. We can fully understand the present only in light of what has happened in the past. We can interrupt the course of an ongoing event effectively without knowledge of basic causation, but we cannot ensure effective prevention. For example, we can halt the course of an epidemic by closing the path through which the contagion is spreading, but the basic problem remains unchanged—the cause of the disease still exists. To prevent recurrence, we must isolate, understand, and alter the causative factors.

Three factors determine how causation can be used by workers to define a problem: (1) the wishes and needs of the client, who wants relief from the discomfort of the present situation; (2) the role of the worker, who may be charged only with responsibility for dealing with the current problem; and (3) the nature of the problem itself, which may be one that can be effectively dealt with in terms of the immediate situation or one that must be attacked at the root.

Often there is variance between what the client sees as the problem and what the worker sees. The original definition, however, must be based on what the client sees, as this is what appears relevant to the client at the time. Defining the initial problem differently often results in losing the client.

The concept of a client's problem is not static but changes as work progresses, just as in the total life experience coping with one demand leads to another. In addition, we rarely deal with a single problem but rather with a constellation of problems, each related to the others. The worker's task is to focus on the primary problem, which will open the way to consideration of those peripheral to it once an initial solution is reached.

It can be useful to think about problems in three frames of reference:

1. Immediate problem: The one about which the client is most concerned, which is causing the current difficulty, and in terms of which the client perceives the need for help. This is usually only one aspect of the whole. (For example, Willy Jones comes into juvenile court for breaking the windows of the Garcias' house when bouncing his ball against their wall.)
2. Underlying problems: The overall situation that created and tends to perpetuate the immediate problem. (The high-density population area where Willy lives has inadequate play space for growing children, and Willy has too little supervision from his working parents.)
3. Working problems: Those contributory factors that stand in the way of both remedy and prevention and must be dealt with if change is to take place.
   - The anger and frustration of Willy Jones and the Garcia family.
   - The absence of free space in the neighborhood.
   - The ignorance and apathy of the parents.
   - The inadequacy of service programs such as YMCA/YWCA, park department, and so on.
   - The indifference of city officials and real estate promoters.

It is obvious that each of these working problems involves many similar ones that must be dealt with as the process continues.

Setting of Goals

Definition of the problem should lead logically to the setting of a goal. Actually, one is done in terms of the other. The purpose of a goal is to lend direction to efforts. Without such a focal point, activity tends to become aimless, random, and often ineffectual. This does not mean that a goal is rigid and unchanging. Life being a dynamic process, a fixed goal, except in a large overall sense, can be stultifying. If we define health as the capacity for maximum functioning as well as the absence of disease, the overall goal of human services (a healthy society made up of healthy individuals) is too lofty to be useful pragmatically except in determining a philosophical base.

However, there should be a long-term goal for the particular helping services undertaken so that the expectation of achievement can be met. In addition, progressive subsidiary goals will lend focus to the ongoing work. When one goal has been realized, another will loom ahead. An example of this is the situation of the worker who was dealing with the problems of Willy Jones and his neighborhood. The overall goal would be the provision of adequate recreational facilities in the neighborhood. A subsidiary goal would be the involvement of community members in working toward the solution of their own problems. The immediate goal would be determining the point at which the worker could most effectively intervene in order to start the process that would lead to the achievement of these goals. Each step en route would have its own small goal and be part of the progression toward a larger one.

Goal setting is most effective when it is a shared process, when the client has a major voice in deciding what needs to be achieved and how it is to be done. Motivation and independence are strengthened by this involvement. The goal should always be based on what is realistically attainable. Differences between the goals held by the worker and those held by the client should be based on logical differences in roles and tasks in the working partnership. The overall goals should be held in common.

Sometimes what the client sees as a goal promises no solution to the problem. In marriage counseling, one partner will often want the worker to punish the other, to "straighten him/her out"; this may be more important to the client than working out conflicts in the marriage. The worker's initial task in this instance would be to work toward a redefinition of the problem and the goal.

Selection of Alternative Methods and an Initial Mode of Intervention

When the nature of the problem has been defined and understood, when the goal toward which the work is directed has been set, and when the resources within the overall situation have been assessed, alternative solutions and interventions should become obvious. The most propitious solutions should be indicated by the above procedures. Final selection should be based on the following criteria:

1. Maximum feasibility: The solution that possesses the greatest chance of producing the desired results. The worker must think in terms of what is possible and attainable, which, unfortunately, is not always the most desirable. Compromise is an essential element, as we must deal with things as they are, not as we would like them to be.

2. Availability of resources to carry out the plan—either already available or capable of being created. Resources should be considered from various points of view. An important resource is the client's motivation and capacity for carrying out a share of the work in utilizing a particular method of resolution. The question of motivation, that "inner drive, impulse, or retention that causes a person to do something or act in a certain way," can be a puzzling and exasperating one. All too frequently, we see ourselves and others who possess the capacity and opportunity for change as lacking this essential ingredient. Happily, this is an area where much research is under way, and we are beginning to understand better the part that general health, emotional satisfaction, basic drives, reward and punishment, and self-determination play in determining motivation. Therefore, we can appropriately consider whether it is possible to develop motivation in situations where it appears to be absent or limited.

In addition, there are concrete resources, such as programs and services that exist or can be created, and there are intangible resources, such as emotional support, that are essential during the process of change. The battered wife who is emotionally and physically terrorized; who lacks education, working skills, and financial resources; and who has several small children to care for will need a lot of support if she is to marshal the strength to change her situation. We should be extremely careful not to use "lack of motivation on the part of the client" to cover failure of the society to provide what is necessary or lack of skill on the part of the worker.

The capacities—physical, intellectual, emotional, and spiritual—that clients possess are basic resources. What physical health, strength, and stamina can they summon? What level of intellectual achievement are they capable of? What knowledge and skills do they possess? What can they learn? What capacity do they have for relating to other people in a useful, satisfying way? What stress can they tolerate? What emotional stability do they possess? What spiritual strength can they call on?

In addition, what resources to carry out a particular mode of intervention exist within the worker? What knowledge and skill does the worker possess in the type of service that is needed? Is the worker personally committed and competent to deal with the problem posed by this particular client? Failing this, can a referral be made to some other individual or program that can meet the client's particular needs?

Community resources that can be drawn upon to implement a mode of intervention constitute the final category. Here workers should think broadly and flexibly, as there are both informal and formal sources that may be enlisted. Frequently, that which is most needed cannot be found within the framework of an institutionalized service, but is found within private individuals and groups. In isolated rural areas as well as some urban areas, services may be either nonexistent or inadequate, and workers must resort to their own inventiveness.

Initially, the worker will need to determine the most effective level of intervention— with an individual, a family, a group, or a community. Frequently, all four levels will need to be involved in various combinations.

When deciding on intervention strategy, the decision should be made as to the kind of services that are needed, whether specialized knowledge and skill are required, and if services will be secured through consultation, referral, or teamwork.

On the basis of all of these considerations—feasibility, availability, and workability— the worker will select a mode of intervention designed to meet the needs of a particular client in a particular situation.

Establishment of a Contract

From the selection of a particular alternative for action and a particular mode of intervention arises the need to establish a contract between the worker and the client. A contract is an agreement that is entered into with the understanding that there are reciprocal obligations for the parties involved. It may be either oral or written. In a sense, there is an oral contract at the time of engagement: The worker and the client are involved in shared activity toward a particular goal. When the problem has been defined, however, and the mode of intervention selected, it is important to have a specific understanding and commitment, and a written instrument is most useful here. It should be specific, contain an agreement as to goal, spell out procedures involved and roles and tasks of each participant, and specify a time limit for activities. All parties involved should have copies.

Contracts are useful tools. They create a structure within which the client and worker operate and, when properly used, ensure that the client understands what is involved. They can deepen the transactional nature of the relationship and dignify it by establishing it firmly as a working partnership. When the client—as is often the case with adolescents—tries to manipulate or test the worker, a contract provides a firm point of agreement that can be useful. Contracts, both oral and written, need to be used with a degree of flexibility and with openness for renegotiation or clarification should either become necessary. Contracts may be as diverse as those between foster parents and a caseworker to determine how they should serve the needs of a foster child, between a public health nurse and the volunteer committee that sponsors a geriatric service, between a psychotherapist and the individual or group with whom she is working, between a street worker and a neighborhood gang, between an administrator and his staff, between an employer and employee, or between doctor, nurse, or technician and patient.

However diverse, the basic premise of a contract is always the same—definition and delineation of a working agreement between and among people.

Action Leading to Desired Goal

The direction and manner of action should be laid down in the contract itself along with the tasks and roles of the people involved. These tasks and roles must be coordinated—decisions made as to who does what, when, and under what circumstances. Because each task often depends on what has gone before, there needs to be some agreed-on timetable. When the decision is made not to use a written contract, workers need to be very clear about their responsibility for action.

The tasks involved in working with people can be as many and varied as the problems of the people involved and their social organizations. They can range all the way from such minute details as seeing that a building is unlocked for a meeting, to confrontation of the hidden agenda that separates a divided task force that has been charged with a community responsibility, to helping a frightened, disturbed adolescent face the nature of the sexual problems that are upsetting her.

Workers need to be very careful to make a valid assessment of the capabilities of the clients involved and not to expect more from them than they are capable of achieving. Setting a person, a group, or a community up for failure often results in loss of motivation for working toward any change and in a sense of hopelessness.

For example, a child whose learning problem is related to the presence of an incompetent or psychopathic teacher can do nothing to change his situation. Workers would need to think of interventions at the level of school, perhaps involving parents and teachers, to create an action system comprising all of them.

Equally, the householder whose home is being taken over for urban development without adequate compensation could do little to change her situation alone. Other systems would have to be involved in order to change the law or to bring pressure to bear on officials or government.

The nursing home operator, struggling with problems of staff morale, unhappy patients, and poor relationships with visiting medical staff, presents a problem that calls for interventive strategies designed to work inside the system itself as well as with the individuals involved.

The responsibility of workers to carry out their tasks in the agreed-on action is paramount, particularly in working with people who have little experience with trustworthiness. In all relationships there is an element of role modeling, and the example the worker sets is important. When the terms of the action agreement cannot be met, the reason should be carefully explained, but even so, this does not always suffice.

Evaluation

Flexibility is essential in working with people. There is not only constant change in living entities, there is also the fact that interventions sometimes result in unexpected changes, and there is also the possibility of error. It is the worker's responsibility to create a climate where an accepted part of the procedure is objective evaluation or appraisal of what is occurring. In such a climate, worker and client may see the results of what has been done in terms of movement toward immediate and ultimate goals. A continuous and honest review of what has occurred, an analysis of success and failure that attempts to understand the factors involved and the results, should point to continuation, termination, or redesign of the working plan.

Continuation or Termination

Continuation is indicated when the results of the action show movement in the desired direction. Such movement confirms the validity of the original assessment, problem definition, goal, selection of mode of intervention, and contract.

However, the action may not result in progress toward the desired goal. The fault may lie at any point in the process. In engagement, false understanding may have been set up between worker and client. The original data may have been either incorrect or misinterpreted. The problem may have been wrongly defined or an improper aspect selected for initial work. The goals selected may have been incorrect, unreachable, or irrelevant. The alternative selected for action may have been a poor one, and the mode of intervention inappropriate. The contract may have been too demanding, too simple, or invalid, and the action either a failure or inconclusive. A reassessment, then, must take place that involves the familiar process of picking up the pieces and starting over again—not, however, at the beginning. There is the asset of what was learned in the initial phase, and there are the liabilities created by the failure of the chosen problem-solving plan.

Termination takes place when the goal has been achieved and the service completed, when nothing further is to be gained by continuing, when the client requests discontinuance, or when referral is made to another source of help and the original worker will no longer be involved. In termination, as in the other steps of the problem-solving process, the client's participation is of maximum importance. If the helping relationship is at all significant, the way it ends will be important for the client's self-image and capacity for future relationships. The reason for termination should be clear in the minds of both client and worker and, whenever possible, feelings about it expressed and understood.

A part of termination is leaving the door open for future contacts. As we have realized that life is a continuous problem-solving process, we have come to know that people may need help many different times with many different concerns. The desired results of a good helping experience involve not only increased knowledge of resources, but also increased readiness to use them as need be.

Using the Problem-Solving Process
When Ethnic Differences Are Involved

The basic problem-solving process so commonly used in Western society remains for workers the most useful way to approach members of different ethnic groups as well as other clients. As always, it is important to remember that this is the worker's way of thinking and planning and is not necessarily shared by clients. The rational gathering of data, weighing of alternatives, anticipation of outcomes, and selection of the most desirable may not be the method clients have learned to use in their own cultures. Workers must be sensitive to this and respect different approaches while at the same time using, for themselves, their own disciplined way of looking at problems.

A frequently desired goal of problem-solving work is to teach clients this method through example, but this needs to be done selectively with consideration of the needs and wishes of the particular client and the problem being considered.

The first step in this process, engagement, which involves establishment of communication channels and of the worker as a trustworthy and capable person, is vitally important. Contingent on it is the success of subsequent steps. Clients may have trouble accepting that workers of a differing background and experience can ever understand their problems, and workers must demonstrate willingness to do so and to learn. It is often necessary to go more slowly while this learning takes place.

Language differences are barriers, but not impenetrable ones. While it is the worker's responsibility to ensure that written and verbal content is understood, fundamental attitudes that will open or close communication channels are most often conveyed nonverbally. Workers must listen, observe, and learn as they go, for words and actions have different meanings for different people. Such differences can be worked out, and one of the best ways to do this is by demonstrating a concrete ability to help with immediate problems as the client sees them.

The gathering and analyzing of data, assessment, is a process that begins long before actual contact with clients. All assessment must be made in light of ethnic reality, past and present. Newcomers bear the major burden for adaptation to a different culture, and such adaptation can be viewed as existing on a continuum. Even members of a family group, for example, are often at different places on that continuum. Available resources, too, must be evaluated in light of this continuum in terms of whether they are geared to meet the perceived and/or actual need or whether they are so geared to the needs of the dominant culture that they are not relevant.

Workers are continually involved in assessment, and with ethnic peoples, as with all clients, it is important that the clients themselves be involved in the assessment process. The establishment of a climate of trust will determine whether clients will feel free to look critically at both the people and systems involved. Newcomers who may not fully understand, who are uncertain of their futures, or for whom previous efforts to use resources have been unsuccessful often have difficulty in looking objectively at what is taking place.

In *problem definition,* it is particularly important to observe the old mandate to start where the client is and to move at his or her speed. Dealing with the immediate problem as perceived by the client is essential, especially if it is a "real" one such as need for food or shelter. If feelings are involved—and they always are—they must be dealt with, and this can be done more easily if workers have established trustworthiness, effectiveness, sensitivity, and respect for differences in dealing with concrete problems. Different cultures mandate different ways of dealing with feelings, with family situations, and with outsiders. If, on the basis of objective assessment, the worker determines that herein lies the problem and success depends on dealing with this, it must be done in light of the cultural determinants.

A particularly delicate problem to define and work with occurs when the client feels that all of the problems exist because of ethnicity—that she or he is unemployed or does not get advancement, is lacking in education, or cannot live in a good neighborhood because of it. There is often an element of truth in this, but it is not the whole story, and if the worker is going to be of help to the client in improving social functioning, it is essential to face and deal with this.

The next three steps in the formal problem-solving process, *setting of goals, selection of method,* and *establishment of a contract,* again must be considered in light of both individual or group need and ability, of the existence or possibility of creation of essential resources, and of the ethnic reality. The worker's presence in the situation, however, is predicated on knowing more and better about how to deal with the problem than the clients themselves. As one mother in a multiproblem family commented, "We know things are bad. What we need to know is how to change them."

Workers must have a clear idea about what goals are immediate and doable in achieving the desired results, how to take the steps upon which their achievement depends, and what the necessary roles and tasks of the clients are in this process. These need to be viewed in light of the demands of the ethnic culture, but with awareness that the larger culture will adapt to these differences only so far and slowly. Newcomers to a society often must make major changes in thinking and behavior in order to survive, and the worker's task often is to facilitate such change. It is even more important that clients here have the opportunity to be involved in the steps of the process, in decision making about accepting new ideas, for therein lies much of the secret of motivation to help them succeed. What the worker sees as a problem may not seem a problem to clients who are members of an ethnic group wherein such behavior or experiences are a culturally accepted way of life. The task of the worker is to develop a relationship in which the client can be enabled to see the contradiction between what is necessary to allow adaptation to a new way of life and what the past life has dictated.

The final step, *evaluation,* which, as always, should be continuous and ongoing, needs to involve both worker and client. It is both a professional thing for workers to do, and a natural step in the process of solving life's problems, particularly when the decision making and role performance have been shared. It is the worker's responsibility to create a climate in which evaluation can be honest and open.

If evaluation results in termination and if the working relationship is a meaningful one, workers must be sensitive to how the ethnic culture marks such occasions. This is an opportunity to look back, to think and talk about what has happened, and to consider the future. It must leave the door open for future contacts, for life is essentially a problem-solving process and future help may be needed.

Two Case Studies in Use of the Basic Process

Basic Process 1

Two illustrations of this helping process serve to demonstrate how it can be used. The first is a so-called multiproblem family, the Kinkaids. In one sense of the term, every family could be so classified, for certainly life consists of a continuing series of problems for which solutions must be found. However, there are some families for whom the number and severity of their problems is often combined with a lack of coping ability on the part of the individuals and the unit itself or a lack of the essential social resources to make solutions possible. Such problems often cause a breakdown in a family's capacity to function. This breakdown usually shows itself at the family's most vulnerable point, which might be a shaky marital relationship or the incapacity of children to meet the demands placed on them in their life experience.

In the Kinkaid family, Richie, at age 8 the oldest child, was that vulnerable point in his family, and the school nurse was the worker who first perceived his unmet needs. Young Ms. Ishito had become aware in three years' experience in an elementary school that the child who came to her office frequently with colds, headaches, and minor ailments was often in trouble in other aspects of his life—home, school, and community. Richie rarely missed a week without coming. Ms. Ishito became concerned about his pallor, his thinness, his frequent sore throats and colds, and his fatigue, which caused him to fall asleep on the cot in her office and lie there for hours. Mentioning this to his teacher, she learned that Richie was one of the faceless children in class, neither good nor bad enough to be outstanding or remembered—just there, doing minimal work and causing no trouble.

Engagement.   Thus alerted, Ms. Ishito was particularly aware of Richie's tests on the upcoming health screening, and she was not surprised when the examining physician noted swollen tonsils and underweight with possible malnutrition; she recommended a follow-up by the family doctor. Before contacting the Kinkaids, Ms. Ishito secured as much data as she could from the school records about them as a family. Mr. and Mrs. Kinkaid had both been born in Caney Creek, Kentucky. Mr. Kinkaid (28) worked as a clerk in a small variety store. Mrs. Kinkaid (27) was a housewife. There were five children: Richie (8); Linda (5), who was in kindergarten; twins, Robert and Phillip (3); and an infant, Peter.

The classroom teacher reported that Mr. and Mrs. Kinkaid came to Parents' Day faithfully but were not active in any of the school organizations. Richie tested a little above average in intellectual ability but with his absences and his passivity, earned the all-too-frequent comment "not achieving up to capacity." Linda's file indicated the same pattern. Both children had all of their required immunizations.

In considering how to approach the Kinkaids, Ms. Ishito decided that instead of sending the usual form reporting on the health tests and asking the parents to come to the school, she would offer to visit them. She did this for several reasons: the number of young children and the expense of babysitters, the fact that she wanted to talk with both parents together, and her realization that the problem indicated by the children's symptoms might be very broad indeed. Therefore, with the reports she sent a note asking if she might visit in the evening, on a specific date and time. Richie, pleased to be singled out for special attention, faithfully carried the note home and brought back a verbal reply that it would be "all right for her to come." (If the Kinkaids had rejected her offer and had not visited the school, Ms. Ishito could have dropped in one evening, confronted them with the test results, and attempted to involve them in a discussion of what they meant and what could be done about them.)

Assessment.   The Kinkaids lived in a small and simple house, one in a block of six built in an area of much larger and more expensive homes. Theirs was outstanding for its meticulous appearance. Ms. Ishito commented on this to Mr. Kinkaid when he met her at the door, and he came outside and showed her around, talking about his yard and garden. He was a slender, wiry, tense man, clearly accustomed to meeting the public and putting his best foot forward.

Inside, the house showed considerable contrast to the neat exterior. Clean but cluttered, it presented an air of confusion and disorder that was aggravated by the noise of the television, which Linda and Richie were watching, and the sound of the twins, who were obviously being put to bed against their will. When Mrs. Kinkaid joined them, she was carrying the baby and a bottle. She was a very attractive young woman, but obviously tired and harassed. She attempted, halfheartedly, to send the two older children to bed, and when she met with no success, their father switched off the TV and ordered them out. At this point, Ms. Ishito suggested that if the parents agreed, she would be glad to have the children stay to listen, as they were going to be the subject of the conversation. "Remember how you used to feel when the teacher came to visit?" she asked.

It was agreed that they could stay, and Mr. Kinkaid commented that his school was so different from Cherry Street that it was unbelievable. Both the Kinkaids had lived "up the hollow" and ridden the bus to a consolidated school. Determined to leave the hopelessness of Appalachia behind them, they had married immediately after graduating from high school and gone to Cincinnati, where Mr. Kinkaid had gotten a job similar to his present one. He stressed that he had always done white-collar work. They had moved to their present home five years ago because they wanted to live in a smaller town and to escape the racial tensions and problems in the city, where they felt lost. They wanted better schools for the children, and they had selected this neighborhood because of Cherry Street School.

Initially, Mr. Kinkaid tended to do most of the talking, but as the discussion progressed, his wife became more dominant. While he was inclined to pass over problems lightly, Mrs. Kinkaid, in a petulant voice, complained about the unfriendliness of the town and the neighbors, their limited income, the fact that she never got out, and how hard she had to work. This seemed to embarrass her husband, who at first tried to stop her but finally withdrew from the conversation. The two children sat quietly through this as if it were an old story. Richie, sitting next to Ms. Ishito, who had her arm around him, seemed to have relaxed almost into sleep.

The picture that emerged was of a young family struggling hard to function adequately, but with breakdown in crucial areas that promised severe problems in the future.

Definition of the Problem.   As Ms. Ishito talked with the parents, she was trying to assess what they were saying, to raise questions when her understanding was not clear, and to empathize with the deep feelings that were obvious, albeit mostly under the surface. It was apparent that these problems were causing a strain on the marital relationship and between the parents and the children and that what had begun ten years ago as a fairly strong relationship, with potential for a full life, was fraying around the edges. The problems were numerous and on many different levels:

1. The Kinkaids' income was not adequate to meet the needs of the family. Although Mr. Kinkaid was ashamed of this, the problem lay not in poor management, but in the fact that his salary was too low. The burden of indebtedness was climbing, and it seemed that his marketable skills were so minimal that it would be difficult for him to qualify for a better job.
2. While Mr. Kinkaid seemed to be adapting well to the change in setting, Mrs. Kinkaid, perhaps because of her early cultural experiences (and this is often true of housewives confined to the home by the demands of their job), had been unable to establish an effective and satisfying pattern of living in her new community. Her values, attitudes, and ways of living remained those of the mountain town where she had grown up.
3. The family had too many children too soon. Each family unit has the capacity to deal financially, physically, and emotionally with a certain level of demands, but when the demands become too great, the family breaks down. This was evidenced in part by the fact that the first two children had had good medical and dental care, but the twins and the baby had only the minimum.
4. Each of the family members was adapting to these problems in an individual way, but all in ways that were destructive. Mr. Kinkaid tried to shut his eyes to their seriousness and drove himself harder and harder as he became more desperate. Mrs. Kinkaid adapted by giving up. Meals had become sporadic and inadequately planned. The children were not given the care they needed nor the opportunity for stimulation so vital in these early years. In her fear she had become passive, only taking action when forced to, and complaining in a whining way that was destructive to the morale of her

husband and children. The two older children had followed her pattern of passivity and showed signs of intellectual, emotional, and physical starvation.

5. Adequate social resources to meet their needs did not exist. Social planners have never dealt adequately with the situation in Appalachia, where the roots of the problem lay. It has become a sore spot and a testimony to inadequate planning and lack of protection for people and resources. In their present setting, the Kinkaids fell into the category of low-income families for whom medical and dental care is often nonexistent and for whom the only flexible budget item is the money they spend for food. They did not qualify for public welfare programs. Mr. Kinkaid was most reluctant to use what free services did exist because he did not want to be "dependent," and Mrs. Kinkaid's hopelessness presented a strong barrier to learning to deal with the demands of a hard reality.

The immediate problem was where to start. It would be easy to turn away from such a situation, particularly in light of all the other problems involving severe antisocial behavior that demanded Ms. Ishito's attention. Yet the consequences of this kind of situation can be great not only in terms of human suffering, but also in financial cost to the overall society. Although she realized all this, Ms. Ishito could not, at this point, share all of her understanding with her clients. They saw the problem as the children needing healthcare that they could not afford, and it was here that all efforts had to start. Because they saw this need as "respectable" and divorced from welfare, they could probably accept help with it.

Setting of Goals.   The overall goal of both Ms. Ishito and the Kinkaids coincided, which was a strength that the worker could use. Also there was basic affection and trust between the Kinkaids, and they wanted a good life for themselves and their children.

The immediate goal, securing further examination and medical care for Richie and Linda and preventive care for the younger children, was one on which, again, everyone agreed, and when they had talked about the school examination, Mr. Kinkaid said they would call their own doctor.

Selection of Alternative Methods and an Initial Mode of Intervention.
Ms. Ishito replied that of course they could do this, and in the final analysis, they might decide to do so, but she wanted them to know what else was available. They had told her and she knew how hard it was to stretch a salary to cover all of the young family's needs. The town was fortunate in that the Health Department had a good well-child clinic, where examinations were free and shots were given at a minimum cost. Many of the parents of Cherry School District used it and found it helpful. Ms. Ishito had brought several brochures on the clinic, which she gave to the Kinkaids.

Ms. Ishito did not add that this clinic afforded a broad range of services, including a mothers' group to discuss nutrition and how to feed a family well and inexpensively, specialists who worked on both an individual and group basis in helping parents meet the emotional needs of children, and family planning clinics. She saw the mothers' group as possibly providing the opening that Mrs. Kinkaid needed to begin developing a social experience similar to the one her husband found with his fellow employees at work. However, she did not want the Kinkaids to feel that she was taking over their lives, as this would quickly alienate the independent Mr. Kinkaid.

Establishment of a Contract. After considerable discussion and many questions about the nature and financing of the service (Mr. Kinkaid talked about his horror of welfare as he had known it during his childhood in their little mountain town), the parents decided that they would try it. It was agreed that Ms. Ishito would make known the results of the school tests to the clinic worker. Unfortunately, the clinic hours coincided with Mr. Kinkaid's working hours, and so he could neither accompany his wife nor babysit with the younger children. Ms. Ishito offered to go with Mrs. Kinkaid for the first trip and watch the younger children while she and the older ones saw the doctor, if no other arrangement could be made. If they decided to continue, Mrs. Kinkaid felt that her neighbor might agree to babysit when needed. They discussed the kinds of information the doctor required and the questions they wanted to ask.

Action. Ms. Ishito called the clinic, referred the Kinkaid children, and sent the school reports to the clinic. She phoned Mrs. Kinkaid the day before the clinic visit. As she had anticipated, Mrs. Kinkaid had second thoughts and was dwelling on the problems involved in getting there. Ms. Ishito recognized how hard it was for her to mobilize the impetus and energy for her undertakings but encouraged and supported her real desire to give the children the care that they needed.

When they arrived at the clinic, Ms. Ishito remained only long enough to get her client through the first stages and then excused herself to do some errands elsewhere in the building. She did this intentionally. The clinic waiting room was friendly and cheerful, with a coffee urn and a volunteer worker who worked with the younger children as they waited. The twins gravitated very naturally to this group. Other young mothers were there, and Ms. Ishito hoped that without her presence, Mrs. Kinkaid would begin to interact with them. If this did not occur naturally, it was the clinic worker's job to attempt to facilitate it.

On the way home, Mrs. Kinkaid talked about how she had enjoyed being out. The doctor had prescribed vitamins for both the older children, had complimented her on how well they behaved, and seemed particularly interested in their eating and sleeping patterns. He had suggested that Mrs. Kinkaid might want to talk with the nutritionist about how to serve more balanced meals and had said an aide would come to the house if she could not get down to the clinic. He had started shots for the twins and the baby and made an appointment for followup care.

Evaluation. Mrs. Kinkaid felt that, on the whole, the clinic was a good resource that she and her family could use. She wanted to take her husband with her the next time. Ms. Ishito, recognizing the sometimes transitory ebullience that results from doing something about a problem and knowing how difficult it was going to be for the Kinkaids to maintain the motivation to act, supported and encouraged Mrs. Kinkaid as much as she could, and she agreed to keep in touch.

In looking at her initial intervention, Ms. Ishito decided that it had been a good beginning. In addition to providing vital medical care, the clinic offered opportunities for learning and for meaningful relationships that could help to ease the pressures on the family—provided the workers in the various areas involved were skillful enough to keep the Kinkaids involved, and the Kinkaids were sufficiently motivated to use the service.

This intervention, however, left the broader and more basic social problems untouched. Society faces the clear choice of guaranteeing an adequate income to families such as the Kinkaids whose earnings are too small and providing free the essential services necessary to meet their basic human needs, or of dealing with the endless series of problems of increasing severity that result from their semipoverty. In the final analysis, the economic cost of the latter alternative is much greater than that of the first two, to say nothing of the human suffering involved. Where, then, does the responsibility of the individual worker lie? How can Ms. Ishito intervene effectively to help deal with these basic problems, to do more than merely palliative work, and to bring about the changes in the total social system that are essential to ensure that families such as the Kinkaids become and remain healthy units in the total society?

Social change on so broad a scale cannot be effected by one individual working alone. It requires the strength of many people working together and utilizing the tools that a democratic system provides. In her role as a social changer, Ms. Ishito can use specialized knowledge of and experience with the inadequacies of the total system and their effect on both individuals and the society. She has recourse to the various groups she belongs to by virtue of her work, to organizations of teachers or health workers, to groups she belongs to by virtue of her role as a citizen, and to those that she helps create with her clients and colleagues to deal with specialized situations.

The first categories are ones through which she might work for the necessary legislation and the enforcement of that legislation. The two areas of basic need in this family—adequate wages and healthcare—are areas to which the population as a whole is already committed, and the questions that currently need resolution deal with how these goals can be achieved. Ms. Ishito can contribute knowledge and strength to the resolution of these problems.

One of the major problems the Kinkaids faced was their feeling of helplessness and hopelessness. An excellent tool in overcoming this problem was involving the clients in ways to change their own situation—in the struggle for self-realization. The parents' group at the clinic, developed out of a common interest in the needs of families and children, need only take one further step to start moving actively to secure the resources to meet these needs. Opportunity for personal growth as well as necessary social action can be achieved through use of this medium. We can see concrete evidence of results achieved through group action—for example, the vastly changed attitudes toward, and improved care for, retarded children, through group efforts of both lay and professional people; for the elderly, through their own group efforts; for children in foster care, through foster parents' groups; and for a multitude of various special interest groups. When individuals band together with a common interest and acquire the knowledge of how to tackle the system, they can develop the necessary power to effect change. The worker, by virtue of specialized knowledge and skill, can provide the catalytic action often needed to get this process started and serve as consultant, resource person, enabler, and when necessary, advocate.

Continuation.   The outcome of Ms. Ishito's evaluation with the Kinkaids of the results of their initial clinic visit would be a continuation of the process well begun. The worker's efforts would focus on providing the essential personal support to keep their courage high and to work toward changing the basic social conditions that create problems for this family.

Basic Process 2

The problem-solving process is equally applicable in dealing with larger units such as a troubled neighborhood, which Southeast was becoming, and in working with groups of people.

Southeast is an older section of the city, where big homes had been turned into apartments and some low-income housing had been introduced. To the few older white families who remained in their homes and the African American families who had lived there since World War II were added two new groups, the Asian Americans, predominantly Vietnamese, and the Mexican immigrants who were brought into town to work at the meatpacking plant. Both of these newer groups were in search of inexpensive housing. Although the older residents complained about the newcomers taking jobs from them and using too much welfare, these diverse people had managed fairly well together; gradually, though, it became increasingly obvious the young people were in trouble and, hence, so was the entire community.

Complaints increased of teenagers congregating in the parking lots of the small businesses, driving away customers and leaving garbage; of frequent loud, late parties; and of weekend cruising around the streets at high speed. There also began to be problems with vandalism, violence, and drugs in the schools. Gang symbols began to appear on public buildings, and membership in these gangs was apparently based on ethnic background.

There was concern among people in the neighborhood, but no action was taken until an afterschool fight erupted into a minor riot. Then the board of the Family Service Agency, which operated a satellite office in Southeast and included some local residents among its members, voted to hire a worker whose specialty was community organization to help develop a plan for dealing with these growing concerns.

After taking time to know the community (the beginning of *engagement*) based on *assessment* of what was taking place and what resources were available, the worker, Leon Howard, *defined the immediate problem* of getting the residents involved in planning and action. His *mode of intervention* was to develop an initial planning committee made up of representatives from each of the four ethnic groups in the neighborhood, including members of the various social organizations responsible for dealing with such problems. He also wanted to involve parents of school children of all ages.

Accordingly, from the church he had attended he enlisted Margaret Niles, a parent and a real estate agent who would represent the African American group; Juan Garcia, a lawyer who was considered one of the leaders of the Hispanic American community; Thang Bieu, who kept a variety store in "Little Asia" and was known to most of the Asian Americans; and John Ramy, a volunteer for Family Service who had lived in the neighborhood for most of his life and knew most of the white families. Sergeant Shelley, the Police Department's representative in the schools, and Maria Lopez, the City Council member from the district, agreed to serve. The Health Department designated Jane Fister, a visiting nurse, and Linda Ramirez, president of the PTA, as members of the committee. Father Minelli of Saint Stephen's Church and Reverend Charles Federson of the Unitarian Church, whose congregation was known for the diverse people it included, volunteered. Leon also wanted some representatives of the young people, and Shawanda and George, seniors from the high school, were enlisted.

The first meeting was held in the conference room at the Family Service Agency. Because many of the dozen or so people were not acquainted, it began with coffee and cookies and general introductions. Leon presided at the meeting and began by outlining what he had learned about the community, pausing now and then to ask individuals to supplement his report with their own experiences. He concluded by mentioning the strengths of the neighborhood—the absence of pockets of extreme poverty, the good balance of small businesses and residential property, the two small parks, the branch library, the schools, and the churches. The challenge as he presented it was to look at the situation, consider its seriousness, and decide where, how, and whether to intervene. He then opened the meeting for general discussion.

This started slowly with the professionals there holding back somewhat, but finally Margaret Niles spoke of her concern about her children at the school and her worries when they played in the park near their house. She was supported by Thang Bieu, who told of the groups of teenagers who came into her store and disrupted business.

Shawanda and George agreed that the problems after school and in the parks centered around older boys and girls who just took over. Some of them were school dropouts, and many of them were not even from the neighborhood. Sergeant Shelley seconded this, and he told how the police and park departments were cooperating in trying to cope with this. Maria Lopez's major concern was that something be done to keep drugs from coming into the community—was anything being attempted?

There was considerable discussion of these separate concerns, and then Charles Federson questioned whether the separateness of the four groups in the neighborhood contributed to the creation of a climate that tended to foster the development of such social problems. There was general response to the idea, both pro and con, but the feeling emerged that this was a total community situation and that everybody needed to pull together.

Leon then took over and summarized their discussion. He said that, in addition to the specific problems with which they must deal, it seemed that the group generally felt that an underlying contributing factor was the divisiveness of the groups within the community— perhaps this was where they should start. There appeared to be general consensus to have a meeting to which all interested people in Southeast would be invited to discuss these concerns. There would be reports on what was presently being done, and an effort would be made to enlist ideas and support for further action. This was accepted as the first step, and members volunteered individually to undertake the tasks required to implement this—publicity, program, and talking it up to ensure attendance.

Throughout this meeting the basic process for planning change was taking place. The members of the planning committee had *engaged themselves individually* with the situation at the point when they agreed to serve. In the meeting they *engaged themselves as a group* with all the strengths that arise from such a coalition. *Assessing* the situation, they arrived at *definition of an overall problem and goal* as well *subsidiary problems and goals.* In so doing they established priorities and *selected modes of intervention* from the various alternatives available to them, arriving at a series of (in this case unwritten) *contracts* or *actions.* Obvious in their deliberations and actions were provisions for *evaluation* and either continuing or changing the process depending on subsequent results of their interventions.

Major responsibility for keeping this process going rested with Leon, and in so doing he was using the process himself. Although the meeting was a success in the sense that some people became involved and felt that something was being done, Leon had no illusions about the difficulty of the work that remained. Coalitions can present special problems because of all the different interests involved, and Southeast's problems were representative of some of the most severe ones facing current society as people try to learn to live together in a changing world.

Summary

In summary, the basic problem-solving process that underlies all human service tends to look unwieldy, cumbersome, and somewhat rigid. It also seems obvious, because it is the process by which we naturally adapt to the demands of living. To the neophyte human service worker, it may seem awkward to attempt to be consciously aware of the steps in such a natural process, but only as we are aware of it, of what we are doing, and of how and why it is succeeding or failing can we hope to control it.

It is a simple, continuous process, one step growing out of another. It can be short term or extensive, depending on the requirements of the situation. One of its great advantages is that the user of this process learns a way to approach problem solving that can be used over and over again. Workers are teachers of an orderly process of dealing with the demands of living. Its very familiarity as a natural process of adaptation may create problems for workers who need to use it consciously with full awareness of its progressive steps. However, such a disciplined way of practice can be learned, even though initially the reaction of workers may resemble the centipede in the following poem:

> *A centipede was happy, quite, until a frog, in fun,*
> *Said, "Which leg comes after which?"*
> *This worked him up to such a pitch*
> *He lay disconsolate in a ditch*
> *Deciding how to run.* *

*From Mrs. Edward Craster, "The Puzzled Centipede or the Perils of Thinking," in *Under the Tent of the Sky* (New York: Macmillan, 1937), edited by John E. Bruton. Reprinted with the permission of the publisher.

SUGGESTED ASSIGNMENTS

1. Assign a short paper or outline to be used in class discussion in which students use the problem-solving process to deal with a situation in their own lives or with someone they are trying to help. Was the process consciously used? Designate steps in the process and consider its continuous and ongoing nature.

2. Assign students in small groups to design an outreach plan to deal with one of the following:
   a. Racial conflict in a neighborhood park.
   b. A mobile home court where many young, single parents live and where there are indications of neglect and possibly abuse of children.
   c. Old people living—often alone—in a housing project where adequate social services are lacking.
   d. "Throwaway" and runaway youth, many addicted to drugs and suffering from AIDS or HIV, who live on the streets in urban centers.

3. Assign students to develop a contract between themselves and someone with whom they are involved in a relationship—one of their children, a spouse, a teacher, or another person. These can be verbal or written. Utilize this contract as a basis for discussion of contracts and how they can be used.

REFERENCES AND RELATED READINGS

Bartlett, M. (1970). *The common base of social work practice.* Silver Spring, MD: NASW Press.

Brieland, D., Castin, L., & Atherton, C. R. (1985). *Contemporary social work.* New York: McGraw Hill.

Compton, B., & Galaway, B. (1998). *Social work processes* (6th ed.). Belmont, CA: Wadsworth.

Egan, G. (2001). *The skilled helper: A problem management and opportunity development approach to helping* (4th ed.). Belmont, CA: Wadsworth.

Johnson, L. (2000). *Social work practice: A generalist approach.* Boston: Allyn and Bacon.

Kirst-Ashmar, K., & Hull, G. A. (1993). *Understanding generalist practice.* Belmont, CA: Wadsworth.

Zastrow, C. (1999). *Introduction to social work and social welfare: Social problems, services and current issues* (7th ed.). Belmont, CA: Wadsworth.

Developing an Eclectic Approach to Practice

8

Why is an eclectic approach in practice desirable and how is it achieved?

What is the difference between a specialist and a generalist and how are they related?

How are consultation and referral used in practice, and what are some of the factors involved in making them successful?

Eclecticism is, for many people, a dirty word implying lack of coherent, organized thinking and specialized skill. The phrase "jack of all trades, master of none," a saying widely used to describe a generalized worker who can do all things a little and nothing well, is generally considered to describe the eclectic.

By the very nature of the demands of their jobs, human service workers are required to deal with the totality of both individuals and society—and specialists are not always available. To be successful, workers must use elements from many different theories dealing with the human condition. There is much duplication and overlapping in the various approaches to working with people, and the knowledge and skills developed through differing branches of specialized research are not necessarily inconsistent when used together in a larger context.

Out of this eclecticism has come a common core of knowledge and skills that specialists and generalists alike in all of the human services must possess if they are to be successful. This book represents one attempt to define the content of this core.

The significant point is that regardless of how eclectic it may be, the worker's approach must form a consistent whole and be one that the worker believes in and is convinced can be effective. This conviction, combined with the worker's belief that each individual possesses the capacity for change and the worker's personal optimism about chances of success, forms an important factor in determining outcome. Without it, the worker is defeated before getting started.

In determining what to incorporate from various approaches into a total working model, the worker will need to measure principles and methods not only by the yardstick of results, but also in terms of their consistency with the worker's basic value system, view

153

of human beings, and theory of how change occurs. In human relations, the unresolved question of whether the end justifies the means is ever present. If one's philosophy and value system are valid, however, they should help to dictate the means to achieve the ends. Means that are inconsistent with valid basic values are self-defeating. For example, we believe that people have a right and a need to be involved in decisions regarding their own welfare. If we choose to ignore this, if we arbitrarily make decisions and force changes, we may succeed on the surface but fail in the more important aspect—the promotion of individual growth and capacity to deal with life problems.

It is equally important that, in their search for knowledge and skill from a wide variety of approaches, workers avoid faddishness and the swings of the pendulum from one extreme to another. When this occurs, we find overall approaches and techniques being used in situations where they are not applicable. The wide use of "insight therapy" to deal with poverty and its attendant problems is a graphic example of this. Overuse of the nondirective interviewing techniques of Carl Rogers is another.

Misunderstanding and misinterpretation of the theory and techniques of an approach can also lead to gross abuse. Nowhere can we find a more damning example of this than the way in which psychological test results have been misused in the public school system. The past two generations of school children have been classified, categorized, and frequently stigmatized by the misuse of instruments that have limited utility. Tools are only as good as the user, and only the knowledgeable person who possesses a healthy skepticism can effectively utilize the wide range of knowledge being developed in the behavioral sciences.

Development of a Working Model

In human service, the eclectic worker is the one who operates on the basis of a value system that uses knowledge, skills, and techniques that have been drawn from many different sources and organized into a coherent whole. When you consider the complex nature of human functioning and the broad range of services from habilitation to rehabilitation, it is obvious that there is no one practice theory broad enough to cover the entire spectrum. The existence of so many theories is further testimony that each lacks completeness and finality. Difference is an essential concomitant to a vital and growing body of knowledge, and it must always exist and be welcomed. The mind closed to question and change is moving toward sterility as surely as any other closed system.

However, because of these differences, workers are faced constantly with a bewildering array of new theories that purport to offer the sole solution to human problems. Because success in working with people is indefinite and difficult to achieve, workers tend to grasp at new ideas and approaches in an almost faddish fashion, often abandoning the old without either adequate reason or an effective replacement. Rather than flying back and forth like a shuttlecock from one theory to the other with desperation born of concern and the desire and need to produce results, workers must do the following:

1. Determine that there is no single way to deal with all the problems of living.
2. Be open to consideration of new ideas and approaches and committed to ongoing learning.

3. Develop sufficient knowledge to evaluate such ideas or reliable sources on which to depend for this evaluation.
4. Learn to differentiate among those theories that contribute only to the understanding of people and their societies, those that speak to practical methods for working with them, and those that do both.
5. Develop a broad base of knowledge and understanding on which to build, and decide whether to become a generalist or a specialist in practice.

Just as the proof of a pudding lies in the eating, the proof of a theory of change lies in its effectiveness. Does it work? Does it bring about the desired change? These should be the key questions asked, but in human service the answers must always be evaluated in light of the underpinning of all theories about people, the base on which they rest.

Figure 8.1 shows the evolution of a technique from a theory. The bottom line (A) is the worker's basic philosophy and value system, the yardstick by which all intervention into the lives of people must be measured. That measure must include: (1) respect for human dignity; (2) respect for the rights of individuals to have a good life and to be self-determining; (3) a

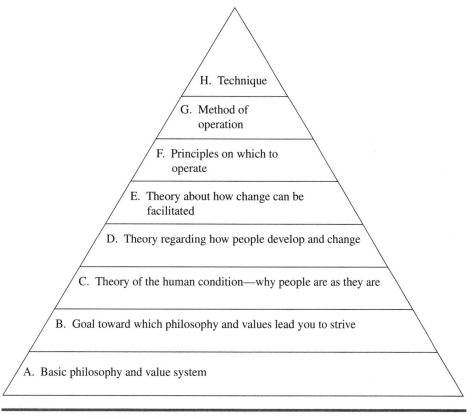

FIGURE 8.1   Evolution of a technique.

sense of social responsibility—concern for the relationship of mutual rights and responsibilities between the individual and the society, with the welfare of its members the primary responsibility of the society; and (4) a recognition that change is inevitable and that outside intervention can facilitate healthy and desirable change.

Out of this basic value system comes (B) the overall purpose—the end result of all endeavor—toward which workers strive. Because overall purposes tend to be broad ("the greatest good for the greatest number," "the realization of a truly democratic society"), workers need to cut them down into attainable goals, both immediate and long-term. These goals constitute steps toward realization of the general purpose. Specific goals can range all the way from such things as improvement of relations in a family, to provision of prenatal care for mothers, to development of a school system geared to meet the needs of all children. The purpose and goals must be consistent with the worker's value system.

Having decided what they believe and where they need to go to implement this belief, workers then need to ask themselves, (C) "What do I need to know about the human condition and about how and why people grow and change?" It is important to differentiate between steps (B) and (C) and the next step, (D), which is the issue of how change can be brought about. There is an increasing tendency to make three classifications of theories regarding the human condition: (1) those that deal primarily with understanding people, (2) those that deal primarily with how to enable people to change, and (3) those that do both.

It is difficult to conceive of a theory of change that does not rest upon some conviction about the nature of people. It is possible, of course, to work as a technician in human service, using accepted techniques or untested folk knowledge with a degree of success. It is equally possible to deny the importance of causality and to focus on and deal only with the "here-and-now" problem.

However, the experience of working through a problem, be it in habilitation or rehabilitation, almost always results in learning what will better enable the client to deal with subsequent problems, and even prevent their recurrence. We need to use the principle of parsimony in deciding what we must know and do in light of the immediate situation. But the most lasting service we can provide depends on our understanding of the roots of the problem at hand and our ability to select from a variety of interventions based on sound theoretical knowledge.

The final four steps in the evolution of techniques deal with how change can be facilitated in light of (E) the worker's theory about how change can be facilitated, (F) principles on which to operate, (G) the worker's method of operation, and (H) the techniques that the worker uses.

Techniques are vast in number. Human service workers make conscious use of themselves in working with people, and there can be a large amount of personal artistry among experienced, skilled, and knowledgeable workers as they experiment with and select among a variety of techniques. The test of pragmatism—do the chosen techniques work in bringing about the desired result?—is paramount. But here, too, techniques must also always be measured against the value base. If we believe, for example, that fundamental and lasting change must come from within the individual involved in the process, coercion is hardly a valid technique, except as an adjunct when essential.

It is difficult to measure success in working with people because of the infinite variety of experiences that all of us are subject to at a given time. The variables are almost endless. It is much easier to validate a technique that is limited in scope and goal than a broad personality theory, but if the technique works, the underlying theory about the human condition must contain some validity. There is always an underlying theory present, even if not articulated, and often not in the consciousness of the worker, as in the use of folk knowledge. We are striving to know what we are doing, why and how we are doing it, and what works in particular situations. Use of such an organizational structure as "the evolution of a technique" is an orderly, coherent way to approach this undertaking. It does not lock the worker into the use of only one approach to problem solving but can be used to validate a variety of approaches as needed.

Illustrations of Models for Eclecticism

Three widely used current approaches in human service will serve to illustrate the development of an eclectic model for human service work. They are crisis theory, behavior modification, and marketing theory.

Crisis Theory. Crisis theory, as used at present, rests on Hans Selye's work in physical medicine on internal balance, crisis, stress, and adaptation and on the work of the ego psychologists, Heinz Hartmann, Anna Freud, Erik Erikson, and others, describing the process of adaptation to the demands of the environment. Crisis theory developed out of work in a public health setting and orientation, with a truly interdisciplinary approach involving medicine, social work, psychology, and psychiatry. The practice theories that have grown out of these two ways of thinking about the human condition emphasize (1) health rather than illness, (2) strength rather than pathology, (3) present and future coping ability, and (4) extending the need for change from helping the client deal with reality as it is to enabling the client to take responsibility for changing the reality itself.

With the acceptance of the ideas that a "problem-free" state is unattainable and that life itself poses a series of recurring developmental crises that must be dealt with, workers began to search for ways to deal more knowledgeably with immediate breakdowns and at the same time strengthen the client for the task of coping with the breakdowns that inevitably will occur. From this and from observation and research on the adaptive processes that people undergo in coping with the hazardous events of life, crisis theory was formulated, with specific goals and specific techniques.

The concept of balance is basic to this theory, for true crisis is an upset in the "steady state" of the reacting individual. Research has defined the duration of the imbalance as limited, as there is an almost immediate effort to recover an operating equilibrium. This period of upset is characterized by a high degree of tension, anxiety, and fear. Three different types of crises have been identified: the normal, developmental ones such as the movement from childhood to adolescence; those related to role change such as first marriage or first parenthood; and the accidental events that occur in all lives such as death, illness, loss of work, and so on. The goal of the worker is to help the client cope with the immediate problem, regain equilibrium, and function anew, hopefully on a higher level than before, for crisis provides significant opportunity for growth. Work is time-limited, and it is focused on the immediate goal of regaining equilibrium. Dealing with underlying conflicts and problems is not the goal of the work (see Figure 8.2).

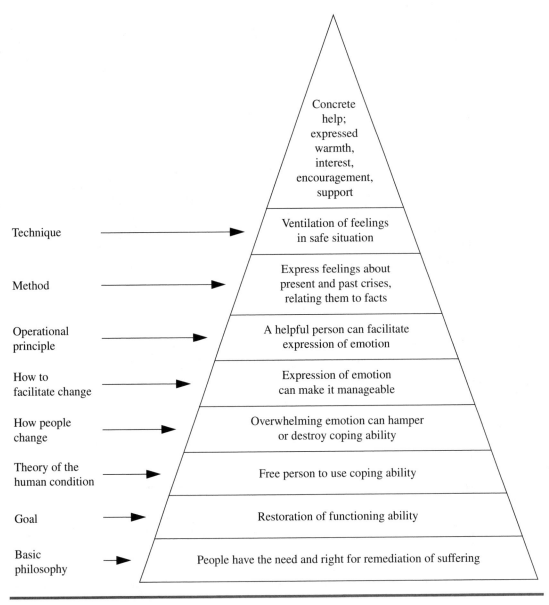

FIGURE 8.2   Evolution of a technique in crisis theory.

Four practice implications grow out of this crisis-theory approach:

1. The worker must be immediately available at the time of crisis when the individual is motivated to deal with the problem because of pain and discomfort.
2. Focus should be on the present problem, but because the old scars tend to hurt again in such circumstances, opportunity should be given for thinking and talking about past crises.
3. Although the worker should provide opportunity for expression of feeling, the rational and adaptive capacities of the client should be supported and strengthened.
4. During the crisis, the worker can be more active (and should be) than in a noncrisis situation, and he or she should avoid creating undue dependency. The worker can give advice more freely and be authoritative without fear of undermining the client's capacity to act.

As the crisis is resolved, the worker and the client must decide whether additional help of a different nature is needed through referral to another source or whether the client will go on alone, hopefully having learned how to deal with crises more effectively.

This theoretical approach can be used with families, groups, and communities as well as with individuals. A family, group, or community can be stunned and thrown out of equilibrium by a critical event, but soon, almost visibly, it begins to pull itself together to start functioning again. The worker who intervenes at this point can count on more openness to change than when an established balance is functioning. A part of dealing with crisis is determining when more extended service is necessary, after the current imbalance has been resolved.

Ann Carlson, medical social worker at Saint Christopher's Hospital, was vacationing in southern Arizona where she shared a cabin with Mrs. Aronson, an older woman just returned from a birding expedition in Costa Rica. Mrs. Aronson was awaiting her husband, who was bringing their camper down from Pennsylvania, and they were going to spend the winter in the Southwest.

The night before he was due to arrive, Mrs. Aronson received a call from the police in a small northern Arizona town—the trailer had been demolished in an accident and Mr. Aronson was in intensive care in the small hospital there. Mrs. Aronson "went to pieces" and naturally turned to her roommate, who naturally fell into her role as a crisis worker.

First, Ann called the hospital directly and talked with the Emergency Room physician. Mr. Aronson was stable, had a broken leg and a punctured lung—they would like Mrs. Aronson there as soon as possible. The town, halfway between Tucson and Albuquerque, had no plane connection. As they considered possibilities with the ranch managers, Ann, who had been planning to drive north the following day, offered to drop Mrs. Aronson at the town, which was only 70 miles off the interstate she had planned to take. It was only a seven-hour drive from the ranch—they could pack and leave immediately, notifying the hospital they were coming.

In the car, Mrs. Aronson subsided into a tense silence with her eyes closed, but she kept clenching and unclenching her hands, and so Ann knew she was not sleeping.

"How about a cup of coffee?" she suggested—the rancher had packed a lunch. "I take mine straight."

Mrs. Aronson busied herself with the thermos.

"So does Fred—I had to get used to that. Daddy always took cream and sugar."

Daddy was her first husband. This was a second marriage to an old neighbor whose wife, too, had died. He had only one son, Danny, who lived in New York and never came home, and a married daughter who refused to come to the wedding—she felt that Mrs. Aronson was marrying her father for his money.

Her two daughters thought she was foolish marrying an old man whom she would just have to take care of—he had bypass surgery several years ago—but she was lonely and the children were busy with their own lives. They would all blame her, and she wondered if this was her fault. They had sold their houses and bought a town house and a camper so they could travel slowly—the children thought they were too old to travel like this. "Will they help now?" Ann asked when Mrs. Aronson finally lapsed into silence. It seemed time to move from expression of feelings to the present reality.

Mrs. Aronson considered this and decided to call Danny first. He had not come to the wedding two years before, but had called to wish them well and sent a check to buy something they really wanted. He could tell his sister and then Mrs. Aronson would call her younger daughter—everything would depend on how Fred was.

Throughout the night hours they talked. When Mrs. Aronson's anxiety became great, they stopped at a filling station to call the hospital and learned that her husband was resting quietly. Ann said they could go directly to the hospital, and she would see Mrs. Aronson settled before she left. They talked about what needed to be done—talk with the doctors, find a place to stay, and call the insurance company about the camper.

While this was not a structured professional relationship, Ann consciously utilized her professional knowledge and skill in dealing with crises. She took action giving direct reality help and support, encouraged expression of feeling about the immediate event and related events, and then as Mrs. Aronson was able to mobilize her own ability and energy to think rationally and plan, helped her to think of steps to be taken—to use her own coping ability.

Behavior Modification.   Behavior modification developed from psychological theory that grew out of the early work on conditioning. Based on learning theory, it has formed the basis for widely used approaches to work with individuals, groups, and communities, and it has generated a controversy in which workers have become polarized for or against behavior modification, without evaluating objectively the potentials and utility of this approach. It is damned as being mechanistic, manipulative, unethical, and applicable only in controlled situations not suited to a free society.

Actually, the basic theory has been known and used by workers ever since someone tumbled onto the fact that the carrot can be effective in getting desired behavior from the donkey. People expect that their behavior will lead to meaningful, satisfactory outcomes, and when the behavior does so, expected and desired reward reinforces the particular way of behaving. It is possible to condition people to give up or to retain and develop certain behaviors through use of reward and punishment without placing the burden of responsibility for change on the client. At present, workers are attempting to understand and develop specific ways of utilizing this basic principle to change behavior that is destructive and to reinforce that which is constructive (see Figure 8.3).

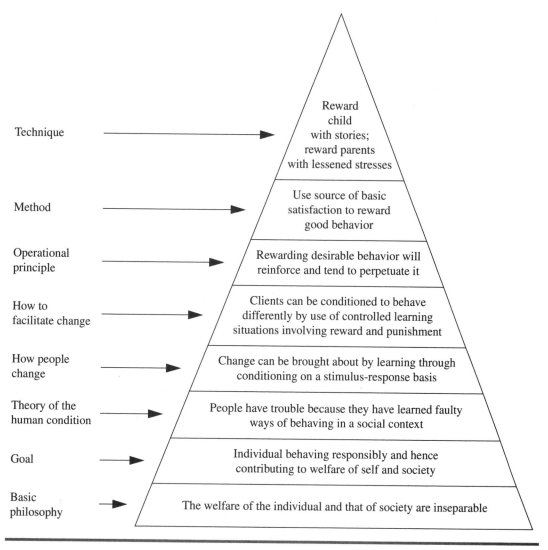

Technique	Reward child with stories; reward parents with lessened stresses
Method	Use source of basic satisfaction to reward good behavior
Operational principle	Rewarding desirable behavior will reinforce and tend to perpetuate it
How to facilitate change	Clients can be conditioned to behave differently by use of controlled learning situations involving reward and punishment
How people change	Change can be brought about by learning through conditioning on a stimulus-response basis
Theory of the human condition	People have trouble because they have learned faulty ways of behaving in a social context
Goal	Individual behaving responsibly and hence contributing to welfare of self and society
Basic philosophy	The welfare of the individual and that of society are inseparable

FIGURE 8.3   Evolution of a technique based on learning theory.

That this way of working can lend itself to manipulative and mechanistic uses is obvious. However, we deceive ourselves if we do not realize that the worker-client situation is one in which considerable power rests with the worker, regardless of the theory of change favored. With the development of new biological, psychological, physical, and social tools for bringing about change, the importance of the personal philosophical base on which the worker operates has become apparent. Depending on how it is used, behavior modification can be a growth experience for individual clients, or it can be destructive, even when the desired behavioral changes take place.

Modern workers who opt to use behavior modification techniques are operating directly with the individuals concerned while also attempting to teach other persons significant in the client's life experience, such as parents and teachers, to utilize this knowledge. It is a method that can be incorporated effectively into a generalist's pattern of working as one approach, because it uses some of the same basic principles used in the generalist approach. For example:

- The techniques used must be suited to the particular client; rewards and punishments are different for different people, as is the behavior that needs modification.
- The orientation is toward solving a problem—the way of behaving that is contrary to the good of both the individual and the society.
- The worker's role is an active one—to interpret, to reward, and to punish.
- The relationship between worker and client is based on acceptance of the client's worth and expectation of the client's capacity for change.
- Effective work involves the worker's insight into the client's past and future, in order to anticipate probable behavioral changes.
- Environmental changes must be made to effect permanent behavioral changes.

Much of the controversy over behavior modification centers on extending its use to control and bring about change in the larger society to the detriment of individual freedom and integrity. Life itself is the great "operant conditioner," and when we change and control social situations we obviously change people also.

Ken and Arlys came to the Family Center for counseling—they were worried about their marriage. Both worked outside the home, although Arlys, who was pregnant with their second child, planned to resign when the baby was born. Both were anxious to have this child. Kenny was in day care. They had just bought their first home.

The problem was that they seemed to be fighting all the time and Kenny was increasingly difficult to manage. Bedtime was particularly difficult—they had always kept Kenny up with them, and now he refused to settle down and then had trouble waking in the morning. It often ended with their disagreeing what to do about it; Kenny would get spanked and go to bed crying, while they argued. Ken and Arlys were strongly motivated to have a good family life but were caught in a situation where she was often fatigued with her work and her advancing pregnancy, and he was anxious about undertaking the additional responsibilities. After they and the worker together decided they were dealing with too much pressure, the worker suggested that they select one item on which they wanted to work. Both immediately said "Bedtime!"

The worker suggested that they use behavior modification as a method of helping Kenny learn to go to bed peacefully. He enjoyed being read to, and so this was selected as the reward. The parents agreed to stand together on this, and it was decided that they would take Kenny to the library to select a book and read to him for half an hour each night after he was in bed. They agreed on a regular hour and decided to take turns with his bath and getting him into his pajamas. They decided to try this for two weeks and then report back. The worker cautioned them that even though they explained that Kenny was going to start kindergarten and needed his sleep, he would be bewildered by the change and probably attempt to manipulate them into returning to the old ways where he stayed up until they went to bed.

The first week was a battle, and the worker talked with both parents by phone, urging them to come in and raise any questions, but they were committed to this—and fought it out on drinks of water, extending the reading time, and dawdling in the bath. By the second week, they were beginning to see results and reported that the best thing was the time they had alone together at the end of the day. This lessening of tension opened the way for discussion of the other pressure points in the marriage.

This is an example of an instance in which all participants in the dispute were altering their behavior and being rewarded for it—Kenny by learning to go to bed at a regular time with minimum protest and being rewarded directly by being read to; Ken and Arlys by learning firmness and a new method of dealing with an old, old problem in child rearing and being rewarded by peaceful evenings and less stress.

Marketing Theory.   Of increasing concern in modern society are pockets of social breakdown where people are not being reached by existing services; where the services are inadequate or not readily available; where individuals are either unaware of their existence or not motivated to use them. Problems may be such things as poverty, unemployment or underemployment, family breakdown, substance abuse, violence, inadequate housing, child abuse or neglect, school truancy, or the like. Whatever the problems, they are of serious import not only for the people themselves but also for the society as a whole.

Workers attempting to deal with such situations not only need knowledge of the problems themselves, but also must be equipped with special skills in reaching out; it is here that concepts of marketing theory can be useful. A program must be developed and then sold to potential users (see Figure 8.4).

Initially, there must be an assessment of needs that will answer the questions: (1) Who are and where are these people? and (2) What do they need? A part of this assessment should be through contact with the people themselves, and a part through organized social

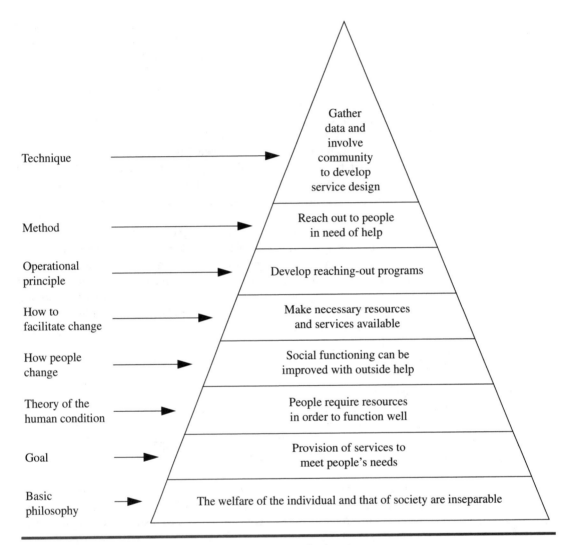

FIGURE 8.4   Evolution of a technique based on marketing theory.

systems concerned with meeting the needs of people and/or that maintain records of social problems, including organizations such as schools, health departments, social agencies, police departments, and civic authorities.

Out of this assessment should come a service design that will take into consideration (1) the kind of services needed, (2) the methods to be used in providing them, and (3) the resources needed to put the design into operation, such as people with requisite training, money, physical equipment, and so forth.

Once the design is created and accepted, there needs to be developed a system of distribution of the services that will make them available to potential users. Distribution will involve such things as accessibility of facilities, geographical location, hours, and manner of access.

Once these steps have been taken, a plan of communication must be created so that people can know of the existence of such services, learn how to gain access to them, and become motivated to make use of them. It is particularly important that the potential users be involved here—as indeed it is every step of the way—as well as workers who have knowledge of the culture of the neighborhood and of any special circumstances that might make people hesitant to use such help.

Finally, consideration needs to be given to the cost of such services to the users—such things as recognizing and accepting the need for help and the risk that it may involve, or the fact that it may violate the individual, personal, or cultural values system, or just the cost in terms of physical factors such as time and organization. For example, cost might involve an abused wife who decides at long last to take the children and make use of a safe house; an alcoholic who acknowledges the addiction and seeks help with it; a family with an uncontrollable adolescent who fear to face what is involved; a blue-collar worker who believes that a man supports his family and solves his own problems but who is faced with loss of a well-paying job. It is important to remember that change is difficult and often painful; change can be hard to accept even when it promises a reward in the long run.

Family problems are often initially evidenced in those most vulnerable members—children. The guidance counselor at Elmwood Elementary school, Raphael Lopez, became concerned about the number of children from the Greenwood neighborhood who had not had their shots, were often in the nurse's office, and about whom the teachers reported inattentiveness, tardiness and absences, and inability to do their work.

When he discussed this with the newly elected council member for the district, Marge Young, she echoed his concern and secured funds to finance a study of Greenwood and its needs. This revealed an isolated neighborhood of families with children and working parents who owned their own modest homes. Employment was largely at the box factory and the railroad yards, with many of the mothers working in food service. Salaries were not high. There was tension over negotiation of a contact with the factory and renewed threats of another strike. The assessment of needs was based on data from members of the community, employers, and social and civic organizations.

Greenwood was a neighborhood geographically isolated by a highway and the railroad tracks. The families were second generation, blue collar, and white; the grandparents had settled the area around the railroad where they worked. There was only one church and no hospital or social agencies, although the downtown Family Service agency had once established a satellite office there, which had been closed because it was not used. Few families were on welfare or even used food stamps—the cultural values stressed self-reliance and keeping problems within the family. The assessment also revealed that while these families possessed many strengths, there were also serious problems that were being reflected in the children. Services designed for them would be the most readily acceptable and would afford an entry to the family problems. Initially, the service design considered a plan for daycare at the church and an afterschool program for older children, but the facilities were hardly adequate.

Then Mrs. Young attended a conference on family centers and presented the steering committee that had been formed to consider plans with an alternative. An old mansion in Greenwood had been given to the state a number of years previously as a home for children, but when orphanages went out of style, it was used for state offices. Because it was too isolated from the central office to make this desirable, the proposal was adopted to create a family center here beginning with a daycare center and gradually bringing in other services as needed, such as a satellite of the Health Department for shots, nutrition classes, homemaking, and counseling as needed. The building was centrally located and accessible to the neighborhood.

A social worker experienced in developing family programs was hired to be the director, with a board consisting of representatives from the community, the major industries and the unions, the schools, the social agencies from the larger community, and the city. Interest in the project was high, as the old mansion was a part of Greenwood. There was good attendance at the open houses and registration for the daycare center. As other services were introduced when need and demand became evident, funding was based on both public and private money, fees based on ability to pay, and support by foundations and service clubs in the total community to cover maintenance and changes in the building and for special programs.

Such change as this represented does not occur overnight, and there are many incidental problems that need to be worked out. Greenwood was fortunate in possessing an available building in fairly good condition that was an accepted part of the community, and the people were ready to accept help with the problem as they saw it. The basis of its success was sound planning and involvement of the total community.

Eclectic workers will make use of these and many other approaches in working with their many-dimensioned clients. The only limitation on workers comes from the amount of knowledge they can master and the amount of skill they can acquire. Some workers may opt to become specialists developing more extensive knowledge and skill in a particular area of thinking and/or work.

Specialist or Generalist?

The role of the specialist is essential in light of the number and complexity of human problems, the proliferation of knowledge about them, and the increasingly diverse fields of practice in the human services, each of which has its own particular body of knowledge and skills.

Not only are we greatly in need of specific services, we also need the kind of meticulous research, testing, and development of new knowledge that specialization makes possible.

The specialist is only effective, however, when the specialization derives from a body of general knowledge about people and the human condition, upon which is superimposed what is known about a particular situation. Practice is always specific, and yet to be done well, it must rest on the basic body of knowledge and skill. This is particularly obvious with the current emphasis on holism in all human service practice—an awareness of the need to look at the total picture to understand and deal effectively with a part of it. Specialization and holism have resulted in increased emphasis on intra- and interdisciplinary teams, and on the use of consultation and referral in order to provide a total service package that better meets the need of the client.

Consultation

Consultation is a process wherein specialized knowledge and skill are made available to those who need it. Usually time-limited, (1) it can involve only communication between the worker and the specialist, with responsibility to carry out recommendations resting with the former; (2) it can involve consultation from the specialist directly to the client; or (3) it can involve the withdrawal of the consulting worker completely when specialized service only is needed.

There are three steps in this process of consultation:

1. Determination that specialized knowledge and/or services are needed on the basis of assessment and problem definition.
2. Selection among available resources. Specialists are, by their very nature, often in limited supply. Technological advances, such as the storing of information on computers, sophisticated communication devices, and extensive modern transportation facilities, have extended the reach of specialists and increased available resources. Workers operating in isolated areas can make good use of this kind of hardware and software.
3. Enabling the client to make use of the specialist's services. Use of specialists is extensive and varied. Their services may range all the way from work with a group of administrators to improve office management, to direct diagnosis and treatment for an individual with a health problem, to developing and implementing a plan for a community to better deal with increasing juvenile delinquency. The worker involved in securing the consultation may act as a channel through which the specialized knowledge and skill are made available to the client, or he or she may refer the client directly to the specialist for a consultation.

Referral

Referral is the process that helps a client move on to use another resource for service. Just as an individual worker cannot be all things to all people, so there is no one social institution that will serve all the needs of a complex individual in a complex society. One of the major problems is that although people may feel strongly that help is needed to effect change, they do not know where or how to get it. If they find themselves at the wrong place, due to the essential specialization of programs and services and the multifaceted aspect of need, people seeking help might find it necessary to go elsewhere, sometimes two or three times. Regardless of whether the need for help is occasioned by a breakdown in some life area, by efforts to enlist support for an idea, or for any other reason, the applicant usually has an emotional investment in it. Therefore, being referred often carries with it elements of rejection, anger, hope, and expectation. The feeling of rejection arises when clients are unable to get the help needed and wanted from the original worker, and must make themselves known and understood elsewhere. An additional step is involved when the impetus for the referral arises from the worker rather than from the client. The worker may not only have to convince the client that further help is needed and available, but also to encourage and support the client in developing the motivation to seek and use referrals.

Referrals can fail not only because of workers' lack of sensitivity to needs and capacities of clients, but also because workers are not sufficiently knowledgeable about the resources available. These may include various specialists, formal institutions, organizations, and programs, and individuals or groups with varying knowledge and skills. Having located an appropriate resource, workers must decide how best to enable the client to use the service successfully. To make this decision workers need to ask the following questions:

1. How much can the clients do for themselves? Whenever possible, it is desirable to let people make their own arrangements—a process that contributes to independence and self-determination. People exist on a continuum, however: At one end are people who can manage even complicated systems alone; at the other end are those who require maximum help. Often, in a crisis when people are upset and off balance, they are less able to do things alone. On the basis of a differential assessment, workers will determine how much and what kind of enabling help is needed. Because our systems have become so very complex, because there is a lag between our technology and the ability of many people to use that technology, workers must often act as brokers, as go-betweens for clients who require help in locating and reaching the services they need.

2. What are the tasks and roles of the referring worker in regard to both the client and the agency or individual to whom the client is being referred? How best can the way be paved for the initial contact, and what information needs to be shared? Clients should always know if information is shared, and workers must keep in mind that legal permission must be secured before certain specialized material can be given out.

Workers need to find a nice balance between encouraging a client to use another source of help and promising too much from that source. The service should be interpreted in such a way that the client does not see it as a total and easy solution but as a resource to be used in working toward the solution. Clients are best served by knowing the reality of the situation, but this does not mean that workers cannot serve as advocates for clients who, for a variety of reasons, do not get the service for which a given program is designed.

In making a referral, workers may choose among several options. The worker can:

1. Select several possible sources of help, explain each, and help the client evaluate and choose among them. This is often done with older people selecting a nursing home, with older foster children who have a choice of foster parents, or with patients who have a choice of treatments for a physical condition.
2. Merely give directions to the client to go down the hall, across the city, or to a neighboring community to see a particular person or service. Physicians frequently do this with patients in need of further evaluation or care; all workers do this with intact clients who can manage for themselves.
3. Give (or enable to be given through volunteers or aides) specific and concrete help on a graduated scale from a preliminary telephone call or letter or even a visit, to provision of transportation, to accompaniment on the initial visit and subsequent visits as necessary.
4. Provide opportunity, as needed, throughout the entire process of referral for the client to express feelings of fear, anxiety, anger, and frustration. If necessary, workers may teach clients how to talk with the person or system to which they are being referred, how to ask questions designed to elicit the information they want and need, and what to do with this information when they get it. Actual role rehearsal may be very useful.
5. Decide what the role of the referring worker should be after the referral has been made. This may be the end of the worker's responsibility, it may mean an ongoing collaborative contact, or it may mean merely a follow-up to see that the referral has been effective.

Making Referrals

What resources are available? How much can clients do for themselves? What are the role and task of the worker in making a referral and of the client in using it?

For the Raphaels, a good resource existed and the worker's activity was clearly defined and structured. The Raphaels were quite capable of using the referral successfully once they were able to accept the necessity for it.

In a play situation, Mary Raphael looked like almost any other 6-year-old—a little more active perhaps and less able to concentrate on what she was doing. It was only in the classroom that her hyperactivity and almost nonexistent attention span became apparent. At the end of the first semester, her concerned teacher asked that she be evaluated by the school psychologist. Dr. Bernard administered individual tests. They indicated the extent of Mary's inability to function and pointed to the possibility of brain damage. He asked Mr. and Mrs. Raphael to come in to discuss the findings and his recommendations that Mary be further studied at the children's clinic and that she be placed, meanwhile, in a special education class at school.

The report of these findings came as a shock to the parents. Mary's behavior had gone unnoticed in a family of three children. She was "just a little more difficult than the others," and when her mother had mentioned to her doctor that she was harder to manage, the physician assured her that, with firmness on her part, Mary "would grow out of it." Mr. and Mrs. Raphael were overwhelmed by their own feelings and had difficulty comprehending what the psychologist was saying. Dr. Bernard told them about the classroom experience, his own observations, and the test findings. He encouraged them to talk about their feelings of disbelief, anger, fear, and pain, and he answered their questions directly and honestly. He emphasized that Mary could be helped with the right program, but that the usual school routine demanded more than she was capable of—and this failure was having a destructive effect on her. He then suggested that they observe Mary at home for a week with the test results in mind, that they visit the classroom and talk with the teacher, and that they then come back and talk with him again. He encouraged them to call him during this time with any questions and to think over and talk with each other about what they saw and learned. He strongly recommended, as a first step, a thorough study of Mary by specialists in the area of child development.

In assessing the Raphaels' capacity to make use of a referral at this point, Dr. Bernard considered the impact of his findings, which verified their greatest, almost unconscious fears, and the necessity of dealing with those findings. They possessed strength both individually and as a couple and were perfectly capable of carrying through on the tasks that the referral would involve—making and keeping appointments, participating in history taking and planning, and following through on recommendations. The immediate task of mourning for themselves and for the child and of adjusting to the initial shock was one that Dr. Bernard hoped to help the Raphaels begin to deal with during this interim. The children's clinic was the only resource available in the community, but it was a well-functioning institution with competent staff. As a worker Dr. Bernard had to enable them to use this or a comparable resource to help both themselves and Mary. Once this was achieved, he, as school psychologist, would continue to work with the teachers toward carrying out the clinic's recommendations. Dr. Bernard's main tasks at this point were to give the Raphaels an opportunity to ventilate their feelings, to give them support in accepting the need for and working toward the next step, and to provide specific and concrete information about how to go about taking that step.

Before the end of the week, the parents called to say that they were ready to proceed with the study at the clinic. They asked that the transfer to a special education class be held up pending the results of the study. This request was not unreasonable or uncommon; perhaps it was indicative of their continuing reluctance to accept the reality of the current test findings and their hope that further study would negate them. They took the name of the intake worker at the clinic and asked Dr. Bernard to send a copy of the test results to him before their appointment.

In contrast to this formal referral procedure, the second example involves bringing in another person in an informal way. In this instance the original worker delegated responsibility for the actual process to another. Several resources were available for the client to choose among.

Mr. Crocker, age 87, lived in a decrepit old trailer at an intersection of the new interstate highway. As the road building progressed, he was isolated between various lanes of highway. In addition, he had a history of heart disease and attendant swelling of his legs and feet that made it difficult for him to get around. He did not eat properly, and the doctor, whom he would visit only occasionally, was concerned about malnutrition. Mr. Crocker was reluctant to leave his home because he had a goat and two cats that would be unwelcome elsewhere.

The old-age-assistance (OAA) worker had been concerned about his living alone and from time to time had raised the question of possible nursing home care, but Mr. Crocker would not even consider it. When it became essential that he find another place to live, there were only limited alternatives. He had no relatives or close friends, and his social life centered on the small grocery in the neighborhood where he shopped. This, too, was being displaced by the interstate. He could: (1) find a place in which he could continue to live alone, in either public or private housing; (2) live with another family; or (3) live in a nursing facility where he could have care suited to his individual needs and still have considerable freedom.

Mr. Crocker had no means of transportation, and the worker was anxious that he personally survey what was available and be able to choose between alternatives, however limited. He was an independent, rather irritable old man, accustomed to living alone and to his own lifestyle, and any change would be difficult. The worker, therefore, prevailed on him to accept the services of a young man who, as a part of his class work, was serving as a neighborhood aide. After considerable discussion of the laziness, long hair, drugs, and general uselessness of the young, Mr. Crocker reluctantly agreed to use him as a driver.

The OAA worker first met with the student, Fred Carpenter, explaining the needs and the limitations on income and providing him with lists of approved nursing homes, public housing facilities, and suggested areas in which to search for private ones. The three of them then met and Mr. Crocker added his suggestions to the list. They talked about his pets and the problem they would pose, but as he naturally wanted to keep them, both Fred and the worker promised to make every effort to make this possible.

Although Mr. Crocker was irascible, frequently snarled at his young companion when tired or discouraged, and continually made disparaging remarks about people and the world in general, which Fred found difficult to take, they seemed to get along fairly well. When the student became too discouraged, he would come in and talk with the worker, thus ventilating his own feelings. They searched for three weeks and finally settled on a boarding situation with an old couple who lived on the edge of town in a ramshackle home, had a little land, and were anxious to supplement their own income. They did not mind the pets, and Mr. Crocker could either eat alone in his room or with them. He could bring his own few pieces of furniture.

While this was not the solution that seemed most desirable to the worker, who recognized that another move would probably have to come in the near future, it represented what Mr. Crocker was able and willing to do at this point. His newly acquired knowledge of available facilities could help to make the next move easier. He was perfectly capable of making his own decisions and had made good use of the help of the neighborhood aide. The OAA worker's ongoing responsibility would be to keep in touch with him in the new living situation and try to help make it work so long as it met his needs. In this referral, the worker's task was selecting a resource, providing ongoing supervision and support, and participating in planning and carrying out the plan.

The final example illustrates a situation in which the resources are quite limited, the client is so damaged by his life experience that he has great difficulty in using even what is available, and the worker must play an active role in helping the client both with manipulating the environment and also by using a strong supportive relationship. Some of the most difficult of all referrals are those faced by social workers and employment counselors in placing clients with limited capacity in jobs. Finding work in a complicated, competitive society when unemployment is high, particularly among unskilled workers and minority group members, can be extremely difficult. Persistence and optimism are potent factors in determining success. The competent counselor anticipates these problems and copes with them insofar as possible by (1) prior spadework with prospective employers so that they have common agreement of what the job both provides for the employee and requires of him, (2) not making blanket referrals with the resulting high chances of failure, (3) knowing the client well enough to match him or her to the job, and (4) providing the support necessary to maintain the essential, reality-based optimism that is so crucial in motivation.

Tony Morales was laid off when the packing plant for which he worked was automated. At 55, he was married, the father of four, and had held his job for ten years, longer than any of his previous ones. Although the work was steady and paid enough to support the family, he disliked it intensely but had been afraid to quit. He was one of the many who lead lives of quiet desperation and over the years had acquired the habit of drinking before work and at lunch to mask his unhappiness. During the long months of idleness while the family lived on unemployment insurance and afterward when his wife took a job and they applied for public assistance to supplement her low wages, he felt even less adequate and started drinking more heavily. At first he had made the rounds of the employment agencies and been sent out on jobs, but he experienced failure after failure, either not being hired or getting only short-term work.

Al Roberts, the family assistance worker, set two related goals—to try to help Mr. Morales deal with his own feelings of inadequacy and worthlessness and to help him find employment. He felt that time was of the essence because his client was rapidly developing attitudes and a way of life characterized by apathy and indifference. He worked with the counselor at the state employment service in assessing both the availability of jobs in the area and the basic capacities of Mr. Morales. Based on the findings of these two undertakings, they utilized a federally funded program to retrain him for work in maintaining and servicing laundromat machines. As he possessed good manual skill, he was capable of doing this work and obtaining satisfaction from it.

This process required of Mr. Morales the motivation and capacity to use referrals to the training program and the employment agency as well as to prospective employers, no easy task for a badly demoralized man. A strong, reality-based relationship with his worker was of vital importance in developing and maintaining this ability, and success was a fragile thing, for at best he was a highly vulnerable employee in a shaky labor market.

Summary

Because of the complex nature of people and their societies, human service workers need to be able to use a wide repertoire of methods to work effectively. On a broad generalist base of knowledge and skill drawn from many different theoretical approaches and organized into a consistent whole, workers may opt to become specialists on the basis of field of practice or method concentration. Out of such specialization comes the need for collaboration and referral to various programs and specialists.

SUGGESTED ASSIGNMENTS

1. Assign students to select a technique used in working with people (see Chapter 9) and trace it back through the steps designated in Figure 8.1 in order to understand its theoretical base and why we use it. Compare and discuss these papers in class.

2. Assign a brief and specific case situation in which help is needed and have students develop a plan for providing this, selecting the approach and the techniques to be used.

3. Assign students to assess the same situation in terms of the kinds of consultation and/or referral needed and also the worker's responsibility when these are not available.

4. Assign class role plays of the referral process, stressing the importance of different techniques in different situations.

REFERENCES AND RELATED READINGS

Aquilera, D., (1998). *Crisis intervention: Theory and methodology* (8th ed.). St. Louis, MO: D. V. Mosby.

Epstein, L. (1992). *Helping people: The task centered approach* (3rd ed.). New York: Mc-Graw Hill.

Ivey, A., Pedersen, P., & Ivey, M. (2000). *Intentional group counseling: A microskills approach.* Belmont, CA: Wadsworth.

Meyer, C., & Mattairi, M. (1995). *Foundations of social work practice.* Silver Spring, MD: NASW Press.

Netting, E., Kellner, P. M., & McMurtry, S. L. (Eds.). (1997). *Social work: Macro practice* (2nd ed.). Reading, MA: Addison-Wesley.

Turner, F. (1996). *Social work treatment: Interlocking theoretical approaches* (4th ed.). New York: Free Press.

Lewis, J., Lewis, M., Packard, T., & Souflee, F. (2000). *Management of human service programs* (3rd ed.). Belmont, CA: Wadsworth.

Wills, C. C., & Federico, R. (1998). *Social work day to day: The experience of generalist social work* (3rd ed.). Reading, MA: Addison-Wesley.

9

Utilizing Skills and Techniques

> *How are six major skills—differential diagnosis, timing, partialization, focus, establishing partnership, and creating structure—used in developing plans for service delivery?*
>
> *What are techniques, and what is their place in the delivery of human services?*
>
> *What are the basic factors that need to be considered in the creation, selection, and use of techniques in working with people?*

Those who would climb a mountain would do well to sit down first with binoculars and survey the terrain to select the best path for reaching their desired goal. They can then pick up ropes, crampons, and ice axes, and start out with direction and purpose. Workers who have mastered a valid theory have a pair of strong binoculars. They have the knowledge necessary to consider alternatives and exercise options both in direction and in methods of procedure, and they can visualize a goal and probable outcome.

Human service workers who possess a solid base of theory concerning personality, social interaction, and modes of intervention, and who have set an attainable goal, must then consider what particular path they will follow and what tools they will need. Their selection and use of tools will be determined by theoretical base, personal style, the needs of the client, and what is available. Valid tools and techniques evolve by an orderly procedure from an equally valid theoretical base. Practice models and techniques grow out of social and personality theories—theories of the human condition that value the person as an individual and in social relationships. It is essential to remember that workers utilize themselves in their work. They must consider their weaknesses as well as their capacities and strengths in selecting methods, techniques, and procedures. Because each individual is different, all workers must develop their own styles and their own ways of handling the tools of the trade. This is the element of artistry that is a vital part of such work.

Complete objectivity is unattainable, just as complete negation of personality is undesirable. Only robots or machines are exact duplicates of each other and operate exactly alike. While it is necessary in using certain procedures, particularly certain types of testing and therapy, to minimize as much as possible the factor of the worker's personality, it is always present. One must be oneself, and by knowing and accepting oneself, one can then consciously utilize one's own capacities in working with other people. Maturity, gender, wit, physical condition, warmth, freedom of expression, intelligence, and many other characteristics underpin the individual style of a worker.

Just as our mountain climbers, knowing themselves to be weak in rappel, would probably select a terrain that would require as little use of it as possible, so workers, knowing their own capacities, would consider alternative ways of providing necessary help to clients if they have problems with specific techniques.

Thus basic theory and style combine to form a foundation for the helping process, from which specific techniques of implementation have been and are being developed. No list, however, can be complete because all workers also develop their own methods. We must remember, too, that there is a difference between a frank and honest assessment of one's strengths and weaknesses—and perhaps even a verbal acknowledgment of this to the client—and a burdening of the client with the worker's own concerns and problems. Again, this is one of those fine lines that workers must tread. How much can they share of their own concerns and still keep the major focus where it belongs—with clients and their problems? There has been a trend in recent years toward more freedom and flexibility in this area, but we can err in that direction also. Like all other judgments that workers must make, this will depend on the individual situation and the needs of the client.

Skills

A technique is no better than the skill with which it is used. The effectiveness of all techniques depends on the worker's mastery and use of these basic skills: (1) differential diagnosis, (2) timing, (3) partialization, (4) focus, (5) establishing partnership, and (6) creating structure.

Differential Diagnosis

Differential diagnosis is that capacity of workers to understand the uniqueness of client and situation and to adapt their techniques to this uniqueness. To make a valid and realistic adaptation, workers must be aware of the specifics of personality and situation involved, and the diagnosis must be objective. Compassion or anger over pain, social injustice, or circumstance, judgmental attitudes or intolerance of behavior, or feeling for the client must not blind workers to the hard reality of the client's self and situation.

Overidentification with clients because of the worker's personal hang-ups is detrimental to objective vision and clear thinking. This is an area in which good supervision and/or consultation are invaluable, as workers often have blind spots about their own personal needs and problems that can cause an inability to be objective about clients' similar problems.

This is particularly important in working with people from varying cultural backgrounds whose ways of thinking, feeling, and behaving may be quite different from the worker's own. A middle-aged foster mother who has raised children of her own might find it quite difficult to accept help from a young, unmarried caseworker, unless she and the worker have very carefully defined the roles of each and recognized the areas in which each has expertise.

Differential diagnosis also, and perhaps most important, should involve an assessment of the client's level of functioning. A recent study of printed forms given to clients in a public welfare program revealed that they were largely designed to be understood by people with a college education and would be meaningless, without careful interpretation, to people lacking such formal learning. A person's level of functioning may be lowered under stress, in cases of illness, and in unfamiliar settings where unusual demands are made on him or her, and workers must be cognizant of these situations. Efforts will be unsuccessful unless they are geared to the capacities of the individual client.

Timing

Timing can refer to two different aspects of workers' tasks. The first is the personal tempo by which workers live and operate and the effect that it has on their capacity to relate to people who have different patterns. Do they move too rapidly or too slowly for the people with whom they are working? The client's inability to keep pace with the worker can result in a complete breakdown of the work in which both are involved. We can observe this both with individuals and with groups, and workers who are unaware of this difference of life tempo risk losing their clients.

An obvious example is the speed with which people learn. Workers who do not gear their teaching, their explanations, and their interpretations to this factor risk the loss of a client's understanding and involvement. This is particularly true with people in highly specialized occupations such as medicine, who not only have a vocabulary of their own, but are also often under pressure to work rapidly. Equally, clients who can move at a pace faster than the worker's may be lost to boredom.

A second aspect of timing refers to what Shakespeare called that "tide in the affairs of men" that must be utilized at the strategic point if the momentum is not to be lost. Again the selection of this crucial point in time is a matter of judgment that the worker must make on the basis of both generalized knowledge of people and specific knowledge of the particular situation. A good example of this is the timing of advice, which should be given only in response to a verbal or nonverbal cue that the client is receptive. The man whose anger at authority makes it impossible for him to hold a job will probably not be able to even hear advice from the worker until he has dealt with his protecting anger and underlying fear that the problem does lie, in part, with him.

Partialization

Partialization is necessary because problems rarely occur singly or with only one dimension. They are often of such magnitude that they seem unmanageable. Their number, diversity, and complexity may be overwhelming and may leave the client temporarily unable to act. The client literally does not know where to begin. The worker's responsibility is to assess the totality, help break it down into manageable units, and help the client think about and decide where to begin. So common and obvious is this situation among some groups that a term has been coined, "the multiproblem family" or "the dysfunctional family," to designate the poor health, malnutrition, mental retardation, marital difficulties, school dropouts, delinquent behavior, personal disorganization, and violence that characterize them.

Partialization involves the setting of priorities—the determination of what needs to be done first. A single problem may act as a keystone, and when this is dealt with the others tend to fall into place. Unemployment or underemployment often is that keystone. Better work, more money, better family relationships, better nutrition, and better health may follow in that order. It is essential, therefore, to identify the problem that is the keystone.

Focus

Focus refers to the worker's skills in concentrating both worker's and client's efforts on the significant aspect of the situation that requires work and in retaining that focus until some conclusion has been reached. It involves thoroughness of consideration and may be applied to understanding one aspect of the problem under study or one alternative for solution. This can be illustrated by looking at the worker's task in dealing with almost any committee that has been formed to study a highly charged social issue about which its members feel strongly, such as a committee of students, faculty, and parents created to consider the problem of fighting in the parking lot after school. One of the major tasks of the worker is to keep the discussion focused on the problem rather than getting sidetracked on the feelings and side issues raised. Individuals under stress or unaccustomed to thinking in a disciplined fashion often find it difficult to keep focus on the major concern.

Establishing Partnership

Partnership refers to an association between worker and client in which each understands the role and tasks of the other, and in which both form a coherent whole that has purpose and direction. It is based on understanding and acceptance of the differences in these roles and tasks. It is a relationship of complementarity rather than similarity.

The helping services are founded on the belief that, both ethically and pragmatically, people must be involved in solving their own problems and that effective and lasting change comes from within. Clients must help themselves as much as they are able and make all decisions of which they are capable. The only justification for the worker's existence is an ability to supply what the client lacks. The worker must know how the client's concerns can be effectively addressed and must be able to help the client use this knowledge. Without this ability, it is a case of the blind leading the blind—a pooling of ignorance.

Although the worker must make the judgment about the type of partnership needed, how it will be developed and used, and where it will go, this can only be done effectively with the maximum participation of the client. One example of this is the partnership that must develop between the worker who is teaching behavior modification techniques to the parents of a lively 5-year-old who has learned that he can effectively upset them by demanding drinks of water and three bedtime stories every night. In this partnership, the roles of teacher and learner, of enabler and doer, of supporter and dependent are clear.

Creating Structure

Structure refers to the setting and boundaries that are most conducive to the work that needs to be done. Again, the worker is primarily responsible for defining these, but the client should share in the decisions. Structure involves such things as physical setting; the necessary "hardware" so significant in this technological society; where, how often, under what circumstances, and for how long worker and client should meet; delineation of rules (spoken and unspoken) that govern this undertaking; the systems that need to be involved—all the basic parameters that must be established and the basic logistics that must be settled. A major part of structure—and probably the most important—is the orderly process of problem solving that the worker utilizes.

It cannot be too strongly emphasized that structure must be flexible because we are working with people and their societies and they are dynamic and constantly in the process of change. Even the most flexible structure, however, must have a firm foundation.

Techniques

The basic skills considered above are implemented through use of various techniques or methods or procedures. We will examine some of the major techniques here.

Small Talk

Frequently, at the beginning of a contact—interview, discussion, conference, or meeting—inconsequential conversation that has no part in the real business of the relationship will be used as an ice breaker or to put client and worker at ease. In a committee meeting, group, or class, this could take the form of introductions, a cup of coffee, a speaker's introductory joke, and so forth. Small talk has a utilitarian purpose because it offers clues and affords opportunity for the preliminary judgments that are made by all participants about the nature of the persons involved. It can, however, create more anxiety than it allays, particularly if carried on too long, or if used to evade the real purpose. It is a part of the worker's task to assess the utility of this form of communication, use it as needed, and get down to the work at hand at the propitious time. In a crisis situation when feelings run high or immediate action is essential, use of small talk is usually contraindicated. If used, it should be with sensitivity to the situation and the pressure of anxiety, fear, or anger under which the client is laboring. The immediacy of the crisis will have some bearing, as will the client's familiarity with the worker.

How the client defines the worker's role must also be considered. A uniformed police officer appearing at the door usually creates enough anxiety to make immediate identification and explanation of the purpose of the visit desirable. However, small talk and social amenities are frequently initiated by the client's need for such communication. When the worker is making a home visit, most clients find it more comfortable to break the ice with inconsequential talk, and in ongoing contacts this can become an almost ritualistic part of interviews that the worker deals with and then puts aside for the real purpose of the relationship.

The purpose and nature of the relationship itself will determine the extent to which social amenities are a part of the worker's role; the worker should always be aware of how they are being used and what they mean. (In alerting a new worker to the problem inherent in socialization, a rural county welfare department director told the following story: A worker visited an elderly man who lived in an isolated area. As it was lunch time, the man urged the worker to share a sandwich and coffee, which she did. On her return to the office, she found an imperative memo to see the director immediately. He had received a call from the old client berating him for sending workers "to eat him out of house and home.")

In socialization, as in all things, a happy medium, knowledge ably arrived at, is the desired goal. Certainly, from our greater freedom in use of self comes the ability to engage in a greater amount of socialization within helping relationships. But when we do this we must be prepared to understand all the possible implications and deal with the results.

Ventilation

The term ventilation covers a variety of techniques. It involves bringing to the surface, giving expression to, and opening for consideration those feelings and attitudes that need to be broached. It generally refers to feelings that are profound enough to affect the functioning of the people involved and prevent rational consideration of the problem at hand.

Feelings cannot be ignored; they must be dealt with. Positive emotions are accepted and dealt with fairly easily, but negative ones may present more difficulty, particularly in a culture where extreme emotional expressions such as anger and hate are frowned on. Only when workers are able to create a relationship in which it is safe to express any feeling, regardless of its intensity or nature, will they be able to help clients to deal with reality.

Human service workers often find themselves wishing that they could suspend their own and their client's emotions while they utilize their rational capacities to deal with the problems of living. Emotions seem to obscure the real issues and impede solutions. Actually, the feelings themselves often constitute the basic problems that must be dealt with. Mrs. Allen is a case in point.

A neighboring university was considering Dr. Allen, a brilliant mathematician and department chairman, for an administrative position. When the team assessing his suitability visited the Allen home, they found considerable tension between the couple and an uncertainty in Mrs. Allen about her hostess role that raised concern about her ability to fulfill the social obligations of the new job. Because of his eminent suitability of the position, they arranged for an old professor and close friend of Dr. Allen's to raise this question with him. As a result, the couple went for help to a family counselor who, after interviewing them together, talked with Mrs. Allen alone. Here her initial anger was quickly dropped, and she talked at length about feeling inadequate to handle the demands that her husband's increasing importance made on her. After securing her bachelor's degree she had worked for many years as a secretary to put her husband through his graduate work. Her identification was with the "girls" in the secretarial department rather than with the professionals with whom she now socialized. Behind these feelings lay her child-hood in an ambitious middle-class family in which the parents were never totally satisfied with the achievements of their children, leaving her with a feeling of basic inadequacy and inability to be comfortable with other people, whom she felt were always critical of her.

In this instance, ventilation of these feelings was far from sufficient; it was only the first step, for reversing a lifetime pattern is not done overnight. But it was an essential step in helping Mrs. Allen accept and start learning to deal with her problem.

Mr. Ziegler, on the other hand, had to deal with a transitory emotion that, once expressed, left him free to proceed with the practical details of straightening out his tangled financial situation. He was obviously laboring under great feeling when he came into the credit counselor's office, and it required only the seemingly casual comment, "You really are shook up today," to release an explosion of anger toward the loan company and the small print, not understood, in the time-payment contract that had been his Waterloo.

It is not difficult to get people to express feeling; the problem lies in knowing how much feeling to encourage and how to deal with what is expressed. The worker must be aware of the fact that mere expression of feeling, continued for too long, tends to feed on itself and assume unreasonable proportions. To leave the client wallowing in anger, self-pity, remembered pain, and fear is to do a disservice. In a sense, expressing feeling is clearing out the underbrush that prevents forward movement; the worker must be prepared to help the client move into the here-and-now situation, deal with the problems that occasion or are occasioned by these feelings, and concentrate energies on working toward change.

Human service workers are still predominantly white, middle-class people who frequently enjoy a fairly high degree of affluence, social prestige, and security. And—in the better paid and more powerful positions—they are usually men. We need to recognize and, if necessary, deal with the anger this may cause in clients and in other workers who lack these rewards. These feelings can be exacerbated when insensitive or inadequate workers disregard the reality of what it means to be poor, a member of a minority, jobless, handicapped or old, or a woman subjected to sex discrimination. Workers recognizing and undertaking to deal with these angers and depressions must know and face honestly their own feelings before they attempt to cope with those of others.

Support

Support is another term that encompasses many different techniques. In general, it means to encourage, to uphold, to sustain. Workers must first know what they are supporting—an internal strength, a way of reacting, a decision, a way of behaving, a relationship. Once they have decided this, they must select a technique that will meet the need and express it in a way the client can understand and use. Techniques can range all the way from listening to the client talk, to sharing responsibility, to action. Most of what workers do should be supportive; even confrontation and questioning are done with acceptance and concern for the client's need. In giving support, workers must not make the client's success or failure in the area of being supported a matter of the worker's "personal" feeling. If a worker does so, clients will have difficulty in sharing and dealing with the failures that are an inevitable part of life because they will feel that they have failed the worker.

> The scene was a Gestalt therapy session, and the young man in the "hot seat" had just finished describing a dream. The other members had attacked his explanation of its meaning vigorously and had related this to what they saw as the destructive, unpleasant aspects of his behavior in the group. When he sat, crushed and weeping, they crowded around him, placing their hands upon him, raising him up, and physically supporting him with their bodies.

> Mary Williams, 16 and long the scapegoat for her family's problems, was supported by the worker in a family counseling session when he turned to her and asked rather pointedly, "What do you think is the problem in your family?" Here the worker was supporting the girl's right to evaluate and contribute to the discussion and to see things from her own perspective.

A social worker, a teacher, an employer, or a doctor, faced with the necessity of helping a client, a student, an employee, or a patient accept and deal with some failure, will often consciously preface statements about inadequacy by pinpointing and giving credit for some success. Thus the obstetrician who must take issue with his pregnant patient about her weight gain will first indicate the successful results of other tests. Sustained by this success and support, the patient is better able to accept and work upon the failure.

To be useful, a helping relationship must be supportive, but the element being supported must be realistic. Support on a false basis is more destructive than no support at all, and support alone is not enough. "She always found something good to say," said the mother of a large family with many, many problems, in trying to describe what her worker did that was helpful to her; she finished wistfully, "and sometimes she had to look pretty hard because things aren't very good around here."

A helping relationship by its very nature is supportive through the fact that workers are concerned people in and of themselves.

> Ms. Millis, retired after an active and satisfying career, underwent annual examinations because of previous surgery for cancer. Each time she went to get the results of these tests, she called the agency to ask for a worker to accompany her. She wanted an objective person who could support her in her fear and with whose own

emotional reaction she would not have to deal if the results indicated a return of the disease.

Reassurance

Although it can be considered a way of being supportive, reassurance is important in its own context. It involves assuring clients that the situations with which they are struggling have an attainable solution. Reassurance is a valid tool in that there is no life situation to which some adaptation cannot be made, even though the fact itself—for example, terminal illness or the destruction of a family home by urban renewal—cannot be changed. It is important that the worker reassure (1) realistically, not using superficial overall comforting that ignores reality; (2) at the proper time, giving the client a chance to adequately express concern and grief; and (3) knowingly, with awareness that both general and specific adaptations are possible in all situations. Wisely used, reassurance can be comforting and enabling. Poorly used, it can create even greater anxiety, as the client will feel that the worker does not fully understand the seriousness of the problem.

Reassurance can also be used with respect to the client's capacities, feelings, and achievements. Clients are often reluctant to express negative feelings, particularly in a situation in which the worker has considerable power to give or withhold the help that is needed. Yet the feelings exist and influence the client's ability to use the service. We see patients who meekly agree with doctors although they question the treatment recommended, students who continue with teachers although they feel they are not getting adequate instruction, and poor people who do not raise questions or express negative feelings because they are in terror of losing the basic essentials of life. It is the worker's responsibility to reassure clients that they may air their questions and concerns without fear. We can only reassure in this fashion when the relationship is basically honest.

Clients often need reassurance of the significance of their own achievements and their own capabilities to deal with the problems they face. This form of reassurance in particular must be based on a realistic assessment of clients' capabilities. It is no help to clients to set them up for a failure. Often the factor that enables them to use what they have is the faith of a significant other person or people, such as a teacher or a peer group, in their capacity to change and grow. This faith reassures and supports clients in their efforts to do so.

Johnny Webster brought the employment application from the supermarket to his worker and pointed out the question, "Have you ever been arrested?" Two years earlier he had been picked up with several other 16-year-olds at a pot party and—fortunately—had drawn a suspended sentence. Now he was trying to find a job. "I'll never get one. If I answer 'yes' they won't hire me; if I answer 'no' and I'm found out, then I'm ruined in this community."

The worker reassured him that while this would probably make it more difficult in some instances, it certainly was not the insurmountable obstacle that he pictured. "It's a reality we have to deal with so let's talk about ways in which we can handle it."

Advocacy and Social Action

Human service workers have a long history of advocating for civil rights, better housing and health care, and educational opportunities for oppressed people—women, people of color, gays and lesbians. Social workers are mandated by their Code of Ethics to advocate for all clients to have access to resources, services, and opportunities and for changes in policy and legislation to promote social justice (National Association of Social Workers, 1999). When we talk about advocacy we mean representing, championing, or otherwise defending the rights of others. Social action, which includes techniques such as demonstrations or boycotts, may be used along with advocacy efforts but is typically more confrontational (Kirst-Ashman & Hull, 2000).

The process of advocacy involves working with and/or on behalf of clients (1) to obtain services or resources for clients that would not otherwise be provided; (2) to modify extant policies, procedures, or practices that adversely affect clients; or (3) to promote new legislation or policies that will result in the provision of needed resources or services. Workers advocate for individuals and families, called case advocacy, and for groups of people who have similar problems, called cause advocacy. The focus of both case and cause advocacy can be individuals, agencies, public officials, courts, legislation, and divisions of government (Hepworth, Rooney, & Larsen, 2001).

Workers need to take several factors into account before initiating advocacy efforts. They need to consider whether advocacy is the best way to bring about change or whether another method is going to be more effective (also see Chapter 11). When workers are employed by an agency or other institution, they must clarify the organization's level of commitment to the proposed advocacy efforts. Workers also must make sure that their clients agree with the workers' advocating their causes. Clients have the right to decide whether to advocate and how far these efforts should go. Their decisions may strongly depend upon the workers' giving them an honest assessment of both the risks and benefits. Advocacy can result in great changes, and those involved will experience varying degrees of tension and stress (also see the following sections on confrontation and conflict). Workers also cannot assume that advocacy efforts will always bring about the degree or type of change that is needed or wanted. Clarity is needed about what an acceptable amount of change will be, at what point the advocacy efforts will stop, and who will decide these matters. Clients must seriously consider the pros and cons, risks and benefits of advocacy to ensure their interests and needs are best met.

There are many ways to advocate—what technique to use depends upon who or what is the focus of change, what method clients are comfortable with, the skills and abilities of the advocate, and the nature of the problem. Advocacy tactics are: conferring with other agencies, appeals to review boards, initiating legal action, forming interagency committees, providing expert testimony, gathering information through studies and surveys, educating relevant segments of the community, contacting public officials and legislators, forming agency coalitions, organizing client groups, developing petitions, and making persistent demands to officials through continual letters and telephone calls (Hepworth et al., 2001; Kirst-Ashman & Hull, 2000). The worker can use tactics ranging from established procedures for appeal (e.g., review boards) to those that can border on harassment (e.g., making persistent demands through continual phone calls and letters). Prior to engaging in advocacy, workers must address the concerns and questions discussed above.

Perhaps the most recent advocacy tactics available to workers are available on the Internet. Electronic advocacy techniques include using web pages to post information about social injustices, provide "links" to targets of change (e.g., governmental agencies), and accept online donations. Email is also used by advocates as a way to send messages, often in large numbers, to individuals and organizations that are the focus of their efforts to create change. Listservs, chat rooms, and bulletin boards can also be used to share information and discuss strategies.

Dianne is a social worker in a hospital and is told by a patient recovering from a stroke that the managed care company has denied payment for a specialized type of physical therapy that has helped improve her balance. The patient wants the worker to help her get authorization for payment. Dianne discusses advocacy as a way to try to get this done and lets the patient know the possible risk, triggering a review process that might result in even fewer sessions being covered, as well as the possible benefit, getting the managed care company to pay for all the physical therapy sessions. After some thought, the patient decides to have Dianne advocate on her behalf and provides all the important information—the letter of denial, benefits covered under the managed care plan, and the protocol for appealing denial of coverage.

Armed with the facts, Dianne calls the managed care case manager and makes the argument that any type of physical therapy is covered under the company's benefits so the company is obligated to pay for all the sessions. The case manager then agrees to authorize payment for only ten of the fifteen sessions. Continuing to advocate with the patient's consent, Dianne sends a letter to the case manager documenting why the additional sessions should be covered. She includes a letter from the referring physician clearly stating the rationale for the number of treatments, physical therapy notes showing the patient's progress, and a research article from a prestigious medical journal clearly showing that a minimum of fifteen sessions were needed for this type of physical therapy to be effective in restoring balance. Upon receiving a letter from the case manager denying payment for five sessions, Dianne continued to follow the company's protocol for appeal. The next point of contact was the medical director of the managed care company. Dianne sent to the director the physician's letter, the physical therapy notes, the article from the medical journal, and the two letters of denial. Her efforts were rewarded when, after reviewing the information and having further discussions with Dianne and the rehab team, the medical director authorized approval for payment for all of the physical therapy sessions.

Karen was adopted at birth but always wondered who her biological parents were. This became even more important when Karen decided to have children of her own and wanted to know of any possible problems in her biological family's medical history. She became very involved with an organization that worked with adoptees to change laws and agency policies so they would have greater access to information about their biological families.

A worker at the agency created and maintained a website. Karen had a busy schedule but having the website available 24 hours a day enabled her to remain involved and informed. On the website, the agency posted legislative updates and provided links and email addresses to legislators and agency directors nationwide. Adoptees all over the nation were able to quickly, cost effectively, and in large numbers tell their elected officials how to vote on legislation that helped or hindered their cause. The website was also used to post information about how the elected officials had voted on the particular legislation. This created additional pressure on the elected officials to be responsive to the needs of these constituents.

Confrontation

Confrontation may be described as laying the cards on the table and looking at them as they are. It is not a hostile technique but a facing of reality. Workers can confront the client with the reality of the situation, with feelings and behavior patterns that are destructive, with one's responsibility for one's actions, successes, and failures. It is an essential technique because only as client and worker perceive and agree on the reality can they deal with it. Misuse of confrontation can be devastating, destroying all previous efforts. A worker must assess the amount and quality of confrontation the client is willing or able to use, and the worker must be able to give support if the reality is overwhelming. Workers must not use confrontation to express their own anger and frustration, although these are certainly a part of the reality with which both workers and clients must deal.

The current emphasis on "telling it like it is" makes confrontation the tool of today because it offers the opportunity to express all the pent-up angers and frustrations of the moment. But we are learning by sad experience that it is only a prelude. Unless workers are prepared to follow up with concrete plans for reshaping the reality that they have attacked, their efforts are often more destructive than constructive.

Sometimes confrontation can be used to create sufficient pressure and anxiety to produce motivation for change. This is evident on a large scale when individuals band together to face representatives of a corporation or institution with a situation that is untenable to them and that they wish to change. It is equally true on an individual basis.

Mr. and Mrs. Phillips were parents of one child, Andy, who was becoming a problem in the school and the community due to his acting-out, semidelinquent behavior. In their eyes he could do no wrong, and they told themselves and everyone else that this was normal growing-up behavior. When Andy, in a rage over his girlfriend's going to a teen dance with another boy, smashed the windows of the cars parked on her street and broke the picture window in her house, the juvenile court worker confronted him and his parents in no uncertain terms. Utilizing a series of events of increasingly grave nature, he pointed out their relation, direction, and probable consequences. Along with this confrontation, however, the worker recognized the parents' affection and concern for Andy and offered resources from which the three of them could obtain help.

To be an effective force in change, confrontation should be specific rather than general. People can understand and accept the need for change if it is related to a specific source of discomfort. Therefore, when committees and pressure groups attempt to effect change, an essential first step is to define and agree on the grievances for which they are seeking redress and the source from which this relief can come; they may then confront those involved with the need for change.

In certain kinds of therapy, particularly those in which the client's insight into his or her own feelings and behavior is the immediate goal, confrontation has a particular meaning. It refers to that part of the process in which the client relates incidents in the past and present behaviors and feelings that tend to follow stereotyped patterns. When the client is unable to perceive these patterns, the worker may confront the client with them in order to increase the client's awareness of this dysfunctional aspect of his or her way of living and help the client utilize this insight to modify feelings and behavior.

Conflict

Conflict is at once a technique and a whole series of techniques. Defined as disagreement, opposition, or collision, conflict itself is a valid, necessary, and inevitable part of life. Individuals need to know how to fight because when differences occur, feelings tend to run high. While the expression of the emotion is a part of the process, the actual business that results in resolving the disagreement depends on rational consideration. The worker must recognize the factor of emotion, allow for its expression, and use power, compromise, and agreement in the resolution.

"How do you fight?" the marriage counselor asks the couple in front of her, thereby facing them with the inevitability and normality of difference, disagreement, and conflict, and the necessity of understanding and utilizing the process involved. "You must learn how to fight in this arena," the public relations director tells the group interested in pushing changes in laws through the legislative body. "Everybody has a right to a different opinion," the teacher tells her third-grade class embroiled in an argument over where to go on the May outing, "but now we must reach an agreement as a group that we can all abide by."

It is interesting that in a country whose ideology is based on the right of people to differ and to resolve their differences by a democratic process, we have developed a strong pattern that says fighting is not acceptable, particularly in our personal lives, and that a bland surface serenity must be maintained regardless of what turmoil lies beneath. That we must fight to survive is axiomatic and that workers must know how to use the techniques involved, be able to teach them to their clients, and help them become free enough to use them is equally clear. Conflict is an indication of vitality, and its successful resolution, in spite of possible angers, hurt feelings, and grudges, strengthens any system.

 Mrs. Marryett had to be taught how to fight in her marriage. The submissive youngest child in a large family, the lowest one in the pecking order, she transferred her pattern of never complaining to her own home. However, resentment over her husband's high-handedness was there beneath the surface, and when their daughter evidenced trouble in school, the guidance counselor picked up this resentment in their discussions. It was only with considerable support and help from the counselor that she was able to face her husband in a joint conference with the statement that things were not really as perfect in their family as he insisted, and to go on to participate in pointing out the problems and deciding what to do about them.

The new expressway out of the city cut across a neighborhood of old, run-down homes in which families had lived for many years. The value of the homes was too little for the owners to buy elsewhere, and in their fear and ignorance they were a natural prey for unscrupulous real estate developers. The outcry of the residents and concerned citizens resulted in the formation of a housing authority, and Seth Cooper was hired to represent the homeowners. His first step was to bring them together to form an organization, define their objectives, and select a strategy. Together they possessed a strength that as individuals they did not have, and they were able to confront the city with reasonable demands that resulted in the provision of low-cost housing.

Manipulation

Because of its connotations of changing others "by unfair and insidious means to serve one's own purposes," manipulation is a loaded word. In reality, manipulation also means skillful management and as such is a technique that workers utilize constantly. The process itself is a legitimate one and only becomes questionable when it is used destructively. Because we use manipulation, we must face and assess it honestly. The teacher may manipulate a situation to give an insecure student a success upon which he can build; a worker may arrange a "chance" meeting between two amputees or two persons with the same illness. Thus, manipulating is acceptable when used as a tool to provide a constructive experience or to achieve a desirable goal. For example, we are manipulating when we select a particular setting for a conference. The evils of manipulation, as with so many other aspects of working with people, arise when we manipulate to achieve our personal ends or to push people around without regard for their need and right to participate.

Manipulation of the environment is an essential concomitant of working with people. As they increasingly recognize not only the significance of the environment but also the frequent impotence of the lone individual in coping with it, workers are taking greater responsibility in this area. However, in manipulating the environment, workers must always consider (1) the client's right and need to be involved in both deciding and doing, (2) the client's ability to participate, and (3) the distinction between those activities that are appropriate for the worker and those that are appropriate for the client. When the activity calls for special knowledge and skill that the client does not possess, such as reading a chart, making a diagnosis, or searching out laws, participation by the worker will be different. Thus the worker, as the advocate or representative of the client, works in the client's interest and, when possible, teaches the client to use these resources.

Phyllis, an articulate teenager, commented that there are times when everyone needed an adult to help deal with the system. Therefore, when she and several other young people were picked up in a local tavern because members of the group had falsified ID cards to prove age, they secured a worker, in this instance, a lawyer, who knew and understood the operation of the legal system, to help them work out their contretemps.

The Magays lived in a tenement whose plumbing facilities had long since ceased to work properly, and they had exhausted their own resources to deal with the landlord and the city inspector. The worker who became involved not only used his knowledge of how to deal with bureaucracies, but also, through the Magays, helped develop an organization of tenants who could bargain more effectively with the landlord and his representatives and could manipulate the system to their advantage.

It is particularly important to be able to recognize when destructive manipulation is being used and to know how to combat it. Frequently, in meetings, subgroups will subvert the democratic process in order to control the group.

The State International Women's Year Conference met for three days to elect delegates to the national meeting and take a stand on issues. A militant prolife group elected the total slate of delegates from its own members by stacking the conference on the final day. Because of a technicality that allowed all registrants to vote and made no requirement of participation in deciding issues, this group was able to elect a slate of delegates who were personally committed to working against the stand of the conference on every issue. This situation could have been controlled by foreseeing the possible results of the lack of proper registration procedures.

A large part of the activity of any human service worker is manipulation—skillful management—of resources and persons. This manipulation is most effectively done from positions of power and authority derived from knowledge, status, or strength. Because of the dangers of abuse implicit in this fact, it is imperative that the worker's values be soundly based on the integrity and rights of the individuals and of the society.

Universalization

Universalization is use of the commonality of human experience and the strengths of others to cope with situations similar to those which are troubling the specific client. It can be used (1) to soften the overwhelming impact of a situation with the realization that others have faced and dealt with similar problems, (2) to share and compare knowledge about ways of dealing with problems, and (3) to lend the strength of others to the individual with the problem. The worker who utilizes this technique must be sensitive to the particular situation and the needs of the particular client. Each of us not only is but feels unique, and overreliance on this technique may brand the worker as insensitive and lacking in understanding of the client's particular needs. Timing is of particular significance in use of universalization.

When young Alice Brown, on her first job as a statistician in a large insurance office, sought out her supervisor to say that she felt she could never learn to do the work, the supervisor sympathized with the feelings, helped mop the tears, encouraged her to pinpoint the specific incidents that had caused the feelings, and only then remarked comfortingly that most of the new employees felt that way at some time or other and that generally it was a passing thing.

A group of young mothers, meeting at the well-baby clinic to talk about their concerns and problems with their first children, found it particularly encouraging when the worker produced tables on behavior expected at certain ages, emphasizing the flexibility of these norms and the individual timetable of each child. As one mother said, "You knew what to expect and how other parents had dealt with these concerns, and you could answer your sister-in-law when she bragged about her baby having four teeth when yours at that age had none."

The support that can be secured from an individual or group with similar experiences derives in part from elements of universalization. This is most evident in groups whose membership is based on a common handicap, illness, or concern.

Edward Milton, a vigorous, active man of 57, underwent surgery during which a colostomy was performed. Adaptation to this was particularly difficult for him because of its impact on his self-image and because it demanded such radical changes in his whole style of life. His immediate reaction was severe depression. After helping him overcome his feeling that he "didn't want to run around with a bunch of cripples," the worker introduced him to the members of the Ostomy Club, who were well equipped to help him face and cope with the problems that his physical condition imposed.

Advice Giving and Counseling

Advice giving and counseling are two of the most frequently misused techniques of workers. Webster's dictionary, with unexpected humor, pinpoints the problem by saying that advice giving and counseling are based on "real, or pretended, knowledge or experience and wisdom." Actually, they are activities that are used much too freely, with very poor timing, and without valid assessment of the client's capacity to hear or use them, and they are often used to meet workers' own needs to be experts. Workers can become too personally involved in the success or failure of the advice given and frequently tend to base it on a value system that is personal and incongruent with the client's lifestyle.

Despite these problems, advice giving and counseling are valid techniques and, wisely used, can be effective. Workers must be sensitive to the clues clients give that indicate they are asking for, or need, advice and direct suggestion. To be most effective, these should be based on knowledge, objective analysis of the situation, and judgment of the client's capacity to accept counseling.

Using the authority of knowledge as a basis for these activities implies that workers who use them know more about how to deal with clients' concerns than clients know themselves. Advice giving and counseling should be based on objective and realistic evaluation of all the factors involved, including the actual wishes and desires of clients.

It was reported that a physician teaching a course on human sexuality was attacked for lecturing about homosexuality when he himself was not gay. He responded that he had never been pregnant either, but he could teach about pregnancy. It is true that experience may provide unique learning, but unless accompanied by other knowledge, it rarely affords the wide range of wisdom essential for the authority that is taken when a worker advises or counsels clients. Unfortunately, there is a trend toward thinking that experience per se provides all essential knowledge to deal with a particular situation. While its importance cannot be negated, experience does not represent the totality, and it may actually lead to a narrowing rather than a broadening of insight.

Workers frequently have the frustrating experience of proposing solutions and giving advice that the client either agrees with verbally and does not follow, or carries out in such a way that it fails and then says in essence, "See, I knew it wouldn't work." It is a moot question whether workers should give advice based on personal experience, labeling it as such. In general, it is probably not a good idea to say, as did one worker who had raised a family of children, "With my oldest son, I always set midnight as a curfew and insisted that he be in then." This lends a personal element to the situation that can lead to trouble. Certainly, workers use what they learn in their personal experiences, but when logical discussion of solutions is under way, it is better not to personalize the situation.

In the final analysis, the success or failure of the technique of advice giving depends on the client's capacity to use it and the worker's ability to make a valid assessment of this capacity. Clients are most frequently able to use advice and counseling successfully in these situations:

1. In crisis situations, when their own ability to deal with the problem is inadequate, and they are suffering anxiety, pain, fear, and other pressing emotions.
2. When they have a well-founded confidence in and respect for the giver of the advice, either as a person or as a representative of a particularly responsible group, such as social workers, ministers, doctors, lawyers, supervisors, and the like.
3. When their cultural conditioning or life situation is such that they tend to depend on others rather than on themselves for direction and solution.

4. When the advice is given in such a way that the client's integrity and right to be self-determining are respected, and it jibes with their needs and wants.

5. When circumstances are such that they have no alternative.

Advice is most helpful when it deals with means to achieve ends rather than with the ends themselves. Generations of social workers have recorded, with great self-satisfaction, "I advised Mrs. Brown to clean up the house" (this may be recorded fifty times in one file), instead of confining their advice to ways in which this could be achieved if, indeed, Mrs. Brown wanted to achieve it and if it was really necessary and desirable. As one client put it, "I don't need her to tell me what's wrong—I know things are wrong. What I want her to tell me is how to go about setting things right."

When Mr. and Mrs. Masterson had reached an impasse in their battle, even though they were determined to preserve their marriage, they turned to the worker asking for specific advice about what to do. At this point, he was able to suggest specific action—finding a different home for Mrs. Masterson's mother, budgeting, talking over and making joint decisions as to how to deal with the children.

Elizabeth Smelser asked for help from a telephone crisis service when she was depressed, drinking, and had taken several sleeping pills. The worker not only instructed her quite directly to waken her landlady, but also offered and arranged to get emergency care to her.

With her group of 9-year-old Camp Fire youth, Thelma Campbell used advice to point out that an overnight in the city park was not a good idea. She based her advice on the danger in this poorly patrolled section. She combined it with suggestions of alternative places they could consider. She also introduced a discussion of behavior appropriate on an overnight, rather than telling them directly what they should and should not do.

Activities and Programs

In trying to establish communication, create a working atmosphere, resolve problems, and create opportunities for developing the many different kinds of potential for growth inherent in individuals, workers may opt to use adjunctive activities and programs. These can be used to meet needs that are difficult to deal with through other media and extend the reach of the worker. They permit expression on a nonverbal level or in a game situation of feelings that are difficult to express and deal with directly.

The list of activities is limited only by the ingenuity and resourcefulness of the worker in adapting them to the needs of particular clients. Music, dancing, games, drama, handicraft, naturecraft—all provide additional resources. The worker who uses these techniques must develop knowledge and skill in selecting the medium best adapted to the needs of the situation. This requires knowledge not only of the client and the situation, but also of how well the medium selected meets the needs of the particular situation. When involved with therapeutic and growth-producing groups of all ages and conditions, workers tend to turn naturally to programming and activities that can serve many different purposes. To the greatest extent possible, the group should participate in selecting the activities. When well chosen and planned, activities tend to further the goals of the members and worker.

Brad Sills was a probation worker; he numbered among his boys a group of seven between the ages of 10 and 12 who could be defined more as neglected and pre-delinquent than delinquent in behavior. They tended to be underachievers and to lack confidence in themselves. Although they were loners, the group gave them protection and support among their peers. They chose to call themselves "Rejects" because of their common trouble in being part of any official group endeavor in the school. Reflecting the current trend, the boys chose hiking and camping as their main interest, and with Brad's help, they planned and carried out an eight-day backpack trip into a wilderness area. This common experience with its shared triumphs and demands welded the boys into a group that carried status, and it gave them an experience in following through on a project successfully and in the meaning of interdependent relationships. They began to see their group name as a badge of honor rather than descriptive of their failure.

With individuals as well as with groups, workers use such activities to good purpose. Play with children is a widely used and respected technique. Nonverbal adults can sometimes respond to overtures when there is a common activity through which they can express themselves. In a group-living situation such as a home or hospital, the withdrawn, nonverbal person who feels lost as an individual can often begin to relate to another person through the medium of activity.

Mr. Martinez, whose paralysis following a stroke made it necessary for him to live in a nursing home, was angry, depressed, and withdrawn from the overtures of his fellow patients. Mr. Felton, a volunteer with many years experience, made this isolated, lonely, bitter man a special focus of his efforts and, in time, by capitalizing on the latter's skill as a bridge player, was able to inveigle him into playing cards. At first he played solitaire; then he agreed to make it a doubles game with Mr. Felton, and from there they progressed to cribbage and eventually to a bridge foursome that involved other patients. In this instance, the activity provided the medium through which the client could begin relating to people again.

The new executive of the stenographic service, Jane Phillips, came into an office rife with dissatisfaction, suspicion, and alliances among small conflicting groups. A direct, comfortable person, she chose to start her first staff meeting with the seventy-odd employees with a game called "gossip," in which a chosen statement is whispered from one person to another with the final hearer repeating it aloud. The physical closeness, the informality, the laughter, and the discrepancies in the final product of this exchange paved the way for an open discussion of channels of communication, sources of dissatisfaction, and suggested changes.

Logical Discussion

Logical discussion is a technique that utilizes the ability to think and reason, to perceive and appraise reality factors, to see possible alternatives, and to anticipate and evaluate consequences. It is most effective when the feeling elements in the situation are under control and the cognitive strengths of the client and worker can be brought to bear on the concern at hand. However, logical discussion cannot be successful if the feeling aspects of the problem are ignored. Time and again planners face programs and solutions to problems that founder on the rock of feelings, and this is particularly true when plans are being made for other people without their participation. The competent worker—administrator, therapist, or aide—will allow for expression of feeling reactions along with logical discussion, but such expression should not become the major focus.

Mr. and Mrs. Braeburn opposed the necessity of placing his senile mother in a nursing home, but having weighed the effects of her presence on the family, they reluctantly concluded that it was essential. Discussion and realistic evaluation of both the situation and possible alternatives for solution were facilitated when opportunity was given first for recognition and ventilation of their feelings.

Andy Roberts ran a small machine shop with ten employees. It was an informal business with considerable intimacy and friendship among the workers. When young Paul Jones, the newest employee, was arrested for child abuse, feelings ran high among the men, but Andy, after talking with the probation worker, felt that nothing could be gained by firing Paul. Over lunch he sat down with the men and raised the question of keeping Paul on—some had threatened to quit if this were done. After considerable expression of strong feelings, they were able to discuss rationally the probable results of his being fired and to agree, at least grudgingly, to keep him.

Discussion techniques, when used with groups, are significantly related to the structure and function of the particular group in which they take place. They also are used with individuals.

Reward and Punishment

Reward and punishment, or positive and negative reinforcement, are techniques that workers have been theoretically reluctant to use: (1) because of questions about whether they are a valid part of the worker's responsibility; (2) because of the judgments involved; (3) because of a philosophical belief that they are a result of the event and need not be externally imposed; and (4) because they so often meet the emotional needs of workers that workers are afraid to use them. Actually, reward and punishment have been used extensively on a more or less intuitive basis. It is hoped that with the development of the theoretical knowledge underlying the use of behavior modification techniques, they may be employed more definitively with greater understanding of the causes of behavior and greater ability to anticipate and control the circumstances.

Behavior modification poses a specific model, and the worker who opts to use it needs specific learning, particularly regarding the behavior to be reinforced and the methods of reinforcement. However, as theoretical knowledge of behavior and causation grows, as diagnostic tools become more accurate, as methods of working are tested, and as the correlation of these methods with causation and change is established, we will be better able to develop classifications in which designated symbols point to specific methods of such treatment.

Thus the principles of reinforcement are being more widely used with greater understanding than in the past. As with all techniques, this awareness of what we are doing and why is imperative. Without it, we often succeed in reinforcing that which we would prefer to extinguish.

Linda, at 5, has a well-established pattern of screaming and throwing tantrums whenever she is denied anything she wants. Initially, when she used this behavior, her parents, delighted with their first girl after four boys, thought it was "cute," and gave in to it and unknowingly reinforced it to the extent that they now have a serious behavioral problem on their hands with a child who has learned to manipulate in a destructive manner.

Justin was an unhappy, withdrawn patient in the men's ward in the state hospital. When the behavior modification approach was adopted by the staff, efforts were directed to reinforce those scraps of behavior he exhibited that expressed his need and capacity for relationships with others. These were rewarded with tokens that, in turn, he could exchange for small items at the canteen, and in time he was able to use himself more effectively with others. Essential to these efforts was agreement as to the behavior to be reinforced, the method of reinforcement, and the presence of knowledgeable workers, ward aides, and others to judge and to act when this behavior was exhibited.

Role Rehearsal and Demonstration

In the complexity of modern life, individuals and institutions are called on to make many changes in the roles they fill. Often these are unfamiliar roles, the demands of which, as well as the anxiety occasioned by the change, may create difficulties. The worker, whose view should encompass the general aspect of the situation as well as the part the client plays, can enhance functioning by rehearsing role performance, either through discussion or through actual role play. The parents participating in an unfamiliar juvenile court hearing, the patient who cannot talk with the doctor, the group wanting to make a presentation to the city council, the committee testifying at the legislature or working out a labor conflict all can benefit by use of this technique. The worker may choose to demonstrate how these actions can be carried out without using actual role play. In this instance, clients learn through identification and by using the model the worker creates. This is a useful technique for lessening anxiety when approaching an unfamiliar or stressful situation, for opening new aspects of it for consideration, and for developing new insights into its meaning.

Living in an increasingly complicated society is particularly difficult for people of limited intelligence, and yet current studies in the care of the retarded indicate that in many instances the most successful and satisfying placements are within the community itself and not in an institution.

At the age of 18, Allen faced the problem of having to return to the community after ten years in a school for the mentally retarded. He was fortunate in that he was educable and his studies had been focused on practical living problems. The worker who was assigned to prepare him for discharge utilized extensive role rehearsal of buying, making change, using a telephone directory and a bus schedule, following simple instructions, and performing the many other tasks of daily living that are automatic for most people. As part of a group of five boys and girls, Allen went into the community, either alone or with the group, to try out his skills and then returned to discuss his experiences with the others.

Role rehearsal—by discussion, by actual setting up of role play situations, or by demonstration—can be used extensively when learning is required. By participating in the simulated situation, the client has the advantage of assuming and developing some of the feelings the actual event will call into play, which can then be identified and discussed. For the retarded, such as Allen, who often carry visible physical evidence of their retardation, the reaction of other people can be brought out in role play and dealt with there. Studies of Head Start children and their parents several years ago indicated that these families often have no awareness of how to use the facilities that are the joint property of all the members of society.

Conchita Valdez, the 5-year-old child of migrant workers, faced with her parents the additional disadvantage of seldom being long enough in any community to become familiar with it. During the six-week picking season, the Head Start worker who drove Conchita and the other migrant children to school took them on frequent field trips to see and use community facilities. In the classes, they learned to relate to each other and to work with people in a group, to use books and games, and to create for themselves. The worker also got to know the Valdez family well and, capitalizing on their desire for a good life for themselves and their children, helped them to develop the social skills that would enable them to deal more effectively with the larger society when moving frequently from place to place.

Simulated or actual experiences or demonstrations all have the advantage of not being heavily dependent on concepts or use of words to communicate ideas. People with little skill in using language can often benefit from this type of learning, whereas a more verbal approach would be meaningless. With a group of foster mothers whose common problem was children who tested their acceptance with severe misbehavior, the worker arranged demonstrations behind a two-way mirror. They observed childcare workers dealing with these behaviors in a small group, and then they discussed and role-played their own methods of handling similar situations.

Crisis

The creation of crisis can be used as a technique by knowledgeable workers to produce movement when a situation is stalemated. It can either be created by the intervention of the worker in the situation or be allowed to occur by the worker's refusal to rescue clients. Sometimes it is only when a crisis occurs that individuals, groups, and communities can face and comprehend the inevitable consequences of a situation or behavior, and only as they finally face these consequences can they move to make change. Sometimes workers must "be cruel in order to be kind."

There are ethical implications to the use of this technique that often run contrary to the inclination of human service workers to prevent suffering. Rescuing people and societies from the consequences of their own behavior prevents them from learning how to deal with similar situations in the future as well as inhibiting the development of motivation to prevent their occurrence. Use of this technique rests, as always, on respect for human dignity, knowledge of the circumstances, their meaning and their possible outcome, and skill in handling the requirements of such action. The "tough love" of alcoholism programs is a good example of allowing crisis to occur in order to facilitate change.

Mary was a housewife who had been a silent drinker for years. Her home and children were neglected, she was physically deteriorated, and her husband was desperately trying to keep working and to rescue her from her frequent disasters. She refused to accept help or enter an alcoholism program until her husband and children, with the strong support of a counselor, stopped pretending that her drinking was not serious and allowed her to be arrested, charged, and sentenced for drunken driving.

The hospital emergency room was understaffed and overworked. Repeated requests for additional funds from the county were always refused. Finally, in desperation, it was decided by administrators of the hospital to close the service temporarily. This created such a public outcry from people dependent on the facility for the care it provided in situations that were often life-and-death matters that the needed resources were provided.

Touch

Since the beginning of time, helping people have used touch spontaneously in some form to give comfort and support, to demonstrate acceptance, and to reassure the frightened. More recently, practice models have developed that emphasize hugging and use of the physical self more directly in working with people. Such contacts mean different things to different people and can be perceived and interpreted to have meanings that are not the intent of the worker. The worker should be especially aware of different ethnic interpretations of touch. If used to meet the need of the worker rather than that of the client, physical contact is definitely contraindicated. On the other hand, because of the deep, primitive needs within people that touching satisfies, it can be extremely useful. In light of recent developments in the area of sexual abuse, workers need to be cautious in using touch. Organizations should provide opportunities for discussion of the concerns involved and develop policies relating to its use.

Mrs. Foster, a middle-aged woman without family and apparently without friends, was facing the final weeks of a terminal illness alone. Concerned about her isolation, the nursing home assigned a volunteer to work with her. She was not a verbal person, not easy to talk with, but the volunteer struggled along. Noticing one day that Mrs. Foster was turning her head restlessly against the pillow in her chair and that her hair was matted and tangled, the volunteer offered to brush it out. "You might as well," the patient replied. When she finished, the volunteer commented that it would now be more comfortable. Mrs. Foster, obviously struggling with strong feeling and a lifetime of living within herself, said, "My mother used to do that for me." She began to cry and for the first time talked about herself while the volunteer stroked her forehead and then held her hand.

John was an angry, rebellious teenager forced to come in to see his probation worker, a motherly, middle-aged woman. As she walked with him from the waiting room to her office, she touched his shoulder, guiding him. "Get your f—hands off me, you old bag," he yelled.

Mechanical Devices

Use of mechanical devices, such as tape recorders, video cassette recorders, films, and two-way mirrors, extend the reach of the worker. Workers in training and families or groups that are working on interaction can view themselves in operation and become cognizant of patterns of functioning. Workers in children's programs can demonstrate to parents various ways of relating to children. In any of the teaching responsibilities inherent to working with people, mechanical devices open new ways of learning. For storage and retrieval of essential information, they are invaluable.

There are three principal factors that workers must keep in mind when preparing to use such mechanical techniques directly with people. First, mechanical devices should never be used without the client's knowledge and consent to record situations in which they participate. To do so is not only an invasion of privacy, but also self-defeating when clients learn of their unauthorized use. Second, it is almost axiomatic that discussion should accompany their use, during which the learners have opportunity to question, react to, and supplement the ideas presented. Otherwise, much of their potential is lost. Finally, the worker should master in advance the mechanical details of operating the equipment. The malevolence of inanimate objects is well known and is particularly evident when the operator is on display—leading a discussion, teaching, interviewing, and so forth. With mastering the operation of such devices, chances of mechanical failure are lessened, and this is one more instance where advance preparation pays dividends.

Summary

It would be possible to go on almost indefinitely listing and describing techniques for working with people. Each new practice theory brings with it its own techniques. As workers become more experienced and more sophisticated in use of themselves and outside resources, they experiment with and develop new individual techniques. Those listed here are basic. Beyond that, the sky is the limit, as long as the form and the use of techniques for working with people are measured against the values and knowledge on which the helping services rest. These techniques are a part of the essential artistry of working with people who, in the final analysis, are unique, and often require unique techniques.

SUGGESTED ASSIGNMENTS

1. Give students a brief case history of a multiproblem family from which to develop a working plan utilizing the basic skills of (1) differential diagnosis, (2) timing, (3) partialization, (4) focus, (5) establishing partnership, and (6) creating structure. This could be a major paper.

2. Assign students to select and research a technique about which they have some concern, in the use of which they are experienced, the validity or ethical base of which they question, or the use of which they do not understand. Have them present this technique in class, outlining meaning and raising questions for discussion.

3. To develop conscious use of self in working with people, assign students in pairs to role-play client and worker for the class using techniques of confrontation and reassurance in difficult situations such as removal of children from a home, denial of a client's request, expression of anger, and so forth.

4. Have students select a current controversial social issue (e.g., proposed legislation that would increase benefits to populations at risk) and design an electronic advocacy strategy to support their position. This assignment includes having students research relevant organizations that have a presence on the Internet and then present to the class about how these organizations use the Internet for electronic advocacy efforts.

REFERENCES AND RELATED READINGS

Cournayer, B. (1999). *The social work skills workbook.* Belmont, CA: Wadsworth.

Egan, G. (2001). *The skilled helper: A problem management and opportunity-development approach to helping* (7th ed.). Belmont, CA: Wadsworth.

Hepworth, D., Rooney, R., & Larsen, J. (2001). *Direct social work practice: Theory and skills* (6th ed.). Pacific Grove, CA: Brooks/Cole.

Kirst-Ashman, K., & Hull, G. (2000). *Macro skills workbook: A generalist approach.* Belmont, CA: Wadsworth.

National Association of Social Workers. (1999). *Code of ethics.* Available online: http://www.naswdc.org/.

Perlman, H. (1957). *Social work: A problem solving process.* Chicago: University of Chicago Press.

Shaefer, B., Horesji, G., & Horesji, G. (2002). *Techniques and guidelines for social work practice.* Boston: Allyn and Bacon.

(See also practice texts in readings for Chapters 7 and 10.)

SELECTED RELATED WEBSITES

Boston College Electronic Advocacy in Social Work
http://www.bc.edu/bc_org/avp/gssw

Mental Health Net
http://mentalhelp.net

Mind Body Medicine: Implications for Social Work
http://www.geocities.com/HotSprings/Chalet/5410/

The Social Work Cafe
http://www.geocities.com/Heartland/4862/swcafe.html

Social Work Web Ring
http://www.socialworksearch.com

Working with People in Groups

What characteristics are shared by all groups? What are group dynamics? What is the worker's role in the group?

What are the differences between natural and formed groups?

Why are teams increasingly important in work with people, and how are they used?

Modern human service workers use groups extensively in two distinct ways: (1) in direct work with clients and (2) in collaborative work with colleagues and institutional and community groups. The qualities of a group experience lend an extra dimension to practice.

During the course of a lifetime, people share many different group experiences, some constructive, some destructive, often without occasion for ever being concerned about what a group is or what actually happens within it. Although the experiences may be fulfilling, enabling, or frustrating, many of us never know—or care—how this comes about. If workers plan to use work with groups in a knowledgeable fashion, they need to know the dynamics involved.

People have a basic need for group experience. From our earliest beginnings we have banded together for help, survival, and security. In the past hundred years, we have begun to study groups to try to understand what they are and why they are useful to us in our development and functioning. At present, groups are used in all aspects of human service work, in all fields of practice.

Definition

A group can be defined as a system of relationships between and among people. As such, there is interaction; there are common goals, values, and norms; there is a social structure; and there is cohesion among members. As mutual aid systems, groups meet basic human needs for security, for meaningful relationships with others, and for opportunities for growth and development. They provide a useful mechanism for social control and for facilitation of personal and social change. Within the group the individuals find acceptance, support, expectation, and opportunity to share experiences and knowledge with others who may have similar experiences, to be confronted with differences in a safe setting, to evaluate themselves and their own ideas against those of others, and to move toward problem solving.

The person without group identification is often a troubled person, lacking security and the support of others who share similar ways of looking at and dealing with the demands of living. The need for group identification is not met by superficial congregations or, necessarily, by the number of groups to which people belong, but through meaningful group experience where there are significant relationships among the members. In no group does the unity and cohesion essential for groupness occur simultaneously with the bringing of several people together. In no group does an individual become a group member merely by being present.

Groups can be further defined as *natural* or *formed*. Natural groups are those that develop in an unplanned way in the so-called natural course of events. The family and the tribe are good examples of this. Workers come to these groups as outsiders. Formed groups are those that are consciously created in order to deal with specific circumstances that are of interest and/or concern to several or many people. Their number is almost endless and can include such things as social groups for purposes of square dancing or play reading; task groups such as committees, boards, teams, panels; development groups designed to enable members to grow; or therapeutic groups that deal with personal problems. To these groups, workers may or may not come as outsiders. Often they are the instrument of group formation.

Common Characteristics of All Groups

There are certain characteristics—the characteristics of any social system—inherent in groups regardless of size or method of formation:

- Groups have a common purpose that dictates size, structure, composition, goals, tasks and roles, process, and life span.
- Groups have to deal simultaneously with the tasks that grow out of keeping themselves going and those that lead to realization of their purpose.
- There is interaction among group members.
- Members have different positions and status within the group.
- Each member has an assigned role that is essential to maintaining the balance of the group; the group will exert force to restrain members within designated roles in order to protect that balance.
- Each group develops its own values and norms.
- Each group has both an inherent tendency to maintain the status quo and an inherent tendency to grow, develop, and change.

Natural Groups

The two natural groups human service workers use most frequently are the family and what sociologists call the reference groups. To these groups, workers come as outsiders.

The Family

The family is the primary group. It is unique, but it also exhibits the characteristics of all groups. However, one must be aware of its special elements.

Purpose.   The family is a social institution sanctioned by society and charged with responsibility for (1) nurturing the young, (2) meeting the basic survival and emotional needs of all its members, and (3) acting as the first level of socialization and social control. Regardless of the form the family takes, which may vary greatly in different cultures and with changing social conditions, these basic purposes seem to be universal.

Nature of Relationships.   The family provides a kind and degree of intimacy that is rarely present in other groups. The level of emotional involvement is high, and intensity of feelings tends to be great.

Duration.   In contrast to most groups, which are time-limited, the family evolves with the expectation that it will be a lifetime grouping. Even though the rate of family breakdown is higher than ever before, this expectation remains the norm and is often the reality.

Range of Differences in Members.   The family takes in people at all stages of development from infancy to old age. At present the trend seems to be for the generations not to live in the same household, but they are still encompassed in the family group.

Significance.   The family or family surrogate is probably the most significant group to which any individual belongs, and it has the greatest and most lasting influence on personality development. There are often two primary families, the one into which people are born or adopted, and the one they participate in forming when they reach maturity. The significant family may be limited to the nuclear family made up of parents and children, or it can encompass the extended family, which includes a wide range of other relatives.

Reference Groups

It is said sardonically that our families are wished on us, but we can choose our friends. This element of choice operates in our reference groups—those to which an individual belongs that have significance by virtue of the group members' common interests, values, behavior, attitudes, goals, and experiences. Reference groups may be selected because of their social value or prestige, but whatever the reason, they rank next to the family in importance for members. The growing child's peer group, for example, may constitute the initial exposure to attitudes and values that are at variance with those of the family. Such groups exert considerable influence on individuals, good or bad, and can be extremely useful in working with people.

Initially, human service workers tended to shy away from using these two primary groups. Problems in functioning were considered to be individual matters, and workers often removed individuals from the group in order to work with them. With developing knowledge of group dynamics, however, workers realized that returning a changed individual to an unchanged group usually meant that the individual reverted to the original behavior—the balance of the group depended on keeping that individual unchanged. When a family or reference group member is in trouble, it usually means that there are significant problems in the group itself, as in the street gangs that exert destructive pressures on members leading to drug abuse and violence. Workers have realized that relationships among group members can be a potent factor in working successfully with people.

Working with Natural Groups

Workers coming as outsiders into natural groups are faced with the tasks of making a place for themselves as a unique part of the group and assessing already established relationships between and among members—relationships that usually have a high degree of intimacy. They will need first to free themselves of expectations of normalcy based on their own personal experiences and then to develop ways of understanding and making use of the complex web that is the natural group. These tasks are complicated by the fact that such relationships are dynamic and seeing and evaluating is done in a moment of time; the relationships are intangible and expressed only through attitudes and behaviors; and changes in natural groups tend to come slowly and painfully.

As we have become increasingly aware of the complexity of our world, we have learned to make and use diagrams to picture intangible relationships in ways that are understandable. Sociometrics is the science that attempts to explicate such relationships and human service workers use sociometric charts and diagrams both in their own thinking and directly with clients. Such things as sociograms (which indicate what is occurring in communication or closeness at any moment in time), genograms (which chart the relationships existing in multigenerational levels of families), and family histories are useful tools in trying to make use of group relationships by attempting to make concrete what previously has been intangible (see Figure 10.1).

Equally important is flexibility on the part of workers to work with individuals separate from the group or with various combinations of individuals—as with parents alone, with parents and a child, with the total nuclear family, the total extended family, or the total peer or social group. This can only be done effectively if workers are cognizant of the significance of the singling out of a part of the group.

Formed Groups

Bringing individuals into a group is not always easy, particularly when the rationale and impetus for the group rest with the worker, or with the society through its social institutions, rather than with the potential group members. The first, and often the most difficult, task is to get people involved. It is important that these potential members be homogeneous to a degree—that they share a commonness of interest, problem, circumstance, and so forth that will serve as a potentially cohesive force in getting and holding them together. One of the strengths of the group, however, lies in the heterogeneous character of the individual members, each of whom brings different perspectives and different strengths to the common undertaking. The worker will need to strive consciously for a balance of these two characteristics among the prospective group members. It is this balance of heterogeneity and homogeneity that makes democracy so essential to maximum group functioning. Mem-

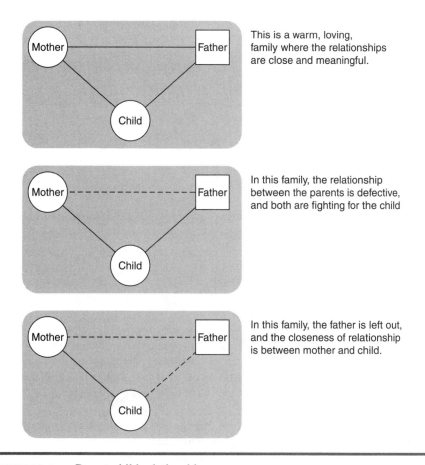

This is a warm, loving, family where the relationships are close and meaningful.

In this family, the relationship between the parents is defective, and both are fighting for the child

In this family, the father is left out, and the closeness of relationship is between mother and child.

FIGURE 10.1   Parent-child relationships.

bers must be able to use their differences to advantage and must be made to feel free, safe, and undefensive in order to do so. The climate of the group, which ensures this freedom for everyone, is a significant factor in attainment of maximum group functioning.

Group formation should be planned on the basis of established need and with input from potential users or consumers so that the service will be relevant to their concerns. This input can be either in the form of personal involvement of consumers in the initial stages of planning or in their helping with accumulation of data to determine need and interest. The success of the effort to get a group off the ground will depend, to a large degree, on how the worker deals with both this type of information and with the necessary logistics of time, place, transportation, and opening up of communication channels. Although people in general are much more knowledgeable than they used to be about group participation, it is often necessary to do a selling job. Use of media for communication, notices, letters, and invitations can be effective, particularly with motivated consumers, but for individuals who are not knowledgeable about group experience, there is no substitute for personal contact, which provides opportunity for a give-and-take discussion about the planned group and its relevance to the individual. Beginning commitment can develop here.

The first meeting is vital in determining whether and how the group will actually materialize. This is true of both voluntary groups, such as educational ones, and involuntary groups, such as a planned group of problem boys from a juvenile court. In the first meeting, individuals involved look at themselves and each other and at the worker in light of personal needs and expectations. The transactions that take place here will determine whether people return, whether they can begin to commit themselves, and whether they can risk themselves with each other and with the worker. The second meeting is equally crucial because the initial euphoria that accompanies a new experience is diminished, and members are faced with the vision of the work ahead and the realization that nothing comes quickly and easily.

Good planning is essential in successful group formation and the following guide attempts to stress the essentials.

Guide for the Formation of Groups

I. Preplanning

    A. This is the stage in which the individual or the "initiating set" of two or more people decides that there is a problem about which something needs to be done and that a group may be the way to do it. Need is established by brainstorming, a survey, and/or observation, all of which should include input from potential consumers. The basic questions to be decided here are:

        1. Is there a problem?

        2. Is the problem one that can best be dealt with by a group?

        3. What is the purpose of the group?

    B. The next step is to determine the kind of group, in terms of size and composition, that will best suit the purpose and need. Although fifteen is generally considered the maximum number that can be included and still have fairly intensive interaction, an educational group could be larger, and many groups will be smaller. Consideration should be given as to whether the group is to be voluntary or compulsory, and whether it will be a closed group or will be open to new members after the initial meetings.

    C. Preliminary decisions must be made as to structure. This again is related to need and purpose. A formal group might have prescribed roles (such as officers), a constitution, specific meeting dates and places, and a ritual that is mandatory. Certain needs and purposes would demand a less structured group that provides maximum freedom for members to interact spontaneously. At this point some thought should be given to the worker's position in the group structure—will the worker lead directly or be an enabler for the leader?

    D. The relationship of the group to the host or sponsoring institution (if applicable) must be determined. Such institutions constitute the group's immediate environment, may be the source of its funding, and may make provision for its staffing. Linkages with the sponsoring institution must be established and maintained. Frequently, they provide sanction for the group's existence and purpose.

E. The next step is the location and commitment of the necessary resources to establish and maintain the group. This includes provision for essential equipment as needed, space, special needs such as babysitting, special facilities such as audio-visual equipment, and so forth, and provisions for paying for these resources.

F. Potential members must be identified and contacted. This initial contact serves the dual ends of (1) interpreting the purpose of the group and its probable activity and membership and (2) informing potential members of the time and location of the first meeting and inviting attendance. As previously stressed, personal contact by the worker or co-worker is the best way in which to answer questions, develop interest, and secure beginning commitment. In cases where group members are children, it is usually important to talk also with parents or parent surrogates. Not all groups require this kind of reaching out in the initial stage. Letters, the telephone, public announcements such as posters, flyers, and radio and TV spots can be used. Again, the purpose and composition of the group are the deciding factors in selection of the techniques for reaching the potential members.

G. The initial session must be carefully planned. Almost inevitably, except in compulsory groups, not all potential members will become members. The rate of attrition will be lessened, however, if the worker plans this important first session with two things clearly in mind:

1. Why is this group being established? What is its purpose? Do special activities need to be designed to serve the members? What is the anticipated number of sessions? What are the goals of the group?

2. What is known about the prospective members? Special personal characteristics such as age, gender, and family composition are important. It is also important to know what it is that qualifies the prospective members for membership in this particular group and whether they have had prior group experiences, good or bad. Occupation and/or school attendance are significant and, depending on the kind of group and its purpose, the worker may need to know the nature of the individual's capacity for social functioning.

II. The first meeting. In some types of developmental groups, members are left very much on their own in the initial stages and evolve their own group. However, the worker should be clear as to how this first meeting should move and whether to be obviously active. It is helpful to visualize five steps in this process:

A. Arrival of members. This will involve direction to facilities such as meeting room, babysitting, and so on; introduction to the worker and/or others if desired; name tags if desired; refreshments if desired (maybe here or later).

B. First total group activity. What is it to be, how is it to be started, and how is participation to be encouraged?

C. Transition to working on major tasks. How will the group move from the initial introductory activity into the major work of the meeting? How will the purpose, roles, tasks, and goals within the group be defined and responsibilities designated? How will the contract with the worker be defined? How will conflicts be resolved and decisions be made?

D. Future plans. Will there be subsequent meetings? When, where, and how often? Will additional members be solicited? What resources are needed to facilitate the work of the group, and how are they to be secured?

E. Ending. How will the session end? At a predetermined time? If cleanup is required, who will do it? Is there homework to be assigned? Is the worker responsible for providing transportation for members?

III. Flexibility and readiness to change plans if necessary. Because groups are unique and dynamic entities, the best laid plans of the worker might not be appropriate to the situation. Therefore, the worker must be prepared to "read" the group and be adaptable enough to change if necessary.

The Worker and the Group

Workers who opt to use groups in human service will need not only to be aware of the process that takes place within them but also to determine where they will stand in relation to the group itself. The group is the agent of change, not the worker, and the worker must be at the same time a member of the group—a part of the system—and yet apart from it. There must be a verbal or nonverbal contract between the worker and the group members based on mutual trust; within that framework, both worker and members find their place. Contracts may need to be revised, these relationships may need to be reworked during the life of the group, but throughout this entire process, the basis of mutual trust must persist.

The roles of workers in groups are almost endless and infinitely varied according to the nature of the group itself. They can be included under four headings:

1. *Teacher.* The group worker as a teacher imparts knowledge and develops interest and learning skills.
2. *Therapist.* The purpose of the group worker as a therapist is to heal and cure and to use the group process to facilitate this.
3. *Enabler.* The group worker as an enabler makes it possible for the group to function, to make decisions, and to do the work for which it was designed.
4. *Role model.* The group worker as a role model demonstrates by personal and professional behavior the manner in which groups can be used.

In addition, the workers have to decide what position they will hold in relation to group leadership. They can be either the actual leaders or facilitators for the designated leader, who may or may not be elected by the group. In addition to the designated leader, natural leaders will doubtless emerge, and one of the worker's tasks may be to assure compatibility between the two.

Leadership is all-important in determining the kind of experience the members will have. Theorists in this area have divided group leadership into three categories: (1) democratic—where decisions are shared by the group; (2) autocratic—where all decisions are made for the group; and (3) laissez-faire—where there are no controls at all. The strongest group experience for members is that based on democratic leadership, but the manner and extent to which leadership can be shared must be related to the purpose of the group.

In meeting the demands of the various roles required of them in groups, workers will consciously behave in a variety of ways, using their knowledge and skill in understanding human behavior and group dynamics, as well as concrete know-how about the availability of resources and the ways in which to use them to meet group and individual needs. To be effective in performance of these roles, workers will need considerable self-awareness because they will be representing a set of values and norms and affecting the other group members by conscious and unconscious modes of behavior as well as by use of the authority they represent.

Nguyen Kwanh teaches socialization and work skills to a group of retarded adults in a sheltered workshop. These three men and two women are classified as trainable and have all been institutionalized for a period of years. Nguyen is a warm, accepting teacher, using demonstration and support on an individual basis. She limits, mediates, confronts, and guides. She uses the group strengths to support the efforts of individuals and is a part of the group, but with a very specialized position and status.

Robert O'Connor is a therapist working with a group of professed alcoholics in a community chemical dependency program. He is in a definite leadership role in which he confronts and interprets aggressively on a basis of acceptance and concern. The group assists him in these behaviors as well as in support of the individual members. In addition, Robert's role is an enabling one: He opens the way to the use of resources for necessary physical care and family and employment counseling.

Anna Napoli is a community organizer employed by a neighborhood association. As such, she forms committees and task groups to deal with community concerns. She acts as a planner, enabler, teacher, and adviser. Her leadership role is peripheral, as her purpose is to free and develop the groups and the community for self-leadership. She is the professional staff person who provides knowledge and skill that enable the committees to plan and to act.

In addition to the worker's role in the group, each individual member has a role to fill, and these roles must be complementary in order to achieve the desired wholeness that is the group's strength. One of the major internal organizational tasks of the group is to decide who does what, when, where, why, and how in relationship to all the other members of the group. Roles and the behavioral norms they carry are subject to negotiation both early in the life of the group and, when necessary, throughout its existence. This negotiation takes into consideration not only the personal qualities of the individuals that affect their relationship with the other individuals and with the group as a whole, but also each group member's specialized knowledge and skill. Roles can be considered as (1) structural—those mainly concerned with internal life of the group, such as chairperson, leader, secretary, or (2) task related—those arising out of personal characteristics of members, such as specialized knowledge, humor, and personal warmth, and affect the life of the group.

Conflict resolution and decision making are equally important to group life. The healthy group provides opportunity for the existence of differences, for open expression of ideas and discussion of issues, and for decision making based on the maximum participation possible in light of the purpose and structure of the group. One of the major tasks of the leader is to get closure—to move the group to a decision and to an action to implement that decision, whether it is when and where to go on a picnic, how to change community attitudes toward adolescent behavior, or what a family will do about its faulty communication patterns. Edgar Schein's six ways of reaching group decisions (to be discussed later in this chapter) constitute a reminder that the decision-making pattern of a group can be both constructive and destructive to realization of the group's fullest potential. Although the purpose and nature of the group will determine to a large degree how much authority the leader has and how it is used, it is evidenced in how group decisions are reached.

As a result of its internal organization and its external relationships, the group reaches a contract both among its members and with its environment. Usually this contract is unwritten, except in institutional organization plans, and often unspoken, but it represents an understood agreement among the members, between the members and the worker, and between the group and its host setting, as to the manner in which the group will work and the purpose for which it is constituted. It is also well to remember that groups do not exist in a vacuum, and that some sort of larger social sanction is essential if the group is to survive. This is as true when groups are used by private practitioners as when used by workers in various public institutions.

Extensive use of group methods is not a panacea. Groups have power, and this power can be used for destructive as well as constructive purposes. Power can be destructive to individuals within the group, and it can perpetuate or exacerbate personal problems. The tendency of a group to push its members toward conformity with group values and norms can be destructive to creative thinking and behavior. The tendency to isolate or punish nonconforming members can be dangerous. The tendency of all groups, as social systems, to move toward rigidity and closure can be stifling and can only be combated by awareness, by provision for new input, and by use of opportunity for self-actualization of the group.

Responsibility lies with the worker to see that the group experience is a good one for all of the members involved, that the purpose is constructive, and that the group is changed or disbanded if it becomes ineffectual or destructive. The initial composition of the group should be given serious consideration, and the vulnerability of the potential members assessed. Paramount is creation of a climate that is nonpunitive, that can accept and adapt to individual differences, that provides support for the individual even though one's ideas or behavior might be unacceptable, and that is flexible enough to work toward change and self-actualization of the group.

In the final analysis, the key words in the use of groups in human service work are *differences, similarities, participation, collaboration,* and *wholeness.* Group strength grows out of the ability of the group to achieve cohesiveness around a common purpose and to make use of the differences of the people involved through development of a pattern of interaction that allows for maximum participation and working together as a totality.

In addition to natural and formed groups, workers are required to work with total institutions, communities, and larger political and social entities. In viewing these larger groups, human service workers are concerned with the adequacy with which they are performing their primary function, and the nature and effectiveness of the linkages among the parts. These groups are even more complex social systems than the smaller groups considered previously, but human service work in them is subject to the same set of values, generalized and specialized knowledge, and skills.

Human Service Teams

In addition to using groups to work directly with clients, human service workers use them to work with each other in the interest of clients. The form this most often assumes is the inter- or intradisciplinary team. The modern emphasis on teamwork in human services grew out of five major developments:

1. *The proliferation of knowledge of human dynamics and the necessary resultant specialization.* The breakthroughs in scientific knowledge that marked the nineteenth and early twentieth centuries included new knowledge about people and their institutions. The philosophical belief became prevalent that both could be studied and understood and that this was an appropriate activity out of which could come a better life for all. Theorizing and experimentation generally took place within specific disciplines, and, as knowledge accrued, specialists in their mastery and use developed.

2. *The modern emphasis on holism in human service, and the development of theories and techniques enabling workers to think and practice in terms of the totality of the human experience.* This development naturally followed the era of intense specialization, wherein the tendency was to compartmentalize people and deal with only one aspect of their functioning. The team provides a framework within which specialists can work together to provide services that are planned and carried out in light of the total life experience of the person.

3. *The increasing complexity of present-day society.* The expanded number of options available, the rapidity of social change, and the sophistication of the system and of technology all demand mastery of extensive knowledge and practice skills in order to be effective; often these are beyond the reach of the individual worker. While such skills and knowledge can be secured through the use of resources, as they were secured in the past, the current need for such specialists seems greater in light of volatile social situations.

4. *The strength and extended reach of the team approach.* Use of a team of specialists not only provides more and better knowledge, it also presents opportunities for the "mind-on-mind" interaction out of which new ideas and new ways of operating grow. This could be described as the emergent quality of teamwork, wherein a team engages in a creative process that represents the best use of such a model.

5. *The freedom to use differential diagnosis in determining where the team approach is indicated.* Not all situations demand or even lend themselves to the use of teams. There are strengths and liabilities to the model that must be considered. The assets can be summed up as better use of specialists who may be in short supply, the opportunity for participatory learning, the provision of more comprehensive service,

and the opportunity for individual and group growth. On the other hand, teams can be time consuming and slow moving, and they can lead to greater rather than less fragmentation of service. The major problems, however, are not inherent in teamwork itself but in the way it is used. Once it has been determined that this is the preferred model for dealing with a given situation, it is the responsibility of the workers involved to see that the team is effectively used.

What Is a Team?

A team is a group of people, each of whom possesses particular expertise and each of whom is responsible for individual decisions and action; team members share a common purpose and meet together to pool knowledge, ideas, and meanings from which interaction plans are made, actions taken, and future plans influenced.

The Team as a Group. A team might better be designated as a task group because it is definitely designed for work of some sort. As a group, it is a social system and subject to the dynamics that govern all systems—it is a whole made up of interrelated parts existing in a state of balance. When you change one part—one team member—you look for changes not only in the whole but also in the individual members. Like all systems, a team has both internal and external tasks to perform. It must organize and maintain itself and grow, and it must relate to its environment and do the job for which it was created.

The parts of the team system are the team members, who are always in the process of affecting and being affected by each other and who are making conscious use of themselves in a structured working relationship with others. Each member of the team is there because he or she has something to contribute that makes the whole complete. In addition, each team member is a constellation of personal and professional characteristics that will determine success as a team participant (see Figure 10.2).

Each team member brings a unique personality made up of values and attitudes, behavior patterns and norms, and a set of past experiences that will determine how he or she relates to others within the structure of the team. Essential qualities are:

- Respect for and ability to work with people who differ.
- Willingness and ability to share knowledge and responsibility.
- Ability to agree, disagree, handle conflict, and deal with differences of opinion, without being threatened or threatening others.
- Ability to stand and act alone when necessary.

Teaming can be learned in adulthood, but it is infinitely preferable that children grow up having experiences where they can share and participate in decision making, where they learn respect for differences as a part of their socialization, and where they become secure enough not to feel that their way is the only and right way. Such socialization takes place in the family, in social institutions, and in reference groups. As teams are widely used in planning and delivery of human services, teaming may be a part of both educational programs and in-service training. Workers must possess not only the requisite personal qualities but also knowledge and skill that contribute to the overall purpose.

FIGURE 10.2   Personalities on a team.

Carl Rogers (1995) wrote:

> The immature person cannot permit himself to understand the world of another because it is different from his own and therefore threatening to him. Only the individual reasonably secure in his own identity and selfhood can permit the other person to be different, unique and can understand and appreciate the uniqueness. (p. 37)

In our preparation for teamwork it is this maturity we are striving for. From its attainment comes the fullest individual and team strength.

In addition to unique personality patterns, workers bring as a part of themselves a set of latent characteristics that may affect the relationships among the team members. These are such things as age, race, gender, and physical characteristics such as handicap or obesity. When you are part of a society that says that old people—or young people, as the case may be—are of lesser importance, or that gender and race affect the ability of the individual to be knowledgeable and effective, it is difficult not to be affected by the dominant attitudes and to respond to others in terms of such biases. Stereotyping may also be a problem with regard to the reference groups with which individual team members are identified, such as religious, social, political, and recreational groups. Team relationships need to be based on the reality of this individual in this situation and not on a preconceived opinion or bias about what is represented by latent characteristics, by group identifications, or by previous experience with individuals possessing these qualities.

Finally, the individual team member must bring two bodies of knowledge and areas of competence. The first is that knowledge shared by all team members—know-how about the team, how it is formed, how it operates, how to make use of it, how it can be changed. The second is the unique knowledge of the specialist about how to deal with the particular problem under consideration from the point of view of the expert knowledge and skill that the individual member represents and that justified her or his inclusion on the team.

How Are Teams Formed?

In the provision of human services, teams are usually found in institutions—federal, state, and local agencies, hospitals, schools—where different specialists are represented. Often they are mandated in the table of organization of the institution. Less frequently, they are developed outside any institution as a way of dealing with a particular community problem requiring input from many different points of view. Teams may consist of representatives of different defined specialties, representatives of different levels within a single discipline, or a combination of the two.

Whatever the impetus for the formation of a team, once its members meet together they become part of a dynamic social system that is constantly in a process of changing and moving toward maturity and old age. Like any other vital entity, a team can be visualized as having a life cycle with certain developmental stages. When we choose to think in this way, however, we need always remember that (1) such stages are not absolute, (2) each depends on those that precede it, (3) each team is unique and develops at its own speed and in accordance with its own pattern, and (4) this growth process is never completed until the team is dissolved.

The process of developing into operational maturity can be visualized as having four separate parts with a fifth added for dissolution and evaluation of the total experience (Table 10.1):

1. *Orientation.* Team members are introduced to each other, to the team situation that they are responsible for developing, and to the task they must perform.
2. *Accommodation.* Team members adapt to the group situation and to the uniqueness of the other members; they learn how to communicate with each other and begin to form a total pattern made up of complementary parts.
3. *Negotiation.* Team members become part of the team but retain individual integrity; unity develops and working agreements are concluded.
4. *Operation.* Team members have concluded their internal organization and now deal with the external task.
5. *Dissolution.* Team dissolves into component parts after evaluation of experience—optional but highly desirable.

When a team has reached Stage 4 and gone into operation, it should be possible to describe it as a "mature" system. As such, it should have certain characteristics:

- It should have a clear definition, understanding, and acceptance of its purpose and supporting goals and be able to move toward these in an effective problem-solving manner.
- It should have developed a unity among its members characterized by psychological freedom that encourages expression of differing points of view and does not demand uniformity of thought and behavior. It should be able to use conflict constructively.

TABLE 10.1   The Life Stages of a Team

Stage	Characteristics	Member Tasks	Team Tasks	Outcomes
I. Orientation (determination of position with reference to setting and circumstances)	Definition of situation Exploration Learning Evaluation	Learn what is expected and relate this to self Deal with lack of familiarity, anxiety, mistrust, stress	Define boundaries Provide supports	Acquaintance with colleagues Understand system Beginning security Beginning involvement and identification
II. Accommodation (adaptation and arrangement to create a whole)	Manipulation Movement and change of positions Power struggles Rearrangements of parts of whole	Find appropriate place for self, both personally and professionally	Provide structure and climate conducive to maximum freedom in and facilitation of adaptation process	Common language and communication developing; values and norms developing; affiliation with team developing
III. Negotiation (transaction and conclusion by mutual understanding)	Bargaining and concluding; establishment of boundaries and content of specialization in relation to other specializations	Use self as a team member—able to communicate, differ, confront, use conflict and collaboration	Define boundaries of purpose and specializations Establish contract Designate goals, tasks, roles	Dependency and differentiation established Unity developed Working arrangements concluded
IV. Operation (purposeful action)	Achievement of complementarity and gestalt	Relate to team and to individual members Use both generalized and specialized knowledge Reach individual decisions Perform tasks	Maintain both internal and external balance and vitality Decision making, planning, and executing work	Collaboration movement toward achievement of goals and realization of purpose
V. Dissolution (separation into components)	Evaluation of process, problems, possibilities, and achievement in relation to purpose and goals	Objective assessment of personal and team performance	Support open and critical evaluation of process and results	Personal and team change Awareness of success/failure and appropriate use thereof

- It should have developed a common language and effective communication patterns.
- It should have defined its roles clearly with a minimum of overlap in a way that makes maximum use of differing expertise and with a flexibility that permits change.
- It should have provided for leadership, structure, and supportive resources.
- It should have made provision for evaluation of its work.
- It should be sufficiently flexible to permit growth.

Team Purpose

Purpose is the glue that holds the team together. It must be clearly defined and be committed to by all members. Without this clarity and commitment, there is no way in which the necessary goals to achieve the team's purpose can be agreed on or the necessary tasks performed in ways that complement each other. In addition, team purpose is the bottom line when it comes to constructive use of and resolution of conflict. Purpose may be designated by the host institution or arrived at by the team, but either way, the first team business is discussion, clarification, and commitment to overall purpose.

Team Climate

Below are several areas that make up the components of the team's climate:

1. Acceptance of the normality of conflict in a group of differing people with differing knowledge and skill and differing approaches to problem solution.
2. Provision for freedom of expression and critical evaluation of ideas in which people can disagree openly, safely, and in a disciplined manner. Such conflict can spark creativity and promote innovation.
3. Definition of the reality of the conflict. Differences may involve ideas, personalities, allocation of resources, procedures, and so forth, but in some instances the real causes may be concealed behind those that may seem more acceptable or safe.
4. Delineation of areas of agreement—and the vital agreement on purpose may be the only one attainable. When such is the case, we start there and build on it.
5. Designation of compromises and alternatives for conflict resolution. These agreements must be honestly accepted and committed to by the team members.

It is obvious that, in each of these steps, the manner in which the team arrives at decisions is vital. A first part of the team's business is to make the initial decision as to how team decisions shall be reached. As mentioned previously, Edgar Schein (1999) identified six different methods for decision making:

1. Decision making by lack of response is one of the least desirable methods and is generally a warning signal that the team is in trouble. It indicates withdrawal, nonparticipation, and noninvolvement, and it can imply lack of commitment to the decision made.
2. Decision making by authority may be appropriate in given situations, but frequent use does not allow for maximum development and use of the strengths of the model. Ability to accept and work with appropriate authority is a characteristic of mature workers and is essential for good practice.

3. Decision making by a minority is another style, wherein a small group takes responsibility for such conclusions. In specific instances again, such responsibility may be appropriately allocated, but when this method is generally used it can mean wrongful use of power and status, powerlessness, lack of involvement of other team members, and subsequent lack of commitment to implement decisions.

4. Decision making by the majority on basis of a vote is the most widely used method and is effective if there is provision for consideration of minority opinion. It is probably most successful when there is commitment to implementation of majority decisions.

5. Decision making by consensus, a natural follow-up for majority decisions, implies that the team members recognize the existence of differences but agree to act as a whole regardless of this.

6. Decision by unanimous consent, in which there is total agreement on the source of action to be taken. Here the team represents a totally united front for whatever reason and functions as a single unit. (p. 58)

There are two levels of decision making in teams—those that are appropriate for the entire team to participate in, and those individual decisions made by the specialist in carrying out his or her designated roles and tasks in accordance with particular knowledge and skill. It is important to differentiate between these two types of decision making.

Team Size and Composition

Structure, size, and composition of the team will grow out of its purpose. Although purpose may be mandated in the institution's table of organization or decided on by the team, team structure is determined by the demands of implementation of the team's purpose—literally, what is needed to get the job done. Small-group theorists agree that the smaller the group, the easier it is to get full participation, sharing of responsibility, more democratic operation, and simpler logistics. Generally, such groups are agreed to consist of five to twenty members. When the numbers are larger, leadership tends to become more dictatorial and subgroups tend to form that may be divisive and disruptive to team functioning. They may develop around a strong leader or be based on friendship or professional identification, on similarity of values and behaviors, or on a conscious attempt to control the group. When such subgroups form and are destructive to team functioning, efforts must be made to deal with them, such as forming task groups that cut across subgroup lines or, in some instances, changing team membership. It is important to remember that when new team members are introduced, there will be changes in the balance of the total team as well as in the individual members. Orientation and adaptation to the working situation are essential. In some institutions it is considered more desirable to replace an entire team—as for example, a highly specialized one engaged in research—than to put in new key people.

Team composition strives for a balance of homogeneity and heterogeneity—sufficient likeness among team members so that individuals can relate to each other, communicate, and work together; sufficient difference so that team members can offer various ideas and approaches to problem solution as well as different knowledge and skills that can complement each other.

Team Communication

Communication among these different individuals is fundamental to successful team operation. Difficulties in communicating are compounded by increasing size and heterogeneity. Team members often come from differing cultural backgrounds in which both verbal and nonverbal modes of communication may vary. Specializations tend to develop their own language, and this shorthand for sharing information within a specific discipline may make communication with outsiders difficult.

The manner in which the communicator, the situation, and the message are perceived will do much to determine whether communication is realistic or distorted. In a working situation in which the communicator is perceived as threatening, distortion often occurs because messages may carry a second level that tells the receiver how to interpret and use the communication. This second level grows out of the relationship between sender and receiver and speaks to relative roles, power and status, feelings, and norms of behavior that exist between the two.

Equally important in team communication is the structure of the team, the presence or absence of subgroups, and the designation of roles. In such working groups, people tend to speak in terms of role requirements and expectations, as well as in terms of identification with a particular subgroup. In some teams, for example, where it is the accepted practice that power speaks only to power, communication may be limited and primarily among members of the team's most powerful group.

Establishment of an open communication network within the team is one of its first and, often, most difficult tasks. A climate of openness and honesty where people can speak freely without fear of attack or retaliation, willingness and ability to ask for clarification and use feedback, and awareness that this will be an ongoing task throughout the life cycle of the team will do much to pave the way for better understanding and operation.

Team Roles

A team is a system of interlocking roles, the definitions of which are never finalized—as the team changes and grows, role requirements will also change. (See Chapter 3 for discussion of roles in the workplace.) New team members learn the expectations of their roles and modify them according to ability and perception. The two most important factors in role designation on teams are (1) agreement as to role requirements for a particular position and (2) agreement as to the boundaries of that role. Without these there can be no complementarity of team action.

Three major roles are of particular significance in teamwork: (1) the specialist roles, which are defined according to specific knowledge and skill; (2) the generalist role, which is defined by the need for the client to have someone who will integrate the entire team effort; and (3) the leadership role.

The specialist role is one that each team member fills by virtue of unique knowledge and skill. Defining these roles so there is a minimum of overlap is one of the biggest problems facing teams, particularly in areas such as counseling where boundaries created by specific content of the discipline can be unclear. While there must be prior agreement about who does what, when, and how, in special situations—emergency or otherwise—it may become necessary and desirable for one team member to take over what is ordinarily the role of another. Some teams stress the importance of interchangeable roles. In preparation for such flexibility as well as for better working relationships with other specialists, each team member is encouraged, as a part of orientation, to become thoroughly familiar with the work of the others as far as is possible (see Figure 10.3).

The generalist role, sometimes called the case manager's role, is an integrative one, designed to meet the need of many clients, and is occupied by a single individual who is responsible for representing the total team. This role is frequently assigned to one of the specialists—such as the social worker or nurse on health teams—whose own training stresses

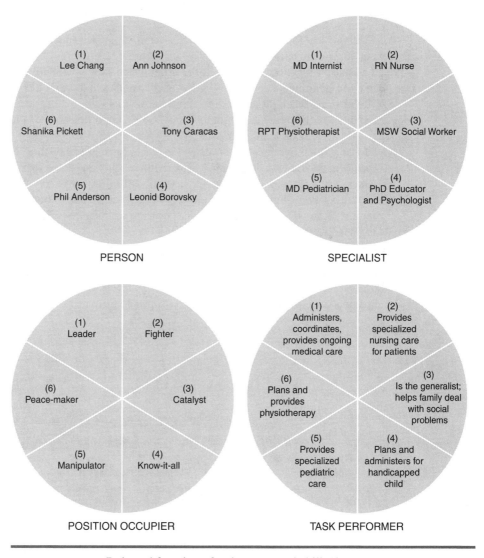

FIGURE 10.3   Role and function of a six-person rehabilitation team.

such brokering work. Without such coordination, the client can fall into the cracks between the specialties and go unhelped. This is particularly essential where clients lack the ability to integrate personally the efforts of the different specialists. The generalist is a person who "speaks for" the team and, as such, must be conversant with all that is done, able to see gaps that may exist in the totality, and able to act as a bridge between the client and the specialists (see Figure 10.4).

The leadership role on the team may be designated, situational, or natural, and frequently it is a combination of these. It is important that team members be flexible enough to allow for changes or for the emergence of natural abilities of individuals in leadership according to the demands of the situation. There are certain ongoing leadership functions that are essential to good team operation:

1. The logistical functions—provision of support personnel, space, equipment, budgeting, and organization.
2. The liaison functions with the host institution or the community—fitting the team into the environmental systems, working out policies and support.
3. The chairing functions at team meetings—providing information, keeping discussion moving and focused, bringing it to a conclusion, supporting participants as necessary so all points of view are expressed.
4. The administrative function involving evaluation—and sometimes supervision—of the team, the individuals, and their work, with recommendations for retention of personnel, changes, promotions, raises, and so forth. Because of the nature of specializations, supervision often cannot focus on the specific content of performance, but it must focus on the actual performance of team members, both as individuals and as members of the team.

Leadership involves use of power, and it is related to position and status on the team, three concepts that have significance in all groups. Power, or the ability to act, may rest with an individual or with a subgroup; in either case, it is a fact that must be accepted and dealt with. Position is the place the team member occupies in the pattern of team life and relates to the function performed. Status is the rank accorded that position. Status may lead to the

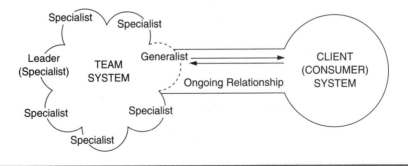

FIGURE 10.4   The developing role of the generalist (case manager or coordinator) on a human service team.

formation of undesirable subgroups within the team—there are generally lower, middle, and upper status groups—and often the middle groups tend to identify with the upper, creating a sense of powerlessness in the lower groups that can be destructive to good team functioning.

There is ongoing research that deals with the circumstances in which people work and how to make them happiest and most productive. We know, for example, that people work best when stress on status and hierarchy is minimal, when controls are neither autocratic nor laissez-faire but based on sound democratic principles, when the work situation is humane with a sufficiently flexible structure to accommodate individual needs, and where there are clearly defined expectations and equal reward for equal performance with minimal use of special and, particularly, unearned privilege.

A good team is a microcosm of democracy and, as such, is a growth experience for its members and an effective way to increase their effectiveness in this day of specialization.

Working Process of Teams

Teams in human service are basically work groups, and as such they use the problem-solving process—definition of problem; designation of purpose and setting of goals, tasks, and roles; selection of intervention from among a variety of possible alternatives; ongoing evaluation and revision; and finally, termination (see Figure 10.5). Teams are usually set up because a problem exists or it is known that one will exist. Because teams must be accountable to the community or institution that sponsors them and because team members' decisions as to problem and solution may not always coincide, their problems with both internal and external communication may be acute. It is necessary to be very clear about what is happening both within the team and between it and its environment.

A team can be as small in number as two people, but the dynamics are the same. Such teams are presently being used in home-based family service, where the purpose is to stabilize the family system and empower the parents to do for themselves. Consisting of a paraprofessional and a professional with a master's degree in social work, the team may be assigned by the court to prevent the placement of children outside the home.

Such a team was assigned by the judge to work with Marilyn, a 20-year-old single parent of Sean, age 4, and an infant, Linda. She had been reported to Protective Services for leaving the children alone in the home in the evening. Acting as home builders, the team would be available 24 hours a day, seven days a week, for a period of six weeks, at the end of which time there would be further evaluation of the situation. The role of the paraprofessional was to help Marilyn deal with the nitty-gritty of homemaking—housekeeping, childcare, use of money. The social worker's task was to see that the necessary resources were available, but primarily to work with Marilyn in helping her deal with feelings of despair and a poor self-image.

Sean was born when Marilyn was only 16 and still in high school. His father, Tony, was also a student, and he and Marilyn had planned to marry when they graduated. He remained with his parents and Marilyn stayed with hers, although her family situation was difficult. After graduation they decided against marriage; Tony went on to the university, and Marilyn moved into a place of her own and

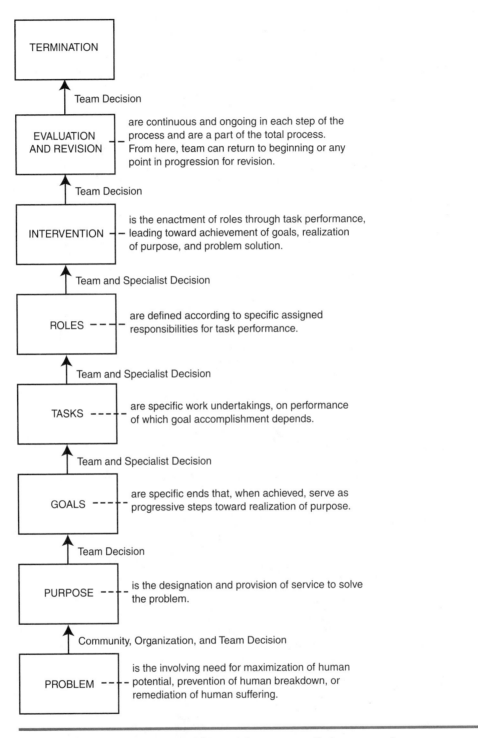

FIGURE 10.5 Steps in the problem-solving process of a human service team.

found a job as a waitress, and Sean went into daycare. With some supplementation she managed fairly well, but when Linda was born as the result of a casual relationship, she was personally devastated and unable to cope. She felt that she was trapped in an impossible situation, that there was no hope of any change, and that though she loved her children she just could not seem to manage. Lonely and frustrated, she began to go out to a local bar after the children were asleep and was reported by the neighbors.

In such a situation, clarity of role definition by the two team members and constant communication between them would be essential. It would be natural for Marilyn to share her fears and frustrations with the paraprofessional as they shopped or house-cleaned together or to discuss her homemaking frustrations with the counselor, but the result would be constructive as long as both were clear as to the purpose of their intervention, the goals of each as an individual worker and team goals, and their roles and the way they carried them out.

A Yardstick for Team Analysis

Each team—like each person—is unique and individual. We can, however, generalize to the extent of pinpointing vital areas in the life space of all teams that determine the success or failure of the teamwork. Each team must be able to answer certain questions as they apply to the team's unique self. Each must be prepared to devote time and energy throughout its life span to keeping the answers up to date.

   I. Purpose
   - **A.** What is the overall purpose of this team?
   - **B.** Who defines it?
   - **C.** Is there common understanding and agreement regarding its meaning among the various systems and individuals involved?
   - **D.** What is required to implement its purpose?
   - **E.** What is required to change it?
   - **F.** Do the working goals grow naturally out of it?

   II. Composition and Structure
   - **A.** Who makes up this team?
   - **B.** How is this decided?
   - **C.** How are both original and additional members selected and involved?
   - **D.** How is membership changed?
   - **E.** What provision is made to enable the individual to become a team member?
   - **F.** How are the roles of the team members defined?
   - **G.** How is the effectiveness of both their uniqueness and their complementarity assessed?

   III. Internal System
   - **A.** What is the underlying value system of this team?
   - **B.** How does this team work to include and/or exclude a member?

Summary

As awareness of the dynamics of group processes increases, so does our use of groups as media for delivery of human services, both directly with clients and indirectly in work with colleagues. Groups extend our reach in the development and use of knowledge and in the variety of practice skills available. Workers who use groups need to be aware of not only their complexity and possible problems entailed, but also the values that can be derived from that use.

SUGGESTED ASSIGNMENTS

1. Assign a research paper on the use of groups as media for dealing with human problems. Students may opt to research groups in general or a particular kind of group.

2. Assign students to keep a journal during the semester of any group to which they belong (learning, recreation, therapy, support, etc.), wherein they will assess the ongoing dynamics of this group.

3. Break the class up into groups of six people, and assign them to create a team designed to deal with a current problem affecting them. Each group should have a different problem—such things as parking on campus, class attendance, combining work and school, finding childcare, or the like. An observer will report to the class on what happens in the team using the Yardstick for Team Analysis as a basis for observation.

REFERENCES AND RELATED READINGS

Brill, N. (1976). *Teamwork: Working together in human services.* New York: Lippincott.

Corey, M. S., & Corey, G. (2001). *Groups: Process and practice* (6th ed.). Belmont, CA: Wadsworth.

Garner, H. W. (1982). *Teamwork in programs for children and youth.* Springfield, IL: C. C. Thomas.

Hepworth, D., Rooney, R., & Larsen, J. (2001). *Direct social work practice: Theory and skills* (6th ed.). Pacific Grove, CA: Brooks Cole.

Northern, H. (2001). *Social work with groups* (3rd ed.). New York: Columbia University Press.

Rogers, C. (1961). *On becoming a person.* Boston: Mariner Books.

Schein, E. (1999). *Process consultation.* Reading, MA: Addison Wesley.

Shulman, L. (1998). *The skills of helping individuals, families and groups* (4th ed.). Itasca, IL: Peacock.

Zastrow, C. (2001). *Social work with groups* (5th ed.). Belmont, CA: Wadsworth.

SELECTED RELATED WEBSITES

American Group Psychotherapy Association
http://www.agpa.org/

Group Psychotherapy Resource Guide
http://www.group-psychotherapy.com/index.htm

Dealing with Vulnerability, Dependency, and Resistance

How are vulnerability, dependency, and resistance related?

What is the meaning of the "social contract"?

What preparation is required of workers for successful advocacy?

Vulnerability, dependency, and resistance are three of the most important factors in delivery of human services. They often constitute a bugaboo for workers, thwarting their best efforts and leading to frustration on the part of all participants in helping transactions. Their origins lie both within the individual and within society, and reactions to them tend to be both value laden and culture bound.

Vulnerability

In every society there are people who can be characterized as more vulnerable than others—more vulnerable to illness, to unemployment or underemployment, to violence, to social isolation, to failure. They are more vulnerable to the changes that take place in the society, first and longest penalized by them. The most prominent of these are the poor, minorities, the handicapped, the elderly, and children.

To be poor in an affluent society, to be old and slow in a world that values youth and speed, to be a child when family structures are weakening and changing and when proliferating no-fault divorces are mainly concerned with the rights of adults, to be a member of a minority group that is considered inferior, to be so handicapped as to be unable to use available resources—to be any of these is to be isolated, stereotyped, and dehumanized. It is to know that within the society there are institutionalized supports that tend to maintain prejudice and discrimination and to close the doors of opportunity. It is to know the frustration of powerlessness, the bitterness of coping with harsh conditions that tend to be self-perpetuating, the loneliness of being the outsider, and the deadening defeat of unfulfilled potential. It is to be afraid.

People caught in such situations may develop one of three patterns of behavior in coping with their vulnerability:

1. They can mobilize personal and social resources to deal with this reality and, if possible, change it (as in the successful activity of pressure groups of elderly people, minorities, and the handicapped).
2. They can become helpless and dependent—although not always consciously—and force the society to care for them by not caring for themselves (as with many of the crisis-prone, multiproblem families who cling to welfare programs).
3. They can strike out in fear and rage at forces they often do not fully understand and cannot control (as do the violent gangs within the ghettos in our cities).

Human service workers in all areas are in immediate and personal contact with our social victims—the physician in the emergency room, the social worker in the welfare department, the teacher in the ghetto classroom, the public health nurse visiting the old person in an isolated rural farmhouse, the foster care worker facing the 13-year-old nobody wants, the minister developing a food program to feed the hungry.

Workers respond to such situations in various ways. They can "identify with the aggressor," placing the cause for such problems on the individuals caught in them, distancing themselves as far as possible from the people with whom they work, partly out of a sense of hopelessness and frustration, or they can respond with moral indignation. But indignation is not enough; it needs to be translated into responsible action.

In preparing themselves to face this challenge, workers need to be equipped with special knowledge and skills soundly based in a personal value system that assures commitment to understanding these problems in all their magnitude, and motivation to work for their alleviation. Prevention and remediation need to go hand in hand in approaching the needs of the vulnerable people. It is important to know who these people are and where they are found in our present social organization, and how their number and the severity of their problems correlate with changing social conditions. Examples of direct correlation can be seen in the emergence of hunger as a national problem, in the fact that one in every five children lives in poverty, and in the quadrupling of the number of babies born outside of marriage since 1950. The groups of vulnerable people specified here are not necessarily all those who share the two characteristics of (1) being stereotyped, segregated, and discriminated against and (2) finding themselves personally powerless to deal with the social forces operating to maintain them in this position.

Researchers have studied character development in a hostile environment characterized by social injustice, societal inconsistency, and personal impotence. This type of environment tends to place responsibility for the problem situation on the individual rather than on the society. It poses a massive personal task of integration in order to make a healthy adaptation to the demands of a society that denigrates both the individual and the group. To survive in the larger society, members of these groups are forced to come to terms with a potent force that constantly, and in many ways, says they are no good. This is truly an impossible dilemma, and it is not surprising that people react with rage and fear, turning inward against themselves or outward against others. It is surprising that so many of the victims of this situation retain the ability to function adequately and to mobilize themselves and others in a constructive way to try to change the society in which they must live.

One of the less constructive ways that clients may use to cope with this situation is a learned helplessness, which may consciously or unconsciously be adopted as a mechanism of defense. Psychology has come up with some interesting laboratory experiments dealing with the effect of learned helplessness on motivation and capacity to survive in animals. Rats, when physically restrained for periods of time, will struggle frantically for a while and then lapse into passivity. When dropped into containers of water, they give up and drown much more quickly than those in the control groups who have not been restrained and who make much greater efforts to survive. The feeling of helplessness appears to involve physical changes as well as changes in motivation, cognition, and emotion.

Although there is some danger in applying the findings of laboratory research on animals to human beings in a "free" setting, we can clearly observe the same dynamics operating with people who have never developed (or who have lost) the sense of being able to control their inescapable situations. Generally, they too will fight until they learn that their efforts to control outcomes are ineffectual. When the sense of ineffectualness becomes overwhelming, passivity, dependency, and depression cannot be far behind.

The major goal of workers in such situations must be to help clients develop and maintain feelings of personal adequacy that will help them mobilize themselves and others to change the destructive environment. However, workers will have to deal first with the feelings involved and must expect that these feelings will be dumped on them as representatives of the destructive society with which these vulnerable people must cope. These feelings were well expressed by the skinny 10-year-old foster child who turned on her worker shouting, "Don't you come around here bringing me a pop and telling me you love me when next week you'll be gone." Increasingly, workers report their own frustration and concern about the apathy, anger, and possible violence that they must face. The answer does not lie in teaching workers karate or other means of self-defense, as has been done in some welfare programs, although there might be situations in which this could be useful. The answer lies in recognizing the normality and predictability of such reactions and in being prepared to cope with them in a more constructive manner while often, at the same time, being required to administer programs that are in themselves reflective of the destructive forces in the society that created them. Although workers cannot totally defuse a situation with a client who is using a worker as a scapegoat for personal frustrations and the ills of the system, it is possible to be forewarned and prepared to deal more effectively with the situation.

Workers must see clearly what is happening, be prepared by knowing how they as individuals fit into what is happening, and be able to maintain within themselves "an oasis of sanity" in a schizophrenic situation. They need to be equipped with five major tools in working with vulnerable people:

1. Self-awareness. Workers must know how they stand in relation to people who are considered of lesser worth by much of society. They must know that sympathy is important but that empathy and objectivity are even more so.
2. Awareness of the impact of the worker's self on others, and of how worker and situation are perceived by clients.

3. Motivation and ability to deal with the special problems of communication brought on by differences in language and culture.

4. Possession of concrete data regarding the group and the client as a member of that group. As no group is monolithic, individualization is of tremendous importance; stereotyping is not only stupid, but ineffectual, and often leads to denial of basic human rights.

5. Understanding of the social situation that contributes so largely to developing and perpetuating problems, and knowledge and skill in working to change both society and its institutions.

On the basis of these values, this knowledge, and these skills, the worker attempts to remedy the destructive effects of the social situation and to prevent their continuance. A major role in serving clients (which, it must be remembered, is also serving the total society) is that of advocacy in both the legal context of "one who pleads the cause of another" and the political definition of "one who argues for, defends, maintains, or recommends a cause or proposal":

- As an advocate on an individual level, the worker, as a guidance counselor in the school system, might go to bat for a troublesome teenage boy who had been excluded from the school because he got into a fight. The appeal would be based on his legal right to an education, his commitment to improve his behavior, and his participation in a counseling program.

- On a citywide level, the worker, as a health service planner, might spearhead a community effort to develop a maternal and child health clinic in the inner city that is poorly served by hospitals. The clients in this instance would be the people of the neighborhood, and the advocacy would be based on the right of all people to adequate healthcare.

- On a state level, the worker, as a social worker on the commission on aging, might work to ensure adequate inspection of nursing homes, enforcement of standards of care, and improvement of those standards. The clients in this instance would be old people and their families, and the advocacy would be based on the right of all people to safe and adequate living situations.

- On a national level, workers from many different specializations in the human services might work to ensure the passage of legislation to put teeth into the housing laws that permit people to live wherever they wish regardless of race, creed, or color. The client in this instance would be primarily members of racial and religious minorities and the poor, and the advocacy would be based on the right under the law of all people to live where they wish.

As is obvious from the examples cited here, workers cannot be effective advocates without considerable knowledge of the rights to which people are entitled—both inherent rights and those guaranteed under the Constitution and the laws of the country. One of the major problems of human service workers in their role as advocates is that they tend to champion people and causes on the basis of ideals and emotions rather than on the basis of hard knowledge.

Rights are those things to which people or society have a just claim and cannot, in American society, be denied without due process of law (Garrett, 1973). Both individual and societal rights are relative and exist within a state of balance that may fluctuate as relationships are perceived differently, as technology develops, or as conditions change. For example, individuals owning land have the right of private property, but when coal is discovered under that land in a time of energy shortages, the society has a right to use that coal for the "greatest good for the greatest number"—particularly if that land happens to be a Native American reservation! The teenager in our first example has the legal right to an education, but the other students have equal rights in this area, and the school system has administrative rights to operate an effective educational program. A current question, in light of what we know about the nature of human development and the demands of parenthood, is whether young adolescents, 12 to 15 years of age, have the right to have children. Statistics being gathered seem to indicate a correlation between dependency on public support and adolescent parenthood, as well as between child abuse and adolescent parenthood. Public welfare and family counseling agencies express increasing concern over the numbers of young people, still children themselves in many ways, who are taking on the demands of parenthood with no real awareness of what is involved. If the pressures become great enough, society will decide if this is an inherent or a legal right.

This relativity, expressed by Rousseau in *The Social Contract* (2003), dating as far back as 1762, is even more meaningful in our present complex society with its many different people and demands. Rousseau said, "Social order is a right—a sacred right that serves as a basis for all other rights; it does not flow from force. Yet it does not flow from nature either. It therefore rests upon agreements." Such agreements are in a constant process of being reworked, and we are presently taking a hard look at those relating to the rights of individuals and those of groups.

It is easy to see that there are built-in conflicts in the concept of rights, and workers who aspire to be effective in this area must be prepared to understand and deal with them. To be effective, they must either be personally knowledgeable regarding the laws on all government levels that codify and establish most of the rights that we have or have access to resources that will provide the necessary know-how. Increasingly, law schools are emphasizing humanistic aspects of the law; the American Civil Liberties Union is an invaluable resource, and educational programs for human service workers in all areas are including in their curricula knowledge of the legal system and ways to use it.

In addition to knowledge of the legal system, knowledge of the legislative process is of paramount importance. Not only must workers know how to develop, introduce, and support legislation effectively, but they must also know how to be pragmatic lobbyists. One of the major current trends in human service systems is what is known as their "politicization"—the entry into politics in an effort to affect the system in which we live, not only in the interests of the system but also in the interests of its clients. Workers who operate here effectively will do so on the basis of knowing how to communicate innovation, having the ability to form and work with coalitions, and knowing how and when to compromise—all of which must rest on a realistic assessment of social situations.

The role of advocate and that of social changer go hand in hand. Changes involve three different levels:

1. The society as a whole, when conditions exist that are destructive to people. The society gives final and overall sanction to change and therefore must be involved.
2. The large social system, such as political parties and professional disciplines, which may, either unknowingly or because of self-interest, perpetuate destructive patterns. These groups are, in a sense, the gatekeepers of change, which is passed on to the society through adoption and enforcement of laws and policies and through the education of practitioners.
3. Organizations that, for many reasons, may not be responsive to changes in their environment such as population shifts and modifications in public policy, practice method, social values, and organizational styles.

Because societal change is generally a long-term process and comes in response to a multitude of variables, workers will need to be able to mobilize a variety of people and interests in their efforts to facilitate such change. One of the most useful and effective tools is mobilization of vulnerable people into self-help groups. This is one of the great strengths of a pluralistic society, providing, through numbers and organization, power to the powerless. When a number of such groups exist, coalitions among them to work on common interests can provide even greater strength and bargaining power. Such groups are seen at present in the American Association of Retired Persons (AARP) and other organizations of old people, in the various racial caucuses and groups, such as the National Association for the Advancement of Colored People (NAACP), and in the organizations of the poor. Only the vulnerable children cannot use this tool themselves and need people, such as the Parents of Retarded Children, to use it in their interest.

As with individual rights, group rights are a matter of balance between those of the total society and those of the subgroup, and among the rights of the subgroups. When one group benefits at the expense of others, it can lead to a polarization that is potentially destructive to the whole. In developing self-help groups, workers need to keep this reality in mind. In staffing such efforts, the worker's role is an enabling one—enabling people to use their own strength so that the worker bows out and people take over for themselves—which is as it should be.

Organizational change is often equally difficult, as workers may be faced with the need to make changes in organizations of which they are a part, and there is an element of personal risk involved. While it is a generally accepted concept that systems (an organization is defined as a social system created for a specific purpose) tend to move toward closure and self-maintenance rather than toward dynamic productivity, we often forget that there is an equal tendency toward survival, development, and realization of potential for growth and change. No organization is impermeable to the changes that take place in its environment, and environments are dynamic and always changing. Organizations may accept or reject pressures, but they cannot ignore them. For example, the adoption of an affirmative action policy on a national level—and the attachment of this to the allocation of federal funds—constituted an environmental change for organizations such as hospitals and universities that mandated internal change.

A good organization has built-in provisions for self-appraisal and established channels for input from its environment, the consumer, and its own personnel. Changes in policy and personnel that reflect the environmental changes going on around the organization can often be initiated by concerned people within the organization.

The role of the human service worker in serving the vulnerable people cannot be limited to work designed to enable individuals to adapt to the status quo. This merely perpetuates the destructive nature of the situation and the problems inherent in it. There is certainly a place for work with individuals and families struggling to deal with their environment in a constructive way, but along with this must go an all-out effort to make the environment a healthier one.

There is an old story of a social psychiatrist and a psychoanalyst walking together along a river. They came upon a drowning man, jumped in, and rescued him. A little farther along they saw another and rescued him. When they came to the third, the social psychiatrist said to the analyst, "You jump in and pull him out. I'll run ahead and see who's pushing them in."

It is time we ran ahead.

A motorcycle accident in his late teens left Johnny Wilson legally blind, badly scarred, lacking use of one arm, and with impaired judgment when faced with complex issues. His mother got him a job as an attendant at a self-parking lot—he was pleasant with people, reliable, and able to make change, and so his employers were pleased with him.

Essentially a lonely person, Johnny became friendly with a group of high school boys who hung out at the fast-food place where he had lunch. He invited them to visit him on the job. The boys realized almost immediately that he was vulnerable, and while one distracted him, another stole from the cash box. He was brought into court for stealing, a particularly serious charge as he had previously shoplifted small items.

Fortunately, the neighboring shoe repair man had a run-in with the boys over their behavior, came forward, and the police were able to find the real culprit. But Johnny lost his job. His lawyer advised his mother to seek help from a social agency.

Because of his handicap, Johnny was vulnerable to exploitation of all kinds. His divorced father had remarried and moved away; his mother alternated between rejection, guilt, overprotection, and anxiety about his future.

The worker's task was threefold: (1) to help Johnny, to the extent he was able, to protect himself and find friends; (2) to utilize social resources to protect him; and (3) to help his mother deal with her feelings and make practical plans for the future. The first involved helping Johnny enroll with a group of people with mental impairments who were learning social skills; the second, helping him get a job in a sheltered workshop; the third, giving his mother understanding, support, and information about the possibility of a legal guardian for Johnny. Fortunately, theirs was a community where legal aid services, sheltered workshops, and group homes for the physically and mentally impaired were available. Had they not been, the worker's task would have been much more difficult, and her responsibility would have included working for the development of such essential services.

Dependency

In winter, the plains of Nebraska are often swept by snow and ice storms and severe cold. Life for both humans and animals can be difficult. The friend who sat beside the worker's desk was a child of the pioneers who, a short hundred years ago, learned to live with this land. She was six months pregnant with her first child, her husband was out of town, and her tears were occasioned by the fact that the pump on the windmill was frozen, the cattle were without water, and the truck she drove to do the morning chores was stuck in the frozen ice and mud in the barnyard. "Surely there's someone in your family who can help you with this work," the worker suggested.

This occasioned fresh tears. "I want to do it myself!" she sputtered angrily.

This resolute, determined young woman who found it so difficult to say, "I need help," or "I need to depend on someone else" developed from a people within a culture at a particular time in history.

The ethic that lauds independence as the great virtue is so strongly inculcated in our society that it is so difficult to admit and voice the need for help, and the fear and loathing of "dependency" is so great that often only a tragedy makes it possible for people to request necessary assistance. In our society, there is something shameful in admitting that one is incapable of dealing alone with the demands of living. Human service workers—physicians, teachers, social workers, police officers, ministers—are all too familiar with the people who come for help too late and then only when a crisis occurs that permits no other solution.

Why do we protest so greatly what is a natural, necessary state? Why do we deny this part of ourselves and worship the myth of an isolated and independent soul riding alone into the sunset? Like Shakespeare's lady who doth protest too much, is the extremity of our denial an expression of our very need to be dependent on each other?

The whole question of dependence is fraught with emotion and characterized by cloudy thinking and inconsistent behavior. Our society sets no clear guidelines for its members. By creating absolutes of the two states—dependence and independence—we have lost sight of their relative nature and their essential coexistence. By glorifying the kind of competitiveness that must inevitably end in a winner and a loser, we have created a system that does not allow people to relate naturally to each other in a supportive way.

No one is ever totally dependent or totally independent. We are interdependent both as individuals and as societies, and interdependence is made up of both dependence and independence in a state of balance. In themselves, these two characteristics are neither good nor bad; rather, it is the totality, the weaving together, the balance in which they occur, that makes them desirable or undesirable, constructive or destructive.

Humans as a species are characterized by the need for a longer period of nurturing than any other life form. Despite this, there is a drive toward self-determination within the infant, whose dependence is only a matter of degree appropriate to its particular stage of development. If one tries to confine the seemingly haphazard movements of an infant's arms or legs, its face will redden with rage as it opens its mouth to scream. The infant wants to do what it wants to do when and how it wants to do it. The extent of and the manner in which these early strivings develop will depend on the way they are dealt with.

A child can be given total freedom of movement, thought, and feeling or can be wrapped in intellectually, emotionally, physically, socially, and spiritually confining swaddling clothes. The need to free oneself for development in all life areas is built in and scheduled to unfold in accordance with one's own individual timetable. In no sense, however, does one develop from one absolute state to another—from absolute dependence to absolute independence. Rather, one exists in a state of relative dependence-independence according to one's need at a particular time in the life cycle. Given a perfectly healthy individual in a perfectly healthy milieu, a perfectly healthy balance of these two needs would result. In specifying a healthy milieu, however, it must be emphasized that we do not mean one without stress, which is ultimately essential for development, but one in which there is a good balance of challenge and support.

The Flexible Continuum of Interdependence

Using the concepts from systems theory provides an effective way of looking at interdependence. When we define a system as a whole made up of interrelated parts, we are also defining interdependence. Each part supplements and complements the others, and the system that attempts to function without this give-and-take relationship gradually moves toward ineffectualness and eventual calcification through its own rigidity and isolation. So it is with the individual's balance of dependence-independence needs. However, perfect balance is a static concept and can scarcely be applicable to anything as dynamic as life. When we look at individuals, groups, and societies, we see a constant shifting and changing as they adapt to changes in each other.

The healthy system possesses a flexibility that enables it to make these adaptations to both internal and external changes. This adaptability, this capacity for adjustment and readjustment, is the essence of healthy interdependence.

The individual who requires hospitalization is a case in point. One of the secrets of a successful hospital stay is the capacity to be dependent, but it is equally important that upon recovery the patient be capable of giving up this dependence and moving again toward independently making the decisions and performing the activities that were done by others during the illness. Diverse problems arise when the patient needs and wants to remain a patient.

Thus we could say that every system—and the individual is as much a system as are groups—possesses a range of capacity for interdependence, involving a continuum from extreme dependence to extreme independence. Adaptations to the demands of living require the ability to move back and forth freely along the scale, and inability to function except at one extreme or the other tends to be pathological. The person who needs and wants to be totally free of commitments, of give-and-take relationships with others, constitutes as great a problem to self and society as the person who can never walk alone.

Two Aspects of Interdependence

Our interdependent society might be viewed from two different frames of reference: (1) that which revolves around the essential give and take that is required to provide material needs and services and (2) that which relates to self-determination, capacity for decision making, and relationships with others.

Given the myth of the independent individual, which is fostered from earliest infancy in the society, one who is in a position of requiring outside help in either of these two areas frequently finds that admitting need and seeking help creates as much trouble as the actual difficulty itself. The very nature of human services requires that practitioners deal constantly with the problems caused by such negative attitudes toward dependence, with those engendered by individuals who are on either extreme of the continuum of interdependence, and with those that arise from the character of the helping relationship itself, which contains within it elements of both dependence and authority.

The Role of the Worker

Workers themselves are products of this society and culture, which have created an unrealistic monolith and made a fetish of independence. They cannot avoid being affected by these attitudes. In addition, they have within themselves the same dependence-independence strivings that are a part of each individual's identity. They may have selected their jobs because of their own needs to control others and have others dependent on them. Consequently, they sometimes approach their work as a divided person, as did the student who wrote in his analysis of the impact of his own cultural conditioning, "I will always have to watch my own attitudes in working with men who do not support their families. In my home town, that man was the lowest of the low."

As always, the worker's first task is to look at the reality of the situation and consider if it should and how it can be changed. The problem created by society's attitudes is a frustrating one because it not only creates difficulties for individuals in need, but it also prevents the enactment of laws and the development of programs that would create the conditions leading to the growth of each individual's capacity for healthy interdependence. Fortunately, however, we seem to be maturing in our acceptance of not only our own personal needs for outside help, but also the similar needs of other people. The willingness of society in general to be accepting of the reality of human needs and the assumption of greater responsibility for those who are unable to provide for themselves will vary with the times and the situation. When the causes of dependency can be visibly demonstrated, as with children, old people, and the physically handicapped, recognition of the need for social responsibility comes more easily than, for example, with the healthy-appearing adult who cannot work.

Despite these attitudes, recognition of the interdependence of all people seems more pervasive than ever before. The very existence of wide-range planning to enable people to realize their maximum potential—regardless of how limited it may be—bears witness to this. The ecological movement extends this philosophy, and we are beginning to recognize the interrelationship of all life forms. A major problem seems to hinge on developing the knowledge necessary to enable us to create a good society, but if the dynamic developments in the behavioral sciences have any validity, we should find ourselves possessed of increasingly effective tools for this purpose.

However, workers' tasks go beyond developing new knowledge. They must use what we presently know (1) to attempt to create the social conditions that lead to the fullest development of the individual's capacity for interdependence and (2) to utilize sound practice methods that tend to lessen the client's need to function on either extreme of this continuum.

What must the society provide so that its members may develop, to the greatest extent, their potential for healthy functioning? It must provide the basic human needs:

- Assurance of access to adequate material resources—food, clothing, shelter.
- Provision of opportunity for growth in all areas, according to the potential of the individual.
- Provision of a climate that does not overprotect and ask too little, or demand so much that it cannot be achieved, but one that involves a balance of opportunity and responsibility.
- Provision of reward for risk and supports in failure.
- Provision for increasing self-determination and involvement in decision making according to the capacities of the individual.
- Provision of opportunity for satisfaction of emotional needs, and the development of a value system that gives meaning to life.

The reader will note that not only should these six conditions be a part of the entire social order, but that they are also an essential part of family life. The developing child who has these advantages within the smaller family unit has a good chance of developing into a healthy adult who possesses a flexible balance of dependence and independence.

Social Change

It is obvious in looking at the foregoing list that there are many people in our society who do not have even some of these advantages. As a society, we pay dearly in human suffering, in loss of the potential strength that these people represent, and in the actual financial cost of caring for them. It is to the advantage of the total group that its members develop a healthy capacity for interdependence. It is equally clear that the individual worker cannot effect the massive social changes necessary to make this possible. Collective planning and action on the part of clients, workers, and representatives of the general public are essential, for all of us have a stake in the necessary changes. The unique contribution of the worker to this undertaking should be knowledge of how to proceed that is not derived from any one discipline or approach. For example, so simple yet fundamental a change as safeguarding small children from nibbling at lead paint in slum dwellings requires varied knowledge of: (1) drafting and putting through ordinances that will require this protection, such as those in some cities that require covering the painted walls with plasterboard; (2) knowing and utilizing the power structure and bureaucracies in the city to see that the laws are enforced; (3) developing and using channels of communication to enable the people involved—landlords, tenants, and homeowners—to know their rights and responsibilities and how to discharge them; and (4) knowing how to work with people to help them to secure and use necessary legislation and develop the motivation to act. All this, for one small aspect of the problem, and we have not even touched on the basic problem—the absence of decent housing that people can afford.

Social change can and has been achieved, but it can be constructive only when it involves use of a disciplined, knowledgeable action based on assessment of the reality factors involved and development of a strategy to deal with them. Without sophisticated knowledge, we can never understand and deal adequately with complex human beings and their increasingly complicated society and thus create conditions that foster a healthy interdependence.

Relationship Role

In practice, workers will have to deal with the end result of the overall effects of the social system on people, as well as with the limitations inherent in personal endowment. They will work with those who are so severely damaged that they possess little or no capacity for directing their own lives or relating effectively to other people. A part of the initial assessment will involve looking at where the client is on the continuum of dependence-independence and meeting the client on the basis of this reality. The helping relationship should provide a firm floor at the level of clients' needs, upon which they can stand for support as they move toward increasing ability to exercise their own talents to a greater degree.

It is extremely difficult to establish this firm footing for people when there is no way of assuring them freedom from want of the material and spiritual necessities of life and when there seems little realistic hope that circumstances will change for them in their lifetime. Nevertheless, this is the task that workers are faced with, and the kind of relationship that is established must be based on recognition of this hard reality. It must be characterized by acceptance of people as they are and by expectation of what they can be; it must be based on a mutuality of understanding and on an interest in dealing with the personal and social reality that clients are facing.

The worker's initial assessment should establish the client's capacity for self-determination and for decision making, which lead to action, as well as for give-and-take relationships based on flexible interdependence. The dependence that causes the greatest possible concern stems from those attitudes and feelings of clients that make it difficult for them to take responsibility for themselves and their own actions and thus cause them to become overly dependent on someone else in these areas. This has little relationship to economic status—although the poor are most frequently accused of "dependency." Once the level of the client's capacity for self-determination and decision making has been established, the knowledgeable worker relates to it in terms of expectations of what the client can and will do and gears the opportunities presented and demands made to this level.

The client's involvement in the total process supports and extends the capacity for self-determination. The self-help groups that have developed so widely in the past decade or so among many different kinds of people with common interests and concerns are a good example of this. The worker's emphasis is "we will work with you to solve your problems" rather than "we will solve them for you."

Much of the so-called dependency of clients is not a true dependency at all, but a paralysis caused by lack of opportunity or lack of knowledge of existing opportunities. The worker must differentiate between true psychological dependency—inability to be self-determining—and that which is only situational.

There are some people who have never developed their potential for independent thought and action for a variety of reasons. Overprotective parents on all social levels often help to produce this condition in their children. In instances where the traumatizing experiences have been too great, some individuals will never be able to stand on their own feet.

Clearly, not all these people fall into the groups of those whose dependency society is able to accept—children, the aged, and the handicapped. Some of them are healthy-appearing adults who, unfortunately, are emotional children. With them, the worker's task is often to provide the kind of decision making that they cannot provide for themselves.

It seems axiomatic that the more monolithic and undifferentiated we become in our attitudes and thinking, the less real understanding we possess. Life is infinitely complex, and uniformity rarely exists within the whole. Nowhere is this more true than within individuals and their societies; nowhere is it more true than in our understanding of interdependence. To deal with the problem realistically, we must dispel the obscurity of distorted values and emotions and recognize the clear voice of reality that testifies to our essential and unending need to rely on each other.

Asking for help is often as difficult as using help, and this was particularly true for Alice Wickham, the only child of elderly parents who prided themselves on keeping things within the family. She found herself at 30 outside the mainstream of life, alone with her aging father, bitterly unhappy, and facing poverty because the family resources were almost gone. In desperation she appealed to her minister, who referred her to the social agency of their denomination.

Physically and intellectually Alice was employable, but emotionally she was shy, passive, and lacking in social skills, and she was without training or experience. She blamed her parents for her situation, was ambivalent about caring for herself, and was angry and frightened. She tried hard to manipulate the worker into making decisions and plans for her.

Reiterating her desire and willingness to help, the worker resisted this, identifying with the healthier part of Alice's personality, pointing out the skills and knowledge she had from caring for her mother during her illness with Alzheimer's that were much in demand, focusing on what she would like to do, supporting her, but also leaving the decisions to her. Knowing that she could only take small steps at a time, the worker recommended a survey of skills, knowledge, and preference for work that was devised by the YWCA program for displaced homemakers who wanted to get into the labor market. With considerable support, Alice accepted this and was on her way.

The problems around dependency here were twofold—the family's unwillingness to accept and live the essential interdependence of people that enabled them to use outside help, and Alice's extreme personal dependency that kept her from taking charge of her own life and making her own plans and decisions.

Resistance

Human service workers in all fields are generally motivated to do good for their clients and to succeed in such undertakings. It can be a source of dismay and frustration when such efforts are met with resistance, and individual workers will find themselves feeling defensive, rejected, and often angry when it persists. In reality, it is a natural and understandable reaction, one which workers need to identify for what it is; they must learn the possible causes for it and develop strategies for dealing with it.

Webster's defines *resistance* as "an opposing or resisting force." It may be expressed consciously or unconsciously through passive apathy or active hostility. It is a natural force in human relations that can be understood in terms of the adaptive processes and systems theory.

People adapt to the demands of living by developing certain ways of behaving and thinking that meet needs and enable them to survive. As these behavior patterns are internalized, emotional commitment to them develops, and efforts to change these patterns, however uncomfortable they may be, can be seen as a threat to be resisted. An example of this can be seen in the grown daughter who "gets back at" the nagging mother with whom she lives by being chronically late in everything she does. While both may find this pattern of living unsatisfactory and ostensibly want to change, they may resist such change strongly—probably on an unconscious level.

Systems exist in a state of checks and balances between their parts, and any change tends to upset that balance. Systems evidence both a drive to change and a drive to retain the status quo. While the former can be capitalized on to bring about movement, there is always the counter pressure to retain things the way they are. A state of imbalance creates a situation that is not comfortable. These dynamics can be seen in a troubled family system whose balance rests on the scapegoating of a particular child. No matter how much the family verbalizes a desire to help the child improve in school, be less a loner, and be a happier person, there will be resistance to upsetting this balance.

In addition to these basic dynamics, there are other factors that lead to resistance:

1. Involuntary clients required by society or by circumstance to use help may express their resistance through open hostility, indifference, or pretended acceptance. This can be seen in legal probationers, old people forced to go to nursing homes, delinquents, and addicts required to enter treatment programs.
2. Clients whose past experiences with "helping" persons have been destructive or whose current experience is not good. When workers are less than honest, insensitive to what clients are saying, incompetent but protected by the system—or when they feel superior to and often actually dislike the people with whom they work—they sow a bad seed that will be reaped by other workers.
3. Clients who are incapable of healthy relationships, who can only use them as mediums for manipulation and power struggles, and for whom all others are adversaries.
4. Clients who resist all power and authority however expressed—and the power to extend or deny help is present in all relationships in human services.
5. Clients whose cultural experience makes the helping situation intolerable. These cultural differences can range all the way from the expectation of self-sufficiency, to the inability to express a need for or use help, which is fairly common in U.S. society, to attitudinal and value differences of minority cultures, such as Native Americans, for whom human services as structured may run counter to the values of their society.

The Role of the Worker

In dealing with resistance, workers need to know that it is a natural reaction that can be dealt with once it is identified and the possible causes pinpointed. They need to assess accurately the discomfort-hope index and weigh for themselves and with their clients whether there is a sufficiently realistic hope of change to justify the upset and discomfort that accompanies efforts to change. Expectations should be based on reality, and workers—usually perennial optimists—must not promise more than can be delivered.

Confrontation with the fact of resistance is often necessary in working with individuals, groups, and communities. It will be most effective when based on demonstrable facts; these can often be gathered after a designated period of effort in which no change has taken place, at which point discussion can be initiated around what is actually happening.

Workers should see themselves primarily as enablers whose tasks are to (1) help clients to see the inescapable realities—for example, those faced by the involuntary clients; (2) recognize the facts of anger and discomfort; (3) offer support and identify with the desire that things be better; and (4) make the necessary resources available.

Workers should also keep in mind that they are never the agent of change. Basically, clients do the changing, usually pushed by reality and by their own dissatisfaction with what is and their desire for what can be. In addition, there are natural helping networks in all societies, and in those situations where cultural differences are a handicap, workers can often operate through them much more effectively. This means that those workers who are not sensitive to or cognizant of the culture of the people with whom they are working need to go slowly and be open to learning about their clients' culture.

This is nothing more nor less than good practice in human service, geared to the needs of a particular problem in human relationships. Respect for the rights of clients and their involvement in decision making are the basic values on which it rests. Empathy for and acceptance of the right to have and to express negative feelings and to put the resistance into words are essential. The worker's abilities to be undefensive, to acknowledge mistakes both by people and in programs, and to stress and define present working relationships as developing entities are important.

Often resistance arises from nothing more than problems in communication, or lack of clarity as to goals and means of reaching them, with misperception of the total situation. Workers who keep their cool and know their practice should be able to accept and deal with resistance.

Resistance that is openly verbalized is easier to deal with than that which is often not even recognized by the clients themselves.

Andy, a part of whose sentence required involvement in counseling, was openly hostile and determined not to cooperate, and so it was possible to confront him directly in the initial interview. After Andy delivered himself of a diatribe, the worker responded coolly.

"Only you can decide whether you want to make use of this opportunity to look at the behavior that brought you here and whether you want to continue it. The fact is that our service is the only thing standing between you and a prison sentence, and no matter how mad you are at the judge, this is a chance to take a look at what you're doing to yourself—and it hasn't been good. I'm prepared to try to help you, but you have to help yourself."

"What can somebody like you do? You don't even know what it's all about."

This was intended as a put-down, but the worker responded by saying quietly, "Why don't you tell me about it?"

This brought an outburst—Andy had a great need to express his anger and, finally, his fear—and though this was certainly not the end of his resistance, it marked a beginning in the relationship.

The Changs, on the other hand, who came for help because their eldest, Cindy, a bright 12-year-old, was suddenly failing in school, were verbally enthusiastic about wanting to change the way they dealt with her, seized eagerly on all recommendations of the school counselor, but always failed to carry them through. Although they were unaware of it, their entire family balance was predicated on Cindy as a scapegoat for their problems. They resisted looking at the difficulties in their own relationship and at their preferential treatment of a younger boy. After working directly with Cindy, supporting her in her right and need to express her feelings about the family, and with the parents alone, the worker moved to total family therapy not only to get the real problems out, but also to help the parents perceive what they were doing to keep Cindy in the role of the failure in the family.

Use of Resources

Extremes of vulnerability, dependency, and resistance call for maximum creation and use of resources, which will often need to be tailored to fit the individual situation. Flexibility and imagination are called for. Workers will need to be able to set priorities. Vulnerable people are also, in many instances, poor people who are often hard pressed to secure the basic necessities of food, clothing, and shelter. Extreme dependency may arise from fear of being without these. Resistance may be caused by this same fear that any change will result in the loss of such essentials.

It is hard for people—workers included—who have never been lacking in the necessities of living to understand the impact of such conditions on the self, on the capacity of people for relationships and for change. The basic human needs must be met before anything else is attempted.

People are resources, and workers who see themselves as enablers can make extensive use of volunteers, of significant others in the client's life space, and of interested individuals who have come from the same culture, who have shared the same problems, and who can often understand and communicate with a client successfully. The workers' task here is to provide specialized knowledge of needs, of services available, and of the way to reach them.

The following example illustrates how the use of the enabling approach can benefit both the individuals and the community.

Over the past fifty years, the small towns of this nation have been dying. Young people have left the rural areas and often only the older people remain, with few home care services available for them.

Eighty-four-year-old Mrs. Weller lived alone in a dilapidated frame house in such a town. The furnace needed a part no longer manufactured and the toilet had never been connected to the new sewer system. Winter was coming, but she wanted to remain in her home despite the drawbacks of lack of heat and the fact that she could not use the outdoor privy because she was partly crippled with arthritis.

There were no services in the technical sense in the community, but the old age assistance worker went to the village bar, which in this culture was the social center for the whole community. There he found and talked with the unofficial mayor of the town. The man who ran the filling station across from Mrs. Weller's house was handy at fixing things—and someone came up with a part for the furnace. Four men spent a Saturday morning digging a ditch and connecting the sewer. While they were there, they braced the steps and fixed some cracks in the old walls. People became interested and promised to "keep an eye on Mrs. Weller" when the weather got bad.

No money was involved—there wasn't any—but a town mobilized itself and became conscious of the needs of its people, its capacity to do something about them, and the satisfaction that could be derived from its acts.

Summary

There are physical resources, such as programs and services, that can be mobilized to meet the special needs discussed in this chapter, but the greatest resource is the knowledgeable and imaginative use of the worker's professional self. This may be complicated by the fact that workers often find these groups exceptionally difficult to deal with both in terms of knowledge and skills and in terms of values involved. Social attitudes toward and social acceptance of responsibility may vary widely. People may feel concerned about, and yet resentful of, the vulnerable who need special supports. They may resent dependency as a characteristic not in keeping with the accepted valuing of independence; they find resistance intolerable—"people should be grateful for help and willing to do what's best for them—and I know what's best!" Because workers are products of this confusion, they may first need to be clear about their own attitudes.

SUGGESTED ASSIGNMENTS

Divide the class into three groups, each of which will make a study of the factors involved in working with people who are (1) especially vulnerable, (2) especially dependent, or (3) especially resistant to change. Consider elements such as causes, extent, special needs, existing services, and discrimination. Each student will present a paper on the group's topic to be graded, and the group itself will plan and make a presentation. Following each presentation, a guest speaker will be invited:

1. To discuss vulnerability—perhaps a speaker from a program for the homeless to talk about the kinds of people without homes, the extent of the problem, the causes, its impact on people, and what can be done about it.

2. To discuss dependency—perhaps a speaker from the Department of Public Welfare to discuss relief programs of the agency in terms of their creating dependency and, if so, what is being done about it.

3. To discuss resistance—perhaps a speaker who works as a counselor or a therapist to discuss dealing with resistance in working with people who say they want help with a personal problem but are unable to face it or use help.

REFERENCES AND RELATED READINGS

Alinsky, S. (1989). *Rules for radicals.* Newbury Park, CA: Vintage Press.

Garrett, J. (1973). *What social workers don't know about rights.* Lincoln: School of Social Work, University of Nebraska.

Gitterman, A. (1998). *Handbook of social work practice with vulnerable populations* (2nd ed.). New York: Columbia University Press.

Haynes, K. S., & Mickelson, J. S. (2002). *Affecting change: Social workers in the political arena.* Boston: Pearson/Allyn and Bacon.

Hoff, L. (1995). *People in crisis: Understanding and helping* (4th ed.). San Francisco, CA: Jossey-Bass.

Kahn, S. (1991). *Organizing.* Silver Spring, MD: National Association of Social Workers.

Piven, F., & Cloward, R. (1979). *Poor people's movements: Why they succeed and why they fail.* New York: Random House.

Rousseau, J. (2003). *The social contract.* Mineola, NY: Dover.

Rothmar, J. (1998). *Self-awareness workbook for social workers.* Boston: Allyn and Bacon.

SELECTED RELATED WEBSITES

Advocacy, Inc.
http://www.advocacyinc.org/

Gay and Lesbian Alliance Against Defamation (GLAAD)
http://www.glaad.org

Gender.org
http://www.gender.org/

Gray Panthers Home Page
http://www.graypanthers.org/

Medicare Advocacy
http://www.medicareadvocacy.org/

National Association of Social Workers Cultural Diversity Committee Web Page
http://www.uncwil.edu/people/blundor/nasw-cultural-diversity/

Pacific News—Movements of the Dispossessed
http://www.pacificnews.org/

Getting It All Together

No man can reveal to you aught but that which already lies half asleep in the dawning of your knowledge. The teacher . . . gives not of his Wisdom but rather of his faith and lovingness. If he is indeed wise he does not bid you enter the house of his wisdom, but rather leads you to the threshold of your own mind.

—Kahlil Gibran, *The Prophet* (1934)

What are some of the reasons people choose to work in the helping professions, and why is the choice important?

What is the nature of the difference between the Yogi and the Commissar, and how does this apply to those who work with people and their societies?

What is burnout, why is it so common among workers in the helping professions, and what are some of the ways we can deal with it?

And from here on in, you take it yourself! The above quotation from Kahlil Gibran's *The Prophet* speaks to the learner as well as the teacher. There comes a point at which learners must take responsibility for integration within themselves of all that they have acquired—the values, the knowledge, and the skill—and for use of the total self in the practice of human service.

We are a people still strongly under the influence of the work ethic. The person who works is virtuous; the person who does not is without virtue. For many, work provides not only the means of survival but also becomes the basic reason for living, and mandatory retirement becomes a veritable death sentence.

People choose the human services as their work for many and complex reasons. They may enjoy transactions with other people; they may have a strong ethical commitment to ensuring a good life for all; they may use relationships with clients as a way of dealing with their own personal problems; they may enjoy having power over others; they may find the challenges and difficulties intriguing; they may want the reward and prestige; they may just want any job.

For whatever reason people choose to enter the human services, they must know that they cannot avoid involvement of self in their practice. An abiding sense of moral responsibility and a willingness to face and come to terms personally with basic issues involving people are essential (see Figure 12.1).

This moral responsibility is all the greater because it is well established that, even in the most controlled experiment, the situation changes when there is outside intervention. Workers do not stand outside of the system—individual or group—but become, in a sense, a part of it, affecting the balance and facilitating the changes; at the same time, they must retain objectivity about it. Workers who are clear about themselves and what they bring with them are able to deal with this dual demand of human service.

Workers must know where they stand in regard to crucial issues that are a part of the times, such as the breakthroughs in genetic engineering that are taking place; the question of who in an expanding population shall share diminishing resources; who shall be permitted to live—(or die)—when that choice is made; what is the responsibility of society for its deviant members, for those who cannot make it alone, and for those who are "different."

Societies and individuals have always faced such concerns, but modern society not only has increased the reach of people immeasurably but at the same time faces the dilemma of a shrinking world in which interdependence is essential to survival.

We realize as never before that all living creatures on this planet are one, that all of us are affected directly or indirectly by what happens elsewhere in the world. A good ex-

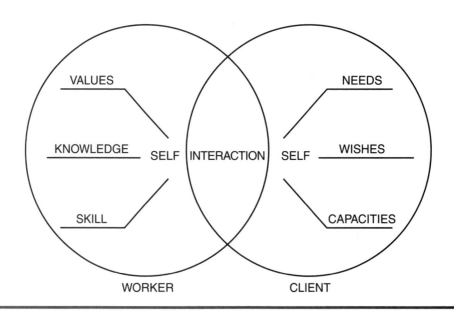

FIGURE 12.1   Interaction of the total selves of client and worker.

ample of this is the chaos in other parts of the world leading to illegal and legal immigration to this country.

We live in an international information society that enables us to share knowledge about, to understand, to make use of, and to influence events that affect all of us. This society demands expertise on the part of human service workers in accumulating, storing, retrieving, and making use of such information. It is estimated that half of all workers will be involved with such activities in the future, requiring additions to the knowledge base of practice, increased skills, and changes in point of view.

A philosophical stance enabling workers to understand themselves in relation to this changing world and its demands is as much a part of the preparation for practice as theories, techniques, and resources—for in human service, the knowledgeable self is the worker's most important resource. Such stances are neither cast in stone nor attained overnight. They will change with changing times and increasing maturity of the workers, but there must always be a solid underpinning of commitment to people and their welfare.

In one of the classics dealing with the spectrum of possible philosophical approaches to a changing world, *The Yogi and the Commissar,* Arthur Koestler (1965) positioned the Yogi and the Commissar at opposite ends. The Commissar believes in

> . . . change from without. He believes that all the pests of humanity, including constipation and the Oedipus complex, can be cured by revolution, that is, by a radical reorganization of the system of production and distribution of goods; that this end justifies the use of all means, including violence, ruse, treachery and poison; that logical reasoning is an unfailing compass and the Universe a kind of large clockwork in which a very large number of electrons once set in motion will forever revolve in their predictable orbits; and that whosoever believes in anything else is an escapist.

At the other extreme,

> . . . colorless, warmthless, but all-penetrating crouches the Yogi, melting away in the ultra- violet. He has no objection to calling the Universe a clockwork but thinks it could be called, with about the same amount of truth, a musical box or a fishpond. He believes that the end is unpredictable and the means alone count. He rejects violence under any circumstances. He believes that nothing can be improved by exterior organization and everything by individual effort from within; and that whosoever believes anything else is an escapist.

Human service workers tend to swing as on a pendulum between the Yogi and the Commissar. Extreme proponents of both theories exist who apparently never realize that one leads into the other and both are essential. Somewhere along that continuum, workers need to find a place for themselves, a place that is compatible with their own basic philosophical stance.

Such compatibility can go far in enabling workers to survive in what can only be described as a high-risk profession. Human services cluster along the cutting edge of change, and such interfaces are always characterized by conflict. The work itself is often frustrating not only because of the infinite number of variables involved, the pressure of human need, and the emotions that exist around it, but also because of the frequent difficulty in seeing both immediate and long-term results. The incidence of what we are calling burnout is very great.

Burnout

Burnout is a word that is currently used to describe a condition that has always existed. *Britannica World Language Dictionary* describes it thus: "To become extinguished through a lack of fuel"—with people, this is literally what happens. For a variety of reasons, workers no longer possess energy for their work and no longer find enough satisfaction from it to balance the disadvantages. The stress that results from being in such a condition, particularly when the worker can neither fight nor flee (the normal reactions to stress), may manifest itself in physical or emotional illness or addiction, in anger toward clients and/or the bureaucracy or supervisory staff who make demands, or in inefficiency in one's work life and problems in one's personal life. Workers experiencing burnout may end up abandoning the job and seeking other employment, often regardless of their commitment to it.

As always, prevention is better than cure. Workers should start out by being aware of the unique sources of stress their chosen work holds. They must be alert to the onset of such problems and prepared to cope with them. They must be receptive to both comments and behaviors on the parts of clients, colleagues, and family members who may perceive the beginning symptoms early. These sensitivities are a part of the ongoing self-awareness essential to human service practice.

There are specific things that workers can do to armor themselves against burnout and to deal with it, if and when it comes:

1. Maintain awareness of the changing social climate and a realistic evaluation of its impact on people—including themselves.
2. Be committed to securing both basic and ongoing learning about their work.
3. Select the field of practice that interests them that they enjoy and about which they are motivated to learn more.
4. Learn to manage their individual workloads efficiently and responsibly and to work with their colleagues.
5. Possess and maintain a personal value system consistent with the value system of human service, even if its tenets may run contrary to accepted social values.
6. Find a personal lifestyle sufficiently satisfying to enable them to distance themselves from their work.

The cultivation of these six areas in the lives of workers provides what, for lack of a better word, can be described as *professionalization*—the process of learning and being imbued with the method, manner, and spirit of a particular kind of work. Without such professionalization, workers are much more vulnerable to burnout, to being ineffective and feeling powerless, to leading the "lives of quiet desperation" that come from being caught in jobs that have no real meaning for them.

Being Aware of Social Change

There are two kinds of social change to which human service workers need to be alert. The first consists of those trends described in Chapter 1 that are a part of the developing social order. Workers must be sufficiently in touch with what is happening to assess realistically its meaning and its impact on the lives of their clients—as well as on themselves. These changes affect social values, attitudes and behaviors, the existence or nonexistence of resources, and the sanction of the service being provided. Sanction of human service is expressed through clients by their use of the services, by the society at large that licenses them, and through private and public funds that support their operation. Such sanctioning changes with the changing society.

The second kind of change is that which workers themselves attempt to bring about in order that the needs of the people they serve will be better met. This includes attempts to change policies and programs in specific areas; to educate people about what is needed and what is possible; and to develop and use power through political, professional, and social organizations to facilitate changes.

In attempting to bring about changes in the status quo, there is always an element of personal risk involved. One student commented, "The bottom line is my responsibility to my wife and child. I'm not going to rock the boat and lose my job."

But there must be boat rockers if we are not going to stagnate. Workers must be very realistically oriented in approaching this aspect of their work, first assessing needs, alternatives, and methods, as well as risks. It is important to survive in order to fight another day.

Securing Basic and Ongoing Learning

Regardless of the level of education and practice to which workers aspire, it is essential that they be committed to both basic and ongoing learning. Earlier it was stated that workers must bring to the job both generalized and specialized knowledge, the generalized being that which all people in human service work need to possess and the specialized being the specific knowledge and skill needed in a particular field.

Regardless of the level, workers should be committed to the development of knowledge and the improvement of practice. Creative thinking does not require a PhD; the ward orderly whose responsibilities and rewards—and educational requirements—are probably low on the totem pole is as capable of coming up with ideas and procedures that will improve service as is the highly trained researcher.

Creative thinking can be visualized as a four-step process:

1. Laying the groundwork. This involves acquiring the essential tools of knowledge and skill that provide the how-to for thinking and the means to stimulate ideas. This must be a continuing process, for knowledge changes and accrues. It is important that workers know how to use research to find the many good ideas that lie hidden behind terminology understandable only to other researchers. Workers should also become competent in use of modern technical apparatuses, such as computers, that have enabled us to stretch our reach and consider alternatives on a much broader level.
2. Mulling over the possibilities. In this, the thinker steps back from the assumptions made earlier and tries to look at the totality with new eyes. This is a dynamic activity, as new input from knowledge and experience is constantly being added and must be considered in various combinations.
3. Achievement of insight into new possibilities for dealing with old problems. Oftentimes this occurs in an instant flash while engaged in some apparently unrelated activity, such as playing, routine tasks, or reading unrelated material.
4. Testing of the idea with the intent of verifying it and putting it to use. If the idea proves to be valid, it must then be made available to the people who can use it.

This kind of thinking adds to our knowledge of people and how to work with them and to the creation of new resources for the betterment of the human condition. This kind of thinking is vital not only to the practice of human services, but also to the welfare of all. It can be used by workers on all levels of education and practice.

Selecting a Field of Practice

Selection of a field of practice with which the worker is most compatible is of great importance in preventing burnout—and just as human problems are endless, so are practice opportunities. Sometimes the choice can be made after workers have gotten their basic training and perhaps some experience, but there are those who know from the beginning where their interests lie and plan their study accordingly.

A major part of the decision is choosing whether to work toward the creation, administration, and maintenance of essential social resources or to work directly with people in dealing with personal concerns. On either level, the work can involve finding solutions for existing problems or the enrichment of the quality of lives that are already fairly adequate.

Many workers choose to go into private practice and become counselors, therapists, or consultants after securing additional specialized training. Many prefer to work with an established agency or group. Opportunities exist for both, and change is always possible as new areas open up with both additional learning and social changes. The challenge for workers is to find the place that suits them best and to try to avoid getting locked into a situation that is not satisfying.

Managing Workload

The most important factor in managing workload is that workers place themselves at the level of expectation where they can be most comfortable and competent. The human services are rampant with ineffectual administrators who have the capability of being effective clinicians, therapists, direct service practitioners, technicians, or support personnel. It is understandable that they move into administration because of its greater rewards and prestige, but hypertension is a high price to pay for such achievement. Mature workers who are self-aware will not put themselves in a position where they are good candidates for burnout.

Learning to manage workload efficiently is one of the best ways to avoid burnout or to deal with its existence. Workers must step back and take a look at their workload, reevaluate and reorganize it so they can handle it better, and feel that they are in control. Realistically, in human services there will be emergencies that will throw the best of schedules into disorganization and take all available time in any given work period. Sufficient flexibility must be built in to handle these crises, but looking at the totality will make such upsets not only less likely but also less taxing and disturbing.

The best way to handle workload is to use the management-by-objectives model, which is nothing more than a common sense, orderly way of thinking and planning, much like the problem-solving process. This is generally visualized in six steps:

1. Setting of goals: What you would like to do—the ideal attainment in your job
2. Setting of objectives: The visible, tangible, concrete, and doable things
3. Activities that must be done: Tasks—what must be done to reach objectives

4. Working out a plan: Strategy for performing these tasks
5. Budget needed for these tasks: The numerical needs in terms of time, people, and resources
6. Evaluation of what has been done: How things are working—well or badly—and how they can be changed

Workers are prone to say they do not have time to go through this process—actually, they do not have time not to. In the long run it is not only a tremendous time-saver, but it also pushes workers to establish priorities by looking at what is most important and the order in which things needs to be done. In addition to the practical usefulness of such thinking ahead, it helps deal with that intangible psychological downer that is the source of so much fatigue and ineffectiveness.

One aspect of the workload that is a frequent source of frustration for workers committed to human service and who want to be up and doing involves accountability for what is being done. This usually assumes the form of some kind of ongoing record. This is not only a practical necessity; it is also an ethical responsibility. Good practice and good recording are inseparable. Agencies and institutions providing human services are constantly in the process of developing new instruments for collection, storage, and retrieval of data, but in spite of this, it remains a time-consuming aspect of the job.

Accountability and Sanction.   Accountability in human services involves being responsible not only for what is actually being done but also for improving the quality of what is done. Implementation of this need for accountability requires constant evaluation and reevaluation of the structure, program, and policy of the various social institutions planning and delivering service, of the practice of the workers delivering the service, and of the results, both short- and long-term, of the service. It requires the development of forms, instruments, and procedures used in collection and evaluation of data; it involves critical analysis of the forms, procedures, and instruments themselves; it requires a flexibility of workers and institutions that enables them to both know and use new ideas and procedures that are being developed.

Accountability in human service exists on three levels: (1) to the clients, users, or consumers of the service; (2) to colleagues and to the organization or agency; and (3) to the society that sanctions the entire operation. Clients who use the services, laws authorizing the existence and support of programs, and lay people who help to support and serve on boards and committees and act as volunteers in the programs are all expressing sanction.

Sanction is also expressed through licensing, certification, and membership in professional organizations, which are designed to ensure competence of workers and responsibility of institutions and to protect both the consumer and the public at large. Here, there is a possibility of conflict of interests, particularly if professional standards and agency practices do not jibe. For example, some of our large public welfare program workers may be called upon to use procedures that they perceive as detrimental to the interests of the client. A consultant at the local Social Security office, called in to deal with the low morale of the staff, learned that when a computer error on a national level caused delay in mailing of checks, workers were instructed to make calls for clients to regional offices with full knowledge that such calls were ineffectual. Such procedures, born perhaps out of desperation and efforts to bring pressure for change, were directly contrary to the ethics of the workers and not of help to the clients. Equally, referring clients for mandatory job training programs to develop skills in areas where there are no jobs would be considered unprofessional and poor practice.

Accountability within the System.   Accountability to colleagues, the employing agency, and the total service system of which the worker is a part involves responsibility for cooperative endeavor within the system itself. It cannot be emphasized too strongly that this overall concept of accountability involves not only responsibility for things as they are, but also for improving the quality of what exists and what is being done. This means that data must be collected that can be used in research to enable better understanding of the human condition and more effective practice methods. The individual worker is responsible for maintaining a record of the basic data needed to evaluate what is being done and what needs are unmet. Such data can be secured by (1) observation, (2) interviewing or discussion, and (3) use of questionnaires or some other devices for securing valid information. For many workers, except those actively engaged in research, the day-to-day recording of information is the *bête noire* of practice. The whole question of how best to secure and store data so that they are not only valid but also usable is a yet unanswered one. In order to serve their purpose, data must be brief (the cost of maintaining records is a large portion of any budget), accurate (although allowances must always be made for the fact that data are filtered through the recorder), and available without too much effort or the consumption of too much time; they must also possess a degree of uniformity that allows for comparison and statistical accounting.

A major concern in the collection of data and the keeping of records about people is the individual's right to privacy and the whole question of confidentiality, of which people are properly assured when they are involved with one of the human services. The legal right to see personal files is assured. There is increasing openness about the fact that information is recorded, and there is shared knowledge of the manner in which it is to be used. Clients are entitled to this knowledge and to the assurance that such information will not be used irresponsibly, without their knowledge and consent, or for purposes other than those agreed on either tacitly or by written contract.

It is important to remember, however, that because of the extensive review process inherent in managed care, confidentiality is not an absolute. Many different helping persons and services are involved, review committees are an increasing part of the effort to assure quality of service, and information must be shared widely. While there is currently much greater openness in discussing personal problems, most people still have a need to keep certain information private. This again is one of those issues in which individualization of the client—helping the client to understand and accept the need to give certain information, how it will be collected, and how it will be used—is a basic essential of good practice.

Involvement of the client in the collection of data is important for another reason—the meaning of the data to the client—which is often just as important as the bare facts themselves. The extent to which it will be necessary for the worker to know this meaning will depend, to a large degree, on the nature of the problem and the kind of service needed.

Getting It All Together **251**

Feeling is fact, but the amount of feeling that must be shared varies greatly. For example, the fact of a divorce shared with a lawyer will be quite different from that fact shared with a marriage counselor. This again is an area where we can say that the client has the right and need to be involved to the extent that is necessary in the individual instance.

In addition, the worker must learn to differentiate between observation and inference in gathering and recording data. One definition of *observation* (*Britannica World Language Dictionary*) is "scientific scrutiny . . . the record of such examination and the data connected with it." *Inference,* on the other hand, is defined as a "deduction," a "conclusion," a "conjecture."

Too often, workers record inferences based on what they think observation means rather than the actual observation itself. At this stage in the development of our knowledge regarding the human condition, inferences can be little more than "scientific guesses." Whether the material recorded is being used for evaluation, for diagnosis, or for research, it needs to be an accurate observation rather than an inference of the meaning of that observation.

To attain the maximum degree of efficiency in the use of self in working with people, workers will usually need to record on two levels: (1) for personal use; and (2) for use by the employing agency and through it by the overall social system. Some of the major uses of recording are for personal improvement, for education, and for supervision of workers. For this purpose, the worker may choose to record the actual content of the interview, discussion, or meeting either on tape with the client's permission or by dictation so that it can be scrutinized and evaluated to improve both understanding and practice methods. While the form of such recording may vary, content should generally include:

1. Identifying data
2. Purpose
3. Observation
4. Interaction
5. Evaluation
6. Worker's role
7. Future plan

Obviously, this recording tends to be lengthy and expensive, and except for teaching agencies, it is rarely used for an entire caseload for permanent files. It is extremely useful, however, for both beginning and experienced workers, particularly if they have good consultation available, as a way of looking at the reality of what is happening between worker and client—whether the client be an individual, a family, or a group.

In the management of the job, workers usually opt to keep a day sheet or log. This is mandatory in some agencies. Sometimes printed forms are developed for this purpose; sometimes the individual worker devises a personal form. These can be used to plan work, as a basis for the preparation of permanent records, as a source of agency statistics and reports that serve to justify programs and expenditures, and for improving the quality of work as well as keeping people informed of what is being done. The human services depend on public support, and such support can only be secured and maintained if the public is accurately informed in a way that they can understand and appreciate. The worker supplies the raw material from which such interpretation is made, as well as information from which studies are planned and carried out. Workers not only need to record their material accurately and usably, but they must also be sufficiently aware of these two programmatic needs—evaluation and public information—to be constantly alert to trends, problems, and possibilities that can be used for either of these purposes.

Maintaining a Personal Value System

Each individual has a personal value system that serves to define what is important, determines goals toward which efforts are directed, and sets standards for acceptable ways in which these goals can be realized. Human service is based on its own set of values, which have both a moral and a pragmatic connotation. For example, not only do we value as a moral imperative the integrity of individuals and their right to self-determination, we also know that this is the most effective basis for enabling people to realize their full potential for development and contribution to the welfare of a democratic society.

People entering human service need more than to be aware of their personal value systems; they also need to be able to assess the consistency of their value systems with those on which the human services are based. The harboring of internal inconsistencies does not lead to personal or job satisfaction or to mental health.

The best human service workers are whole people who can then work with others to help them attain wholeness. Achievement of such wholeness, such internal consistency, is possible and attainable. Workers may not start out with this integrated, interrelated entirety, but through the acquisition of knowledge and experience, through sensitization to a real understanding of the human condition, they can develop it. Then, instead of working in order to survive, they can find the joy and personal fulfillment in their jobs that is the unearned increment of the human services (see Figure 12.2).

Developing a Healthy Personal Life

Since Selye did his original work with the concept of stress some fifty years ago, the idea has grown and developed extensive ramifications. We know that stress is a normal part of life and that the changes that accompany it serve the purpose of gearing us up to deal with a demanding life situation. We also know that stress makes heavy demands on the total person and can require adaptations that may be overwhelming. We know that stress in one life area—physical, intellectual, emotional, social, or spiritual—affects the total person. We know that ordinary events in daily life can be stressful.

Job burnout that is the result of stresses that workers are unable to cope with cannot be confined to the workplace—it affects the personal life as well. A healthy personal life is the best armor possible for enabling workers to deal with stresses on the job. Attaining it is a lifelong process because people change, develop, and grow as the years pass. Modern thinking about people puts great emphasis on the concept of total health. We have stress medicine, which emphasizes prevention of illness and the relationship among illness, stress, and the adaptation process. We have to work toward the healthy body through exercise, yoga, meditation, and proper nutrition. We ascribe importance to the examination and de-

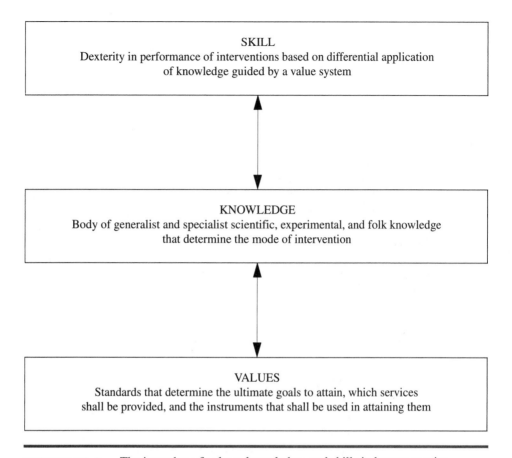

FIGURE 12.2   The interplay of values, knowledge, and skills in human service.

velopment of the emotional and spiritual life as a part of this totality, and we know that lack of intellectual stimulation can be as stressful as too much. Awareness of these trends is sufficiently a part of the total public thinking so that there are resources available to individuals who wish to work toward better adaptive ability.

Workers who are caught in the familiar modern dilemma—where they can neither effectively fight job pressures that are intolerable nor flee from them due to personal or economic reasons—will need to develop the strength of their total healthy selves in order to cope.

Summary

The human condition ensures that we will never attain a problem-free existence, but in the struggle itself lies opportunity for growth and development. There are no greater challenges or satisfactions than those derived from work with people. There is no occupation that has greater importance. Workers who continue to study, to learn, and to use the insights they gain will enjoy the greater freedom in use of self that is the most fulfilling reward of education.

SUGGESTED ASSIGNMENTS

The final class session can be an exercise in termination by looking at the initial purpose and goals, determining how well they were realized, and evaluating them and the methods used to attain them.

Each student will consider how she or he wishes to put this learning to use and where each will go from here. This can best be done in open discussion with seating arranged to assure maximum give and take, with no holds barred in terms of comments about the human services and their future direction in the life of the student, the learning experience provided, and how it could be improved.

This is a good meeting in which to share some refreshment, which will contribute to an informal atmosphere, but its success will basically be determined by the feelings of security and acceptance that exist between students and instructor and among the students.

REFERENCES AND RELATED READINGS

Cherniss, C. (1995). *Beyond burnout: Helping teachers, nurses, therapists or lawyers recover from job burnout.* New York: Routledge.

Collins, S. (1992). *Stillpoint: A dance of self caring, self healing.* Berkley, CA: TLC Productions.

Cooper, G., & Payne, R. (1978). *Stress at work.* New York: Wiley.

—. (1991). *Personality and stress: Individual differences in the stress process.* New York: Wiley.

Gibran, K. (1935). *The Prophet* (11th printing). Los Angeles, CA: Knapp.

Karger, H., & Levine J. (1999). *The internet and technology for the human services.* Reading, MA: Addison-Wesley.

Koestler, A. (1965). *The yogi and the commissar.* New York: Macmillan.

Maslach, C. (2003). *Burnout: The cost of caring.* Cambridge, MA: Malor Books.

Maslach, C., & Leiter, M. (1997). *The truth about burnout: How organizations cause personal stress and what to do about it.* San Francisco: Jossey Bass.

Russo, J. R. (1993). *Serving and surviving as a human service worker* (2nd ed.). Prospect Heights, IL: Waveland.

Shanks, L., & Hughes, H. S. (1999). *A caregivers' guide to Alzheimer's.* New York: Penguin USA.

Veninga, R., & Spradley, J. (1982). *Work/stress connection: How to cope with job burnout.* New York: Ballantine Books.

Weinbach, R. (2002). *Social worker as manager: Theory and practice* (4th ed.). Boston: Allyn and Bacon.

SELECTED RELATED WEBSITES

About Stress Management
http://stress.about.com/health/stress/cs/burnout/

International Stress Management Organization
http://www.isma.org.uk/

Self-Care and Stress Management
httpLL//www.nech.med.navy.mil/hp/stress/managing=stree.html

Stress Management Resources on the Internet
http://www.stresstips.com/stresslinks.html

Stress Management: Ten Self-Help Techniques
http://www.ucc.vt.edu/stdysk/stresmgt.html

SWAN (Social Work Access Network)
http://www.sc.edu/swan/media.html

Index